T0374568

Profiles

PORTRAITS OF INSPIRATION

JIM ANDERSON
WITH LEE MARTIN

iUniverse LLC
Bloomington

Profiles
Portraits of Inspiration

iUniverse books may be ordered through booksellers or by contacting:

iUniverse LLC
1663 Liberty Drive
Bloomington, IN 47403
www.iuniverse.com
1-800-Authors (1-800-288-4677)

Because of the dynamic nature of the Internet, any Web addresses or
links contained in this book may have changed since publication and
may no longer be valid. The views expressed in this work are solely
those of the author and do not necessarily reflect the views of the
publisher, and the publisher hereby disclaims any responsibility for
them.

ISBN: 978-1-4502-3917-2 (sc)
ISBN: 978-1-4502-3918-9 (e)

Printed in the United States of America

iUniverse rev. date: 05/21/2014

For Melissa, Eric, Chad, Cami, Kyrah,
Cole, Raquel and Chris

Acknowledgments

To mentors Jack Shingleton and Dave Ritchie who shape character of all who they touch.

To Eleanor who brought us boys into the world.

To Lee Martin who promoted the initiation of and contributed tirelessly to this work.

And to Cathy whose ability to lift spirits and hearts blesses all.

Foreword

The great dancer and actress Eleanor Powell, when asked about her view of life replied, "What we are is God's gift to us. What we become is our gift to God." Her statement expresses sincere appreciation as well as promotes responsibility to do something positive with our lives.

The gift of life is something we received through no will or action of our own. But its value is largely determined by our will and actions while we live. Though we don't determine all that happens, we have a choice upon how we'll handle it. Our attitude toward it all largely determines the worth of our lives. We can allow trials to break us or make us stronger. We can let others in our lives become positive or negative; depending upon how we choose to respond to them. We can elect to be joyful or sorrowful. Though remaining joyful requires much strength because it is often in the face of difficulty.

The value and work of my life to this point has been very much shaped by the interaction and influence with some gifted and colorful persons. This is a collection of stories about many of them. I haven't included all. But the ones I have described are some of the most important influences. Included are mentors, coaches, teachers, parents, my children, and friends.

The following accounts about others that have motivated and shaped my efforts and experience are true. My endeavors so far are very much direct products of their inspiration, encouragement and guidance. I've profiled each as accurately as I can from my recollections. In some cases I've had to research more about them where necessary outside my direct experience.

I've attempted not to embellish beyond my knowledge

or perceptions. In some cases I've had to infer dialogue as I don't know for certain exactly what was spoken or how it was conveyed. In many cases I was told what the person said. And occasionally I've had to suppose what they might have been thinking during some events or facets of each story. But in all cases I've stayed as close to the facts as I was able.

Beyond the characters and events described the most significant influence upon me is Christ. Though I don't participate in organized religion or follow an absolute doctrine His role in my life is the most positive. Through grace and His influence I've been given opportunities and gifts far exceeding what I imagined or hoped for in youth. While this collection is dedicated to my children, it is written principally in appreciation for the gift of life and the blessings bestowed upon me by our Creator.

Profiles

Rock Me to Sleep

Backward, turn backward, O Time, in your flight,
Make me a child again just for to-night!
Mother, come back from the echoless shore,
Take me again to your heart as of yore;
Kiss from my forehead the furrows of care,
Smooth the few silver threads out of my hair;
Over my slumbers your loving watch keep;—
Rock me to sleep, mother,—rock me to sleep!

— *Elizabeth Akers*

I.

Concrete warmed by the morning sun felt rough against my bare knees and elbows. Prone on my stomach gazing down the hill, I aimed the little toy car toward its target. The tiny vehicle was a cast iron replica of a 1940's "woody" station wagon with black rubber wheels. I figured that if I could aim it accurately the car would coast the ten yards to the bottom of the sidewalk leading to our back door. I gave it a push. As it took off, a sense of excitement overcame me. The urge to race along with it made me jump up. Toddling along behind as fast as my small legs would carry me I descended the slight grade. I had not yet completely mastered walking, let alone the ability to run downhill. While struggling to stay up with the toy, I teetered and stumbled. I fell upon the empty bottles awaiting replacements by the milk man. Pitching forward I landed on the sparkling glass.

The sound of breaking bottles combined with sharp pain

jolted me. I crawled to my feet. Curiously examining my hands and arms I pondered the red fluid suddenly dripping down my body. More focused upon task than trauma, I tottered over to my mother in the garden across the back yard. I called out to her and she looked up, a watering can in her hand.

"Jimmy!" she cried out springing to her feet, "What happened to you?"

The look of alarm on her face is probably the reason this event so was indelibly imprinted in my memory. That and the fact that she recounted the story more than once to me over the years. Dropping the watering can, she bounded up the small terrace from the garden like a cat. Being a registered nurse she knew what to do. She examined me carefully. The smell of moist open earth in the garden was mixed with a new metallic odor of the foreign red substance covering me.

Fortunately I had suffered only surface lacerations from the shattered glass and while they appeared serious, they were easily addressed with iodine and a few bandages. With soft skilled hands and warm concern on her lovely face, Mother comforted and repaired me.

"Jimmy, you must be careful when playing outside, Dear. There are all kinds of things in the yard that can get you into trouble!"

Shortly, I was back outside playing with the little car while Mom cleaned up the glass. The horror of the moment now behind her, she softly hummed the melody of "Mares Eat Oats", a popular 1940's novelty tune as the sunlight glistened on her black hair. With sharp features and a radiant personality, everyone agreed Mother was a beautiful woman. But her deepest beauty was in her heart and it showed radiant to anyone who spent time talking with her. On that morning, at age 32, she was in the full bloom of motherhood with three small boys and a husband and home to care for.

This earliest memory from childhood has remained with me as the first drama connected with her that I can recall. Though she's been gone for many years, I still feel her presence. There was something especially endearing about Mom. Many others felt the same. Forty five years after the broken bottle incident, on a warm humid morning in Florida I stood delivering the eulogy at her funeral. The remarkable outpouring of emotion at her loss from the large audience challenged every bit of control I could muster to finish the short speech at the church. A few lines in particular connected with the audience. As I spoke them, there became an unusual stillness over the group and some dabbed their eyes.

"Everything about her was beautiful. Her mannerisms and her physical presence. The colorful silk scarves she wore so often. Her treatment of friends, family and even strangers. But most significant was her beautiful heart. Her heart evoked the best out of most of us and shone through the best and most difficult of times. It's people like her that make life worth living."

Along the way over the years she graced my life in countless ways. And often I heard others laud her. It seemed almost everyone who came to know Mom learned to love her. What was it that evoked such admiration and affection? It went beyond just the beauty of her physical and personal presence.

Mother's unusually kind nature was a large influence with both family and friends in all our lives. While life during her early years of motherhood appeared ideal, the trials she had suffered to that point and were yet to suffer forged an inner tenacity and steadfast conviction beneath her light hearted and charming demeanor. She longed in her young married life to have a cheerful home. More importantly, she was resolute to be a good mother and promote a happy childhood for her three boys. Her gift for comfort and encouragement were rare. On the morning of my accident she overcame what might have been a traumatic moment for me. And instead she placed on my heart a representative positive memory of her that has lasted for the balance of my life.

II.

Beginning early in her life significant trials had surfaced for Mom. They began at age thirteen. Coming home from school one day she found her mother semi-conscious. The white and pale woman was on the couch in their living room.

"What's wrong Mom? Are you sick?" the girl queried her prostrate mother. Gently shaking her mother's limp arm, she asked again, "Mom. Are you sleeping?"

No response evoked a sense of alarm. The teenager was alone facing a frightening circumstance. Without her fraternal twin Albert, older sister Annabelle or her father to help, she would have to take action on her own then and there. She moved her mother to the bedroom. Struggling with the limp and unresponsive woman, she finally reached the bed. The details described to me years later were sketchy but I know it was not long until her mother succumbed to the cerebral hemorrhage. Mom was to grow up quickly.

The little girl was now 'woman of the house'. She assumed much of that role for her brother and father. Her big sister Annabelle was ten years older but gone from the home. Mom began focusing efforts on keeping the place clean and preparing meals as well as attending junior high school and then high school while earning honor student status. A steadfast responsibility for domestic concerns consumed her. The strict Catholic influence of her family and local parish further drove home principles of duty and dogged determination to 'bear her cross'. At one point she even considered life in a convent. Her brother Albert himself under the same influences became a bother in a Catholic order for years in his young adult life. Mom was on a course of self-sacrifice. This would define much of her identity and role in life.

Because her father was not affluent, she had to work hard and sacrifice much to enter and pay for her college at the Providence School of Nursing in Beaver Falls, Pennsylvania where she graduated in 1940. Beyond that, most of her nursing experience was in a psychiatric hospital. This was particularly demanding work. An unusually good student in high school, it was obvious she was destined to be something special. If times had been different including financial conditions, she was one of those women who may have become a physician or head of a women's college if she so chose. She was that capable. There was a different course for her however. She was to sacrifice her own interests. A common theme for many exceptional women in those times. Through all the years of her life, she carried a cross. It was the cross of putting others first at great expense to her.

There are with me now countless memories of her shining through my life. These memories color my recollections of a Godly woman. The instances are so vivid I can still recall many easily. I remember what she wore at certain times. I recall the fragrances from those moments such as her perfume and her hair. I remember the scenes clearly with her in the center of each. The time of day and seasons are now still alive as the present. My recollections of moments with her seem much sharper than memories of many other times in my life. Perhaps it's because of the great sense of awareness and appreciation for life that I gained from just being near her.

III.

While she was strong, she was at the same time very tender. But Mom was not permissive. She was capable of managing us three boys. In the early years before entering kindergarten, I was already defiant and would sometimes attempt to protest afternoon nap time. When I would resist, she would firmly make me lie down until I grew sleepy. With her humming to me and rocking me to sleep, I would drift off comfortably.

The memory of a highly symbolic dream from those early days of childhood is still with me. She had me lie down next to her on the couch by the windows in our living room one afternoon when she wanted a few minutes rest. Sometime after

I fell asleep, I dreamt I heard noises outside those windows. In the dream I crawled up over her sleeping form and looked out to see soldiers carrying guns. The men were dressed in World War I gear with wide brimmed helmets and old fashioned bolt action rifles. They were moving in crouched positions around the house. I feared for her.

In the dream, I pleaded, "Mama! Hide! They're coming!"

The frightening dream woke me. As I awoke she rocked me for a few minutes before I could describe the dream. She comforted me with words I heard more than once.

"Everything's alright. You don't have to be afraid of anything happening to your mama".

Yet, I always did fear for her welfare. From the very earliest, I had an urge to want to protect her. And there were things to protect her from. Ironically they were not from the outside; but instead inside our home. While there was much good in Dad, his demons, possibly stirred by his childhood experiences became manifested in destructive behavior. None of us ever understood why. It was just the way it was.

Beginning in early childhood I attempted to serve as a buffer between Dad and Mom. Later I grew more challenging and rebellious toward Dad in large part driven by my desire to want to guard her. While I could not rescue her from the dire circumstance, I somehow hoped to. That desire promoted a pattern of rescue behavior that began to carry over outside the home as well. It certainly affected the way I related to women. A pattern that would eventually undermine many relationships with the opposite sex as I often tended toward women in distress. She warned me about that tendency more than once. To no avail.

IV.

The still and humid evening in the summer of 1960 stirred me to sneak out of the house around 10:00 PM. I decided to take a walk. I didn't tell either parent. At fourteen years

I was restless as many young men are when caught in the twilight boundary between childhood and manhood. Prone to sneaking out without being noticed, I would climb from the window of my bedroom on the second floor and descend a trellis from a small roof to the ground.

Soon after I traveled many blocks from the house, lightening began to illuminate the skies. The great purple and gray masses of clouds threatened rain. A fierce wind began swirling through the town. Debris and leaves whirled across the streets. Suddenly a great crash of lightening with thunder struck so near me that I had to run for cover. I sprinted directly for the overhang of a retail building across the street I was on.

Back at the house when the storm had begun Mom ran to close all the windows before the rain could blow in. In doing this, she discovered that I was gone.

"Jim! Jim where are you?" She rapidly hurried through the house calling for me. "Jimmy! Are you in here anywhere?"

Unable to locate me, she went outside in the storm to look for me. Not having any idea where I might be and feeling the need to search right away, she had taken no coat or umbrella. The little woman darted through the streets of the neighborhood calling my name. With no regard for the lightening that was literally crashing around her or tree limbs being torn off by the furious wind she searched frantically for me. The storm and torrents howled around her small frame as she searched. A couple of miles away I held my refuge under the overhang until the storm subsided.

When the wind and rain eased up, I hurried home. Upon entering the house, I found her sitting by the door with the telephone on her lap. She was completely soaked. Her hair hung down limp still dripping a few drops of water on her shoulders.

"Mom, what happened? Why are you so wet?"

"Jim, I have a question for you first. Where have you been and what were you doing out in this storm?"

"It was hot, Mom. I wanted to take a walk to cool down. I went downtown for awhile. I was safe."

"Jimmy, never do that again! I was frightened terribly that you were in danger."

I could see that though she was attempting to look angry, she just couldn't. She was too relieved and thankful I was home safe. Then a feeling of compassion and appreciation overcame me. I sat down by her to talk. The following morning when I stepped out the front door to survey the scene, I could see that our neighborhood was a shambles. Trash, power lines, tree limbs and shingles from roofs lay on the ground. I realized how much danger the little lady had been in while searching for me. She never referred to the danger she had faced. To her it was simply what a mother does.

V.

Over the years there were traditions with her that I never grew tired of. They began in my early childhood when she would take me to White Swan Park or on the train or in the car to Pittsburgh. We would sometimes take walks, or visit the airport to watch planes or go to movies together. We would drive places and talk about all subjects. She never pried but took a genuine interest in whatever I wanted to discuss. I would ask her about her childhood. I took great interest in her experiences or what she thought.

She had her own bedroom and sometimes at night I would go in to talk with her as she sat in bed reading an Ellery Queen or other mystery novel. When leaving I would always kiss her on the cheek and say "Goodnight Mom, I love you." I did this because I knew I was the only person in our house who did tell her that they loved her, or showed her any affection.

One time we were discussing dreams. Because I was studying psychology in college I was interested in learning about others dreams and would try to determine what they might mean. She told me how the night before she had awoken from a nightmare.

"Mom, why do you say it was a nightmare?"

She began. "Well, there was a large tower with a huge bell. For some reason I was in the tower and couldn't get out. I felt trapped at first. But I believed I could survive until I figured out a way to escape."

"How did you think you might do that?"

"It wasn't important. I just believed I could. But then the bell in the tower began to ring. It was loud and had a deep and threatening tone. It began to ring so loud I couldn't think. And I became very afraid."

I could she as she talked and her brow became furrowed the thought of the dream was disturbing to her.

"What happened?"

"That's when I woke up. It was awful."

Dreams are odd. Any number of interpretations can be read into them. In the case of her bell tower dream I didn't attempt to determine what it might have meant. But years later while thinking about it, it became obvious to me that her dream might have had something to do with feeling trapped and oppressed. Possibly by her circumstances in life at that point. I don't know.

VI.

The moon was high in the Florida sky. Waves broke softly on the beach as the small form sat with knees pulled up watching the ocean. A light wind gently rustled her hair as she remained motionless staring out across the water. Around midnight, she had been there alone in the darkness for at least a half hour waiting. Waiting for something she had seen only once before years earlier. But she knew tonight was when it was supposed to happen again. Her deep interest and appreciation for nature and science was the reason she waited patiently and alone in the dark.

Then what she had been waiting for began. At first she saw only one dull lump emerge from the water onto the shore. Then another; and another. Finally, a small army of the sea turtles wended their way up the beach toward where she was huddled. She remained motionless as they passed and surrounded her. Then the digging began. Using their back flippers the turtles hollowed out recesses in the sand. And they deposited their eggs. She was so close to them that she could actually hear the eggs falling into the recesses where they would be covered by their mothers. The distinct smell of the ocean was mixed with the strange odor of the turtles and their precious cargos.

The following morning, she telephoned me in Michigan to tell me excitedly about the memorable spectacle she had witnessed the night before.

"Jimmy, you should have been there. Its one of the most interesting things I've ever seen!"

"Mom, now let me get this straight. You drove out there near midnight and sat on the Jupiter beach alone to watch turtles?"

"So?"

"Why didn't you get Dad to go with you? That could have been dangerous."

"Oh Jimmy, you know he'd never want to do something like that. Besides by nine o'clock he's usually fast asleep in his recliner watching some stupid baseball or football game or whatever."

"But Mom, you remember last year about the murder on that same beach. Don't you think it could be dangerous?"

The year before in 1977 there had been a sensational murder near that same spot she was telling me about. But that mattered not to her. She paid little mind to potential dangers. Especially when it came to adventures having to do with nature.

"When you come down the next time, I'll take you over to Blowing Rock and show you where they came out."

"OK, Mom. But please don't go out there again alone at might."

"Everything's alright. You don't have to be afraid of anything happening to your mom".

VII.

Driving south on I-225 near Denver in 1993, an eerie feeling overcame me. It was unlike anything before or since. It was something like a powerful presence in my car with me. Not of a person or being, but an awareness of something indefinable that was happening. Unseen it compelled me to pull the car off the road and find a telephone to telephone Mom.

The day before I had received a call from my brother Totty who was in Florida visiting Mom and Dad. Totty had called to tell me that while our mother had been competing in a bridge tournament in West Palm Beach, she had fallen and injured herself on the slippery floor beneath her bridge table. However, she had a couple of her friends help her back into her chair to resume play.

Apparently, Mom had broken some bones and didn't know it at the time. After another 45 minutes of play she began to feel faint. An ambulance had been called. Totty had telephoned from the hospital to tell me that she had broken her arm, a bone in her leg and even a rib. She was under sedation and would remain in the hospital for a few days before she could go home.

I took an exit off of I-225 and found a convenience store. There was a payphone outside. I used my calling card to dial the number of the hospital Totty had given me. When I reached the hospital operator I asked for Mom's room number. The phone began to ring in her room.

There was a faint "Hello?"

"Mom. This is Jim."

11

"Hello Jimmy."

She sounded distant. Not because of the phone service, but because something was different about her voice. It took me a moment to figure out that she was receiving intravenous administration of Demerol for the pain. She was not herself.

"Mom. Totty called and told me about your accident. How long will you be there?"

"Not long enough."

"What do you mean?"

"I don't want to go back. I want to stay here as long as I can."

"Mom. Totty told me he'd stay longer in Florida to help you when you get home."

"Jim, he can't stay. He has to get back to work."

She was tired and obviously trying to stay alert against the effects of the drugs. We talked about small things. Like the bridge tournament she had been in. We talked about the kids. And then she started to fade. Her last words were unintelligible to me.

I spoke. "Mom. I love you. I hope that you are released from what you're suffering there soon."

There was no response. She was gone to sleep. I hung up.

How prophetic the final words of mine to her would be. It was only a few hours later that evening while she was resting comfortably in a deep drug induced sleep that it happened. A blood clot broke loose within one of her arteries. It stopped her heart while no nurse or anyone else was in her room. By the time the tone of the heart monitor attached to her was heard, it was too late.

Mom departed the trials of this world unexpectedly. She was finally released to the "silence so long and so deep" as described by Elizabeth Akers.

"Tired of the hollow, the base, the untrue,
Mother, O mother, my heart calls for you!
Many a summer the grass has grown green,

> *Blossomed and faded, our faces between:*
> *Yet, with strong yearning and passionate pain,*
> *Long I to-night for your presence again.*
> *Come from the silence so long and so deep;—*
> *Rock me to sleep, mother,—rock me to sleep!"*

A few days later after delivering the eulogy at her funeral and standing alone beside her casket at the cemetery, I spoke to her one last time. Leaning down close to her remains, I whispered, "Goodnight Mom, I love you." I kissed her casket and then turned to join the rest of the departing procession.

Rupe

Here rests his head upon the lap of Earth
A youth to Fortune and to Fame unknown
Fair Science frowned not on his humble birth
And Melancholy marked him for her own
Large was his bounty and his soul sincere,
Heaven did recompense as largely send:
He gave to Misery all he had a tear
He gained from Heaven (t'was all he wished) a friend
No farther seek his merits to disclose,
Or draw his frailties from their dread abode
(There they alike in trembling hope repose)
The bosom of his Father and his God

— *Thomas Gray*

I.

The long black '46' Chrysler eased into the driveway shortly before dinner. It was early September and the sullen drone of the locusts in the tree tops indicated the transition from summer to fall. The tall figure, weary from a long day standing and laboring over his dental patients had come home to eat before returning to his office for an evening appointment. He bent down and smiled at me as I sat in the yard examining an ant wandering through the grass. Scooping me up, he briskly rubbed his chin with 'five o'clock shadow' against my grimacing face. The stubble felt like sandpaper. A mixture of perspiration and the smell of ether from his office lab filled my nostrils as the big man squeezed me tightly.

"What have you been doing today, boy?" he asked.

After lifting me high in the air he set me down, walked into the house to say 'Hello' to Mom and retire to the living room to read the Pittsburgh Post Gazette. This was a common routine in the 1950's when Dad worked evenings. He held office hours a few evenings a week for a number of years in those times. Living through a lean childhood into the Great Depression of the 1930's had left an everlasting impression on him. It was his need if not his passion to save as much as he could to ensure that neither he nor his family would face financial hardship as he had in his youth. Life was always tough for Dad. And it was not a function of whether or not he had money. His challenges ran much deeper. Much of it had to do with conditions beginning early in his childhood.

As a toddler, one of seven children of Harry Anderson, a struggling insurance salesman, Dad earned the nickname that stayed with him until he reached his thirties. His family lived in a semi rural neighborhood in Coraopolis where horses, cows and other farm animals were common. A small horse on their property named Rupert had become a favorite of the little boy. Barely able to speak, Dad would attempt to talk about Rupert. He did so much that the kids around him began to make fun of him and call him 'Rupert'. Later they shortened this name to 'Rupe' which followed him all the way through dental school.

There were trials facing Dad as a boy. While his mother Mary was kind and loving, his father Harry was the opposite. Harry Anderson was an unhappy and tormented man. Hotheaded, he demonstrated a mean streak that often boiled over into brutality toward little Rupe. To make matters worse, Rupe was precocious and inquisitive which often annoyed and angered his father. Additionally, the boy was defiant and not easily dictated to by anyone. His father was prone to harsh mistreatment of the boy.

II.

While Dad had many unusual talents and good qualities, there were strong negative influences from his father and relatives before him. The Anderson family roots were Scots Irish. The deeply ingrained history and culture of these hardy, yet oppressed people greatly affected the thinking of my grandfather and my dad. The Scots Irish coming before my grandfather and father had, in many ways, a daunting existence as a result of having been forced out of Scotland and into a hard barren land in Ireland in the 1800's. It was a grueling way of life for these economically impoverished people. Religious discord and persecution; poor land for farming; disease; awful living conditions; and then the famine.

The Great Irish Famine and its aftermath, in Ireland between 1845 and 1849, were prompted by potato blight that almost instantly destroyed the primary food source of many Irish people. The blight explains the crop failure. But the dramatic and deadly effect of the famine was exacerbated by other factors of economic, political, social, and religious origin. The famine's immediate effects continued until 1851. Much is unrecorded but estimates are that around one million people, possibly 12% of the population, died in the three years from 1846 to 1849. Most of these deaths were the result of famine-related diseases rather than starvation. Another one million people are estimated to have fled as refugees to Great Britain, the United States, Canada and Australia during that period, increasing the Irish exodus. Anderson ancestors were among them.

The famine occurred within the British imperial homeland at a time well into the modern prosperity of the Victorian era of the Industrial Revolution. This was at a time when Ireland was, even during the famine, a net exporter of food. The impact upon Ireland was devastating and its long-term effects proved immense, changing Irish culture and tradition for generations. The population of Ireland continued to fall for many years, stabilizing at half the level prior to the famine. This long-term decline only finally ended in 2006, over 160 years after the famine struck.

It's not difficult to understand why the Scots Irish developed an austere and fatalistic view of life. To be joyful, hopeful, or positive was not a part of their mindset or view of life. Even to this day the Scots Irish are often believed to have a higher incidence of alcoholism than many other cultures. A powerful and all encompassing fatalistic way of thinking became part of their way of life. Dad's father and relatives were a product of this. And it flowed directly into our home when we were children.

III.

Harry often kept Rupe home from school to work on the property surrounding their house. It caused the boy to miss enough class that he graduated two years late from high school. On a May afternoon in 1921, the fourteen year old boy had gone on to school despite his father's orders to stay home and clean the horse stall. Coming out of the school that afternoon, Rupe saw his father pull up in his car. Dad's stomach tightened and he grew anxious. He knew there would be trouble. The moment was especially precarious because one of the girls in his class that Dad secretly admired was there watching with some of her girl friends as well as a couple of boys.

"Come here!" his father demanded in a low and menacing tone. Beginning to tremble, Rupe walked over. When his father implored "I told you to clean the stall today" Dad made the mistake of attempting to explain that he couldn't miss a test scheduled for the morning or he'd receive a failing grade. Before he could finish, Harry's fist lashed out and split Dad's upper lip. Wiping the blood from his face, Dad glared at his father and put his arms up to protect himself. Harry took this as an act of defiance. His clenched fists exploded on the boy reducing him to a huddled mass on the ground.

The beating in front of his classmates left Dad bloodied, humiliated and crying as his father departed without him. Unfortunately that was only one of many such moments Rupe endured at the hands of his father. This one was especially significant due to his classmates witnessing it. That moment as well as similar events in those years fostered deep seated anger. Rage began to boil within him. This galvanized a fierce and rebellious nature that would stay with him always. In some ways that anger promoted tenacious determination and will power that would result in much achievement. However, in other ways it fed dark and turbulent emotions that would eventually serve to wreak enormous damage.

IV.

The early December evening in 1925 was cold and snowy. After a basketball practice in his junior year at Coraopolis High School, Rupe trudged through the icy streets in the dark to his house. It was a few miles and without boots his shoes filled with snow and his bare head became wet long before arriving at his destination. As he plodded through the dark freezing night, his mind played over the concerns plaguing him daily. Could he keep his grades high enough to qualify for a college? Where would the funds come from to help pay for college? Would his continuing efforts to work part-time interfere with everything else? This period made an everlasting impression upon him. For the balance of his life, through the great depression, the early years of struggling to build his dental practice, and beyond, he would forever be plagued by dread of the ever present possibility of financial hardship.

But through it all there was a bright spot in Rupe's life. His older brother George. Our uncle George was a kind young man ten years older than Dad who took every opportunity he could to help his younger brother. George recognized that Rupe was a gifted student and athlete. He encouraged him in sports and every other way. Though their father attempted to intercede. However, George's encouragement to the boy to study hard and aspire to become successful in athletics was paying off.

"Rupe, there are colleges that'll pay for your tuition and expenses if you agree to play football or basketball for them."

"Dad doesn't want me to go to college."

"You're going to go to college and Dad can't stop you. You can become a doctor or just about anything you want if you decide to. You have the ability. You'll have to sacrifice some, but you're going to do alright."

These words and George's continual encouragement became a lifeline to Dad. Not long after Dad began college at the University of Pittsburgh, when George was only 32 years of age, George died of pneumonia. George lived in dad's memory the rest of his life. A framed black and white picture of his older brother remained by Dad's bed side always. Dad's firstborn son was given the honor of his beloved big brother's name.

But years later, though highly intelligent, a successful businessman, and well respected within the community, Dad could not overcome the demons from childhood that gnawed at him daily, and invaded his dreams at night. When a boy I sometimes heard Dad cry out in his sleep in the middle of the night. The fear of financial hardship was one of the most persistent fears he struggled with. His own father had gone bankrupt in the 1920's and between Dad's last year of high school and the time he entered the University of Pittsburgh was literally spent without a regular place to live. In Dad's last year in high school, his father lost their house and went to North Carolina leaving the seven children and a wife behind with no home of their own. They were taken in by relatives in the greater Pittsburgh area.

So during the grueling years of high school while working part time, attending school, and earning all star honors on both the football and basketball teams, Rupe became unusually tenacious and self reliant. Some nights after their house had been lost, like many homeless souls, Dad had to sleep where ever he could including friends homes and occasionally even in one of the booths in back of the all night Greek restaurant in Coraopolis. He had to scrounge meals and sometimes did not eat. Not until he attended football training camp after being awarded an athletic scholarship at Pitt did he get enough to eat. Within the first few weeks at training camp, while the other athletes lost weight under the grueling workouts, Dad gained twenty pounds.

V.

If financial fears had been the only thing to torment him, our mother and each of us three boys would have experienced a very different reality in our formative years. We may have had much happier times. However, there were dark influences working on Dad that would little by little take away our father's ability to bring emotional stability and real security to our family. Dad was a man of enormous contrasts. One might say he was dual personality. At times he reflected shades of his father. At other times, he was warm and kind.

As the years wore on, for some reason my brothers and I still do not understand, he became less and less the father he could have been for us. The earlier the memories we boys have of Dad, the better. My first memory of him from age three is especially endearing. He and Totty, my older middle brother had to go next door for a couple of minutes to the Perrin's home, across our side yard. Dad told me to sit and play for a few minutes in the living room until he returned. This was a grievous error on his part. Within the few moments they were gone, I found something to play with. It was the record collection beside the phonograph. These treasures were brittle plastic records called 'Bakelite' of 1940's music. I found they could fly if I threw them hard enough.

The vision of those records striking the walls and furniture are still with me. The delightful cracking sound as they exploded on the ceramic tile of the fire place was especially entertaining. As the front door opened and Dad entered, I was happy and proud that he would now survey my handiwork. He stopped and stood motionless. A look of disbelief and then dismay came across his face as he sat down and rubbed his forehead. His head shook slowly from side to side. He said quietly to Totty "Take Jim upstairs to your room. I need to clean this up before your mother comes home."

Years later I learned from my mother how important those records were to him. He loved that music dearly. A number of the smashed copies were favorites he had collected over the years. I suspect one of the primary reasons he didn't give way to anger was that he knew he was responsible for leaving a three year old alone in the house which he should never have done.

There were other good memories of him. But they were almost all from the very early years as well. I can recall how he would hold me on his chest while lying on the overstuffed 40's era couch as we watched the tiny eleven inch screen of the first television on our street. He was gentle and affectionate in those years. He was often sentimental. Because of his unusual memory, he had committed to memory many poems over his life. He would recite poetry from time to time befitting the circumstances. Our friend Jack Shingletown was highly impressed one fall afternoon on the Betsie River by his cottage in Northern Michigan when Dad chose a poem to describe the idyllic setting they were in. 'Elegy Written in a Country Church Yard' by Thomas Gray was one of his favorites he sometimes referred to reciting certain lines that went with the moment.

The contrasts in him are forever intriguing and perplexing. I saw him demonstrate great gentleness and kindness in the early years. However, in time the things that tormented him would become him. The memories of those moments are ones that I spent much of my life working on putting aside. I choose to remember and focus upon the good in him. Such as the work he did for patients that could not afford to pay him or the work he did that benefitted the community through the Kiwanis Club.

By the time I progressed into my teens, Dad was not only overwhelmed by his emotional challenges but by my strong willed defiance and my own emotional intensity. We were battling regularly and I was doing badly in school. At that point he decided he had had enough. He made a decision. It was then that he decided to send me off to Greenbrier Military School for my high school education. This turned out to be one of the best things he did for me. I am most grateful.

Maples

This morning, after
In my own bed I woke
Bathed full and swimming in yellow light
That hovers in and around
Smooth maple branches in late October
On crisp mornings

— Garth Gilchrist

I.

An oily odor drifted through the window screen. It was accompanied by the puttering sound of an antiquated upright lawn mower. On this early evening in September 1949 I was still too small to see over the second story window sill. I managed to climb onto a chair to look out the window. Down below guiding the power mower, my father without shirt was mowing the lawn. His white back glistened with perspiration. Brownish hair rustled by the breeze as he worked. Tall and athletic, Dr. Raymond T. Anderson was an imposing figure even doing something as simple as yard work. He liked to work in the large yard while we boys were small. Before he could assign us the tasks. Dad was proud of our spacious Georgian home on the hill overlooking the Ohio River Valley. The home that he purchased shortly after World War II.

The gray brick two story had been constructed in the 1930's. As a younger man one afternoon Dad caught sight of it being built. He was impressed. He thought that someday he would have a home like it. When we took residence in

23

1947, mature maple trees had filled the terraced one acre lot around the house. The hill upon which it was situated afforded a magnificent view of the Ohio River Valley. In the cool afternoons of October in the early 1950's, the red and yellow leaves of the stately trees provided sanctuary. I often climbed those maples to look out at the valley. Jumping to the lowest limb, I would swing a leg over the branch and then pull myself up proceeding higher and higher. The dark bark soiling my hands and clothes was inconsequential. A sense of accomplishment and peace would fill me. I'd climb to the highest point and sway with the wind. Scenes of adventures played in my mind while drifting off into an imaginary world in my beloved haven.

I was happy alone in the peace of the maple trees. They became beautiful refuges in childhood and a yearning for being close to nature from that experience carried over the rest of my life. The breeze softly rustling their leaves outside our bedroom window at night giving me comfort before sleep. The early morning sun illuminating the green leaves in July and then multicolored in fall were a glorious sight to greet the day when waking. But mostly, it was the view of the valley from their bows which I recall.

II.

On the beautiful tree lined McCabe Avenue, our street, we lived close by many Italian neighbors. As a small child, the Tarquinios, Sardellos, Savini's and other Italian families taught me to love their unique cooking. Entering their homes I was tempted by the aroma of pasta sauce, fresh bread, and a myriad of other delightful smells associated with the rich tradition of their home style cooking.

"Jimmy, you look hungry! Come. Eat!"

"But Mrs. Sardello, I already had my lunch."

"But you didn't have this, little one. Come. Sit. Just try. You'll see!"

Sure enough, whatever it would be, whether fresh bread, spumoni, or anything they heaped upon me, I loved it. I knew better than to eat at my house immediately before visiting the Sardellos home to play with Joey. In those days and our neighborhood, I was benefited by the continuous warm hospitality in most of my friend's homes.

The "Steel City" of Pittsburgh, was about 15 miles downriver from Coraopolis. It had undergone significant industrial maturation since before the turn of the century and up through World War II. Most of the towns on the Ohio above and below Pittsburgh were blue collar industrial communities with rich ethnic representation including high proportions of Polish, Irish, and Italian, Black, Scots Irish and Jewish residents. Regardless of what ethic group, most of the members of each group at that time were proud to be Americans above their racial or ethnic identities. There was no use of the hyphenated "Italian-American" or other such labels in those times. People considered themselves Americans first and foremost. If they called themselves "Italians" they were referring with pride to their cultural origin.

Coraopolis lay on the south side of the Ohio. Our house sat at a special vantage point high above the valley with a view of at least 20 miles of the Ohio. In those days barges ferried iron ore and then the resulting steel up and down the river to Pittsburgh from Ambridge, Beaver Falls and other mill towns. The mills in those blue collar towns turned out a large portion of the materials that fed the growth of America's post war boom. Eventually one day I would work in one of those steel mills in our town to earn money while in college. Train tracks following the Ohio served the powerful steam locomotives shuttling coal through the valley to fuel the blast furnaces that converted the iron ore to steel. Late at night in our beds we could hear the mournful whistles of those trains signaling their progress up and down the tracks next to the Ohio. Something about the haunting tone of those far off whistles in the valley became reassuring much like the wind in the trees outside the windows of our bedroom. When Mom would tuck me in at night, those whistles would call to us.

"Mom. Where are the trains going?"

"Well Jimmy, some will go just to Pittsburgh or Ambridge and back. Others may go all the way to Cincinnati or even Chicago."

"Are those the trains you take me on sometimes?"

"Yes, Honey. Would you like to go again soon?"

"Can Totty go too?"

"Well, Totty's in school during the day. So, just you and me for now."

III.

With the exceptional panorama from our maple filled sanctuary above the valley, summer nights were especially magic. Gazing down upon the river town below and up the valley toward Pittsburgh we could see the lights of the river boats wending their way toward destinations of Morgantown, West Virginia and points south. The warm night breezes at the top of the valley gently nudged lightning bugs among the bushes in our yard as they blinked on and off signaling to one another. The odor of the peonies and roses filled the yard. Mom would put a blanket out in July or August and have us lie on our backs and look up at the stars as she told us about them. One night she explained the story of the 'Big Dipper' as the crickets lulled me to sleep on that blanket.

"Do you see those seven stars in the line over there? Here let me show you. Look over by that bright one there and then to the left."

"You mean just above the roof, Mom?"

"Yes. There's a story about them."

"Will you tell me?"

"Well, one time long, long ago there was a little girl and . . . . "

The memory of Mom telling me how a little girl showed kindness to a stranger by giving water to him with a dipper is as clear as if it were yesterday.

IV.

Across the Sewickley Bridge spanning the Ohio River from Coraopolis lay Sewickley Valley Hospital, where I was born in 1946. Sewickley was a beautiful old and relatively affluent community northwest of Pittsburgh. Coraopolis on the other hand was an industrial "river town". But Coraopolis had its' own special romance that attended a small river town in post World War II America. Its' steel mills, a few churches, blue collar neighborhoods, old school buildings and a downtown retail section provided the backdrop for the basic struggles of life that people face in all towns, small and large. And I would be there to watch and be shaped by some of them over the years of my childhood.

The haunting train whistles at night, the stars, the steady sure Ohio, the wind in the maples, the fragrance of soft grass, the valley below and all we surveyed from our home on the hill urged me as a young boy to look out beyond myself for meaning. In those days, it seemed that all was somehow interconnected and made sense. And post World War II America was flourishing with confidence and a hope for the future. As children, we learned the values and believed in the goals that most Americans shared. And we children also looked forward to the future as the maples swayed in the winds above the Ohio River Valley.

Dorothy and Tinker Bell

"Toto, I don't think we're in Kansas anymore."

— *Dorothy*

I.

"I bet Angie Monderine is taller than you Jimmy. She's taller than everybody".

"No Larry, she isn't. Let's find out. I'll stand next to her."

The warm September sun shone brightly through the open window onto the varnished oak floor of the Central Elementary School kindergarten classroom. The little girl we boys were arguing about pushed back her long wavy black hair from her eyes as she colored a picture for her mother. Squinting in the bright sunlight little Angie attempted to make a likeness of her mother's face next to an oversized rose. Rose was her mother's name. She would make a picture to please her Mom.

Miss Faucet, our Kindergarten teacher overheard the difference and stepped in. "Larry, bring me the ruler from the top of my desk" Miss Faucet ordered.

Larry went to fetch the ruler. Angie quit coloring and walked over to where I stood.

"Jimmy and Angie, stand with your backs against one another".

Miss Faucet laid the ruler across the tops of our heads and then leaned to the side and shut one eye to determine whether the ruler was level or uneven.

"Jimmy, it appears that Angie is slightly taller than you."

Defiantly I stated, "That's just because she has more hair on her head". I truly believed that.

I was prepared to argue. But Miss Faucet told us that was the end of it. She sent me to straighten up the building blocks in the corner. She let Angie get back to her coloring. Angie smiled to herself. I was troubled by the intervention of our teacher and what I considered an obvious bias on her part. In my mind, she was just taking the girl's side. Thirty eight years later on a warm May evening at a class reunion, Angie Monderine and I would recall this early episode and laugh about it together.

Central Elementary was just down the hill from our house. It was the school where my brothers and I began our formal education. In those days it seemed almost everything was either "uphill" or "downhill" in Coraopolis as in so many western Pennsylvania towns along the Ohio River. Having just begun at Central and being away from Mom for the first time in my life I was trying to prove myself. Anyway I could, I would try to prevail. That became a pattern that followed me lifelong. This early trial was important enough that I told Mom all about it when I got home.

"It's alright Jimmy" she said. "I'm sure it was Angie's hair that made her look taller."

Once I heard confirmation from Mom, it was forgotten. At least for the moment.

II.

Beginning school could have been fun. It should have been. But while Mom had tried to build it up to me, I knew better. I had heard my brothers complain regularly about school and the drudgery it served up each day. Additionally, they told me I wouldn't like it. I showed up at Central on the first day of kindergarten with a less than positive attitude.

However, I did immediately recognize some benefits to

attending school. It was a change in the role I had been playing to that point. I was no longer "The Baby Brother" at school. I was a little boy who had an identity that extended beyond our yard and my mother's protection. I was venturing out on my own. I actually liked some things about going to kindergarten. There were new toys to play with. There was the exploration of interaction with other children. There was the pride of telling my mother, father and brothers, "This is what I did today". That is if anyone other than Mom would listen. While my brothers generally discounted my adventures, my mother and sometimes father tried to encourage me. Most important to me about going to school, there was the opportunity to compete.

While there was not much overt competition in kindergarten there were games. And there were little contests between us children comparing our handiwork. There were opportunities to measure ones abilities against others. And there was running. I soon learned I could run faster than most if not all of the other kids my age. While I wouldn't gravitate much toward sports for years, I was bolstered in self-confidence knowing I could outrun anyone in my class. At least I thought I could. At the same time, while I was enduring routine bullying from my brothers at home, I enjoyed the freedom from intimidation in the sanctuary of the kindergarten classroom. It was a friendly place. It also made the weekends more fun as they offered a change of pace.

Kindergarten began to waken me to a world beyond our house and yard. And I began to understand that getting along in life had more to do with things that extended beyond affluence. There were always going to be challenges. Regardless of one's economic status, support system, even talents. Life was not easy. We had much and my father was well known and respected in our community. Very few kids had the same material advantages we did. But I learned it didn't matter. An early lesson at the age of five outside the kindergarten class room demonstrated this vividly to me.

Mom had bought me a new outfit for school. One day she dressed me in the hounds tooth shorts, a white short sleeve shirt and even a small red bow tie and suspenders. Off to kindergarten I went carrying a new 'Howdy Doody' tablet with me that I was especially proud of. I was the best dressed little boy at school that day. She dropped me off a few minutes before the bell would ring to usher us inside.

"Jimmy, don't get your new clothes dirty. Just stay up on the school porch until it's time to go in."

I didn't mind her advice. Proud of my 'Howdy Doody' tablet, I made the mistake of going down into the school yard to show it off. There was no grass on that open field. Just gravel and hard dirt. From out of no where and from behind me, one of the older kids, perhaps from fifth or sixth grade ran headlong into me from behind. I was knocked off my feet and forward, skidding on my knees and palms. He was gone in an instant not even paying attention to what he had done. I was hurt and bleeding. I began to cry. No one cared. I sat there for a moment trying to collect myself. Finally pulling myself to my feet I limped over near a tree to sit down. Regardless of how well I was dressed, who my father was, or even the status afforded by 'Howdy Doody', I learned that life could knock you down to anyone's level in an instant. And often completely unexpected.

Amazingly, as by serendipity, Mom happened to be driving back in front of the school having just finished an errand after leaving me off. She saw me. Stopping the car she scooped me up and took me home. Somehow she managed to clean me up, bandage me and have me back before much time elapsed. As she would do so often, she came to the rescue and turned what could have been a traumatic moment into one of encouragement.

III.

While there was an increasing trend toward permissiveness in post war America as promoted by the likes of Dr. Benjamin Spock and other authorities on raising children, it was not practiced in our school or our home. Though I was independent and not usually inclined to follow rules I learned something important about how to treat others from my teachers as well my parents. It was that respecting the rights of others had less to do with tolerance and more to do with self-discipline and considerate and responsible behavior toward them. Also, a strong appreciation for America and the values of hard work and self-reliance were imbued to us in those old classrooms. During the fifties I and the other children at Central began the day with a pledge of allegiance to the American flag. Prayer took place in many teachers' classrooms. "In God we trust" meant something to us. And my brothers and I were taught to treat others kids with a certain amount of dignity; especially girls.

In those times we learned about what was right with America's history and we were encouraged to be appreciative and positive about our nation's future. We were taught that decisions and actions have consequences. We learned that self-discipline combined with self-responsibility were requisite to worthwhile lives. I can still recall the face of my second grade teacher, Miss Hood emphasizing the importance of respecting the American flag and what it stood for. The gray eyes of this small thin single lady in her fifties would become steely with pride when she began to lead us each morning with, "I pledge allegiance to the flag of the United States of America . . . ".

Then there was my third grade teacher, Miss Hofaker. Miss Hofaker had suffered polio as a child and was crippled. She was barely able to walk and her legs were deformed so badly she struggled to move even with a cane. I presume she must have been in much discomfort. And she lived alone never having been married. At the time she was in her late sixties and without a car. She had to make it to school each day regardless of the weather on foot. It was painful just watching her walk. It must have been terribly uncomfortable and tiring for her. Needless to say, she was a strong woman who demonstrated great commitment to her purpose in life.

And Miss Gordon, our fourth grade teacher, a plump spinster in her fifties who not only seem to love teaching but regularly emphasized the value of daily prayer. And our sixth grade teacher, lovely Miss Larson, another single woman, though I will never understand how, with sparkling blue eyes. Like Miss Gordon, she was obviously a woman of faith. In her class we not only learned the "Three R's" but we were taught that even the written law was secondary to the responsibility we all had to our Creator. That belief and way of thinking carried great significance in the way many of us conducted our lives. At least in those years.

IV.

"Do you think Miss Reed will send us to the office if we're late?" asked the little girl as we both pressed tightly against the solid brick behind us. The old wall of Central Elementary felt warm and comforting much like the school building inside and out. The structure, having been built in the 1890's, had many edifices and arches characteristic of Victorian architecture. The covered place where Barbara Yahres and I were huddled was a natural shield from the April rain blowing diagonally before our eyes. I knew we'd make it back before class began. But because I felt a strange stirring of intrigue hovered there with my pretty classmate I wasn't ready to go back. Though just ten years old I already demonstrated strong resistance to authority including teachers, parents, and rules. Fiercely independent I saw all as impositions. I wanted to stay out of class until the last second.

Since Central was close to our homes, Barbara and I could walk home at lunch. But not together as we lived in different directions. We children would return when we heard Mr. Gossett the janitor pulling the bull rope to the large sonorous bell in the tower above the school roof, signaling ten minutes till afternoon class resumed. Barbara and I had by coincidence met that afternoon as we were walking back from lunch at our homes when the rain began.

"We'll be OK" I assured her and pressed even closer to the wall next to her. The smell of rain mixed with a fresh spring breeze encouraged me to stay outside until the last possible moment before returning to the stuffy confines of the classroom. When we did return, I watched Barbara curiously wondering why I felt such a sense of adventure being out there with her. After all, she was "just a girl" as I and my buddies often observed. At that early age we had no idea of the enormous capabilities and mysterious power of the opposite sex. A few years later, we would begin to learn.

Barbara Yahres was an enigma to me. While a boy at ten years is not often inclined to respect little girls, there was something special about Barbara that I couldn't help but admire. Smaller than most of the other girls, she had a pixie like quality combined with a tough and fearless nature that demanded admiration. She was a combination of Dorothy from 'The Wizard of Oz' and Tinker Bell from 'Peter Pan'. On one hand iron willed and courageous. On the other mischievous and full of fun.

Barbara had first earned my respect a year earlier in the fourth grade. On that January Saturday afternoon in 1955 I heard the door bell ring in our home on McCabe Avenue. Descending the stairs from my bedroom I went to the front door. Upon opening the door I was surprised to see a little girl bundled in her checkered snow suit with a sled. A wisp of light brown hair cascaded out over bright blue eyes and rosy cheeks. She looked up and without fanfare asked, "Would you like to ride sleds?"

Since she had made the decision on her own to come to my house without invitation, I couldn't help but respect her nerve. She obviously had courage. I told her yes and asked her to come in while I got my coat and sled. As I prepared, my father pulled me aside. In a hushed tone he told me that he was glad I agreed to play with her. "Jim, be nice to her, do anything she wants and let her stay as long as she likes. I can drive her home later if she likes."

When Dad spoke with any dictate, there was never any question. I determined to do anything she wanted that afternoon. We rode our 'Flexible Flyer' sleds as well as the aluminum saucer dish. She was so small we both fit in the saucer as we spun down the steep slope together in our back yard. Though we were still just children, there was some indefinable connection. At least for me. At one point she slipped out of the saucer and smacked her face against a low hanging tree limb. A trickle of blood dripped from her top lip down her chin.

"Barbara. You're bleeding."

"Oh, it'll be OK", she said as she simply scooped up a handful of fluffy snow and pressed it against the little wound until it finally ceased to ooze. There were no tears or even a frown. I was impressed by my tough little companion. If it had been me, I might have used the incident as a reason to call it an afternoon. She was undeterred.

Eventually the sun began to sink low in the west and Barbara decided it was time to go home. I told her my dad could drive her but she declined. In those days there was not often concern about security for children as it was a kinder and more civilized era than we would eventually grow up into. The hearty little girl left and I watched her tiny form eventually disappear down the hill. I realized that it had actually been fun to play with a girl. That was a fact that I would not report to my buddies. My father did telephone the Yahres home when she left to tell her mother she was on her way.

V.

By the fifth grade discord between my parents, being regularly picked upon by my brothers as well as being bored all contributed to me having trouble concentrating in class. And I was becoming more rebellious toward school. My grades were terrible and my father was by that time quite concerned. He was relentless about pressuring me on improving my poor grades and study habits. It became so bad that almost everyday I heard him coming home from work I would run to my room to avoid him. Though his intentions were in my best interest, instead of motivating me he lowered my desire to achieve at school. I resented it more than ever.

Our fifth grade teacher Miss Reed was another single woman devoted to teaching but she was different than the others. She was unusually tough and stern. I can not remember seeing Miss Reed ever smile. She had no time for nonsense of any kind and she did not hesitate to employ the paddle or her hand at the drop of a hat to any boy or girl that made the mistake of disrupting the business at hand.

At school I had some skirmishes with Miss Reed and had first hand experience with her paddle a few times. However, I was so hardened by becoming used to being disciplined by my fathers belt that even the formidable Miss Reed was not a significant threat to me. Her paddle did not begin to approach what I experienced at the hands of Dad. So, I behaved only enough to keep from having her or the principle telephone my father. But I occasionally participated in some delinquent fun in her class when the opportunity availed itself.

One kid in particular in Miss Reed's class encouraged my misbehavior. Donald Cleaver. Donald caused my parents apprehension by becoming my buddy. I suspect that his parents must have felt the same about me. While Donald eventually grew into a fine looking man, as a ten year old his appearance was comical. He had an unusually large pumpkin shaped head with very thick and short coarse brown hair; almost like the fur on a bear cub. His undersized glasses seem to perch on his nose like a bird. His ears stuck out like the handles on a loving cup and his face had some resemblance to a troll doll. And he just enjoyed acting goofy.

Among other notorious achievements, Donald originated what was to become known as the "ape call". With his mouth wide open and his eyes crossed, Donald would beat his chest like a gorilla while delivering a most bizarre sound at full volume. At my mother's first and only exposure to Donald performing this memorable act she was both horrified and amused. She managed to choke out the words,"Isn't that horrible?" before dissolving into laughter.

Donald regularly encouraged my regressive behavior, as I did him. Together in Miss Reed's class, we were a significant challenge; even for her. Often when she stepped out of the classroom for any reason, we would immediately begin shooting rubber bands at one another or perform other antics. Perhaps all of this had something to do with why I never saw Miss Reed smile at me. However, before entering her class in the fifth grade I had heard the same adjectives about her from my older brothers as they described her.

One particularly memorable event when she left the room may illustrate why Miss Reed seemed less than friendly toward me. The classroom had two poles spaced about fifteen feet apart to support the old ceiling. One afternoon when she stepped out Donald and I decided to amuse ourselves by climbing each of the poles to the ceiling. Once up there we silently performed the "ape call", using one hand for beating our chest and the other for clinging to the pole. During this impressive feat, Miss Reed just happened to re-enter the classroom. I can remember well the look in her eyes. She stared up at me at the top of the pole in disbelief. Both of her eyebrows became deeply furrowed and her dark brown eyes squinted. She was obviously not impressed or amused by what she was witnessing. Then her arm flung up at lightning speed with her finger pointing directly at me. Her hand froze for a moment and then slowly descended to where it pointed at my seat. I synchronized my slow decent down the pole with the command of her finger. I can not remember what happened after that because the memory of the heroic event far surpassed the drama of any consequence.

Barbara Yahres too even mastered the "ape call" as well as a few other inane behaviors Donald and I practiced. Occasionally Barbara would do something to gain my attention to make me laugh. Sometimes she followed me around the school yard. She would turn up when I least expected it. Possibly she was just bored and I was a good prospect by which she could amuse herself as I pretended to be annoyed by some of her antics. Actually, I liked her but was not about to let Barbara or anyone else know that. Something that especially earned Donald's and my admiration for Barbara was that while she also experienced the sting of Miss Reed's paddle, she took it like a marine. She never once shed a tear or made a sound. This can not be said for any other member of her gender who experienced the paddle of Miss Reed.

While Donald's and my grades were poor I am certain that one reason both he and I were passed on to the sixth grade, by all rights we should have held been back, was that Miss Reed had had more than enough of us that year.

VI.

In the last year at Central, the sixth grade, our teacher was Miss Larson. I suppose she was of Irish decent though her ancestors could have been from any northern European land. Though in her sixties, she was slim and still had the firm stature of a young woman. She had never been married and had no children. The features of her face were distinctive. Bright blue eyes spaced over high cheekbones. The ridge of her nose curved slightly inward toward her face. The creases accenting the corners of her mouth around her lips added definition to accent a beguiling smile. The smooth line of her jaw and chin complemented the rest of her face perfectly.

Until entering her class, my grades were the lowest they

could be and still be passed on from grade to grade. My interest in academics was for all practical purposes nonexistent. Preoccupied by the discord in our home, and being highly independent as well as daydreaming much of the time, I was a very poor student. In fact, I learned later that I had been apprised as being "slow" by the school officials as well as most of the teachers. Thankfully Miss Larson seemed to think there was more to me and she tried to encourage it. While my grades did not improve much in her class, they did rise. And with that slight rise, I began to feel a little hope that possibly I was not as lost as others seemed to think.

Miss Larson made me feel as though she believed in me. Possibly even approved of me. As a result, I would not misbehave in her class. I don't recall Donald or Barbara pulling anything either. I began to try a little harder to concentrate during the day. Less time staring out the window and more time listening to her. Especially on Friday afternoons during story hour. She would choose books of adventure and mystery to read us. Her lovely voice with inflection and pacing that brought the story to life was mesmerizing. With arms folded on the desk I would lay my head down and close my eyes imagining the stories she read on those afternoons. Occasionally I would cast a glance at Barbara. If she caught me, I'd quickly look away.

What neither I nor Barbara could imagine in those days was how quickly both of us would be leaving childhood behind when we left Miss Larson's class. In fact it would only be six short years until Barbara would be thrust into parenthood. And just four years until Dad would send me away to military school. While Barbara and I would soon fall out of touch with one another I would often remember the valiant little girl that reshaped my perspective about the "fairer sex". Eventually, after more than fifty years I would write to her about the respect she earned from me in those childhood days. I never heard back but it didn't change my appreciation for her.

The Gardener

I.

Watching the gnarled old man toil while carrying the heavy rocks, I wondered how he could work so hard in the July sun seemingly without rest. Occasionally he would stop and lift a bottle of water. Throwing his head back he'd take a drink and readjust his tattered blue engineers cap. Then he'd resume.

In that summer of 1954 much of my time was spent seeking adventure in the woods or hanging out with neighborhood kids. But when Sam Trunzo would come to work on our garden and yard, I'd often stop to watch or try to spend time with him unless Mom would redirect my attention elsewhere.

"Jim! Let Sam alone. He's got a lot of work to do and doesn't have time to pay attention to you", Mom would chide.

"Aw Mom."

"Sorry Dear. But Sam has lots to do and when he's working, you need to let him alone. Besides, he works for other people and has to go elsewhere as soon as he finishes here."

Regardless, I'd watch Sam or talk with him if I could get away with it. Funny about the old man. Though bent and worn from years of hard labor in Sicily before coming to America, he

40

seemed unusually strong and vital. And he was kind. Through broken English laced with a heavy Italian accent his blue eyes would sparkle and he'd smile and laugh often when talking with me. He called me "Jimmy". I liked to hear him say my name in his thick Sicilian brogue.

I couldn't understand much of what he'd say. But I enjoyed the sound of his voice and laughter. I suppose he was in his late sixties or maybe even seventies around the time he worked for us. Hard to tell. A deformity caused a hump between his shoulder blades. He stood maybe five and a half feet. I don't know whether it was natural or whether the years of hard physical labor caused the back condition. He reminded me of Charles Laughton's characterization of Quasimodo in 'The Hunchback of Notre Dame'. His hands and fingers were crooked and his arms looked like bull ropes. Regardless of his age, he was a tough and sturdy old man. However, his handling of the flowers and bushes when tending the garden indicated much gentleness in a man who had a deep love for natural beauty.

He'd talk to the flowers occasionally as he tended to them. Sometimes I'd hear him singing quietly in Italian as he worked. I recall a scene of him working in the garden when there was a family of chipmunks in the stone wall and terraced flower bed he built for us. They would come out and scout around or watch as he worked. I wondered why they weren't afraid of him. In fact, Dad called the chipmunks "The Trunzos" after Sam. Dad had a name for almost everything and everyone. Even the animals around our home.

II.

In our small steel mill town of Coraopolis, there were a lot of Italians. There were other distinct ethnic groups as well with Polish, Irish and western European heritages. But when I was a small boy the Italians seemed the most fascinating. They were passionate. They were colorful. And they dominated much of the culture of the town in which I spent my boyhood. In many ways, their life style was 'old world'. They were proud to be Americans but held to traditions and cultural mores and values from where they or their parents originated in Italy. Sam was no exception.

Sam was from southern Sicily. I'm not certain how long he'd been in the United States by the time he worked for us. I vaguely recall my mother saying something about him coming over before the war. His wife had passed away and he had relatives in Pittsburgh that encouraged him to come to Western Pennsylvania with his two small children. A girl and a boy. By the time Sam became our gardener his daughter was in her late twenties. Her name was Andria and she was lovely with her black hair and olive skin. Sam's son Mike was married and had a little girl. And Sam was obviously devoted to Mike, Andria and his grand daughter.

The old man lived alone in a hovel close to the Ohio River in Coraopolis fifteen miles upriver from Pittsburgh. But as with so many Italian families, he had a close bond with his relatives and children. He often spent holidays with his family in the area. The Catholic traditions including regular attendance at Mass and prayer to the saints were deeply held traditions of Sam and his family. There's no way of knowing how much faith he really had. Regardless, even above his faith, our dad told us that his children were the most important thing to Sam.

III.

Across the river from Coraopolis lay Sewickley. Sewickley was another river town but did not have steel mills. It was an older community than Coraopolis with more affluent residents. There were very few Italians there. But one of the few was Mario Genovese. Mario and his wife and three children lived just off the Ohio River Boulevard a mile north of the Sewickley Bridge. By coincidence, Andria Trunzo met Mario one

February evening at a Sons of Italy event they both attended in Coraopolis.

"Hey, Andria, come here! I want you to meet someone" called Mary Castalone, one of Andria's friends.

"Come here. Come here. Andria, this is Mario Genovese. He's the gentleman I told you about that might be able to help you find a new job. Mario has lots of friends. You remember me mentioning him?"

"Oh, yes. Hello, Mario. I'm pleased to meet you", Andria said smiling shyly at him.

The wavy haired Genovese extended his palm to take Andria's hand and he nodded politely. His dark eyes gazing at Andria, he said, "Hello Andria. The pleasure is mine."

The two spoke for a few minutes and Mario danced with Andria. Later he got Andria's phone number and told her he'd check with his friends to see if they may be helpful in finding her a job. And in fact he did just that the following week. An interview led to a new job for Andria and she wanted to thank Mario. One thing led to another and within a few weeks, Andria had become involved with the handsome married man.

Though the two attempted to be discreet, the affair did not escape the wary eye of the gossips as well as her father. When Sam first learned about the affair, he was heart broken. The first thing he did was attempt to talk with Andria about it to see if she would end it at his urging. In fact Sam spoke with his daughter more than once attempting to discourage her from seeing Genovese. But it was to no avail.

Finally realizing he was wasting his time pleading with his daughter, Sam went looking for Mario to discuss the matter. Sam knew that Mario frequented Segnari's Bar and Grill on State Avenue in Coraopolis almost every Friday night. So, he surprised Mario one night in front of Segnari's. Sam had parked his car down the street from the bar and waited for

Mario to come out. As Mario walked toward Sam's car, the old man got out and walked up to him.

"Do you know who I am?" asked Sam

"I do", responded the younger man.

"You must stay away from my daughter. Go home and be a good father to your children and a decent man to you wife", Sam exhorted Mario.

Mario said nothing. He just stared at Sam for a few moments. Then he smiled and nodded his head walking away.

"I'm not going to tell you again!" Sam called out.

Mario continued seeing Andria despite the warning. Upon learning of the confrontation Andria was furious that her father had talked with Mario. She became rebellious toward the old man.

"Papa! How could you think it would be right to intrude into my personal life?"

"Your personal life is our personal life. Each of us is part of the same family!"

"No Papa. My life is my life. I'm a grown woman! You don't understand and this is not your business."

"I do understand! I understand you are involved with a man who has a wife and three children. What kind of a man would betray his own family in such a way?"

"Again I tell you, you don't know him and don't understand. Please stay out of my business. I know what I'm doing."

"My daughter. Since you were first born your mother and I have built everything around you and your brother. What do you think she would say about this if she were here?"

"She is not here. You must stay out of this and let things go as they will!"

"I tell you now Andria that if things continue it will all come to no good. I tell you . . . . No, I warn you that I love you too much to stand aside and watch you ruin your life."

It was reported later by Sam's cousin Carmen in Pittsburgh

that Sam became distraught with it all. He loved his daughter dearly. He could see that eventually there would be terrible pain and consequences for her. And of course, there was the disgrace for all concerned.

In the Sicily where Sam was born and raised there were basic values and mores that focused upon defending the honor of families. Those mores often came before legal recourse or action in the old world customs. Sam was a product of that way of life. Though now in America, Sam was still a Sicilian. He was not above recognizing the need to take matters into ones own hands if necessary to protect family.

Driving back to his small shack by the Ohio River on one dark rainy April evening after leaving Andria, Sam's mind was filled with chaos. And his eyes were filled with tears. As the windshield wipers dashed back and forth sweeping away the water from the windshield he thought about how his daughter would be doomed by her relationship with the married man. He thought about the children of the dishonorable father and what effect this would all have upon them not to mention his wife. Sam thought about how the honor of Andria and the Trunso family was being disgraced. Since Andria refused to do right and apparently could not help herself, Sam knew he had no option but to do the most honorable thing. And to him, Sicilian ways defined honor. The results of such action would likely bring grave consequences to him personally. But he was not important in the scheme of things. His daughter and the honor of the family was what mattered most.

IV.

A few nights later while hunched uncomfortably on a large stone in the dark bushes near his daughter's apartment house, the old man turned the cold steel revolver over and over in his hands. Racing through his mind were memories of his baby girl and her mother many years earlier in Sicily. He also considered what may happen in the eternal when his daughter

45

would eventually face her creator and answer for her actions. But mostly, he thought of how Mario Genovese had dishonored him and ultimately the Trunzo family by ignoring his pleading to stay away from Andria.

The May night was humid and hot. Perspiration formed on the old man's hands. The smell of juniper was heavy in the air. Occasionally the headlights of a lone car would come down Sycamore Street and then pass the apartment house. Waiting in the dark the anxious father remembered waiting in the parlor of their former home in Italy while his daughter was being born twenty nine years earlier.

Eventually a car slowed to a stop near the walk up to the steps entering the house. Sam pressed lower in his hiding place. Looking though the branches of the bushes he could make out the forms of a man and women getting out of the car but he was not able to determine who they were. Then he recognized Andria's voice.

The couple walked up the steps that went to the apartment. While they were inside, Sam was anxious but became more resolved to do what he must. As he waited for the man to come out, anger and a mixture of sadness overcame him. Again, the thoughts of his child and what must be done to protect her dominated his mind and his emotions. The memory of the look on Mario's face, not taking him serious when Sam spoke to him also played upon his mind.

Eventually the door opened and he heard someone step out onto the front porch and descend the stairs. Sam could see it was the man he had been waiting for. The stiffness in his joints and muscles slowed Sam as he stood and walked around from behind the bushes to face the man. At first Mario did not recognize Sam. But when he did, he attempted to speak.

"Sam, I'm surprised to see you. What have you . . . "

But before he could finish his sentence, Mario froze and became silent as Sam slowly raised the revolver from his side. Mario's eyes opened wide and he began to tremble uncontrollably as Sam pointed the gun at his face. Mario raised his hands and tried to speak. But no words came. Before anymore sound came from his lips, a shot exploded from the muzzle of the .38 caliber pistol. The bullet entered under Mario's left eye and existed through the back of his neck. Then even before he fell, another shot. The second bullet slammed into Mario's chest directly through his heart and lodged in his spine. Mario dropped to his knees and then fell sideways with one arm twisted under his limp body. For a moment, Sam stood over the lifeless form. He looked down at the prostrate figure not certain what to do next.

As lights came on in the apartment house and across the street, Sam turned and walked away quickly. His path proceeded around the back of the apartment house into the dark and then he took the dimly lit sidewalk to the next block. Sam stopped and put the revolver into his pocket then hurried away from the scene breathing hard and trying not to look back. He soon came to his antiquated Ford two door. Proceeding up the Ohio River Boulevard in the car, Sam drove a few miles to a pier where he got out and threw the revolver overhand like a baseball into the black waters of the Ohio River.

V.

It was not even twenty four hours from the time of the murder that detectives brought Sam's son Mike in for questioning. One wily detective informed Mike that he was a suspect for the murder of Mario Genovese. During questioning, the fearful son broke and told the detectives that it was his father who had committed the murder. And then shortly there was a warrant issued for Sam's arrest.

When Sam learned that Mike was under suspicion, even without knowing that his son had already fingered him for the crime, Sam drove himself to the Coraopolis police department and turned himself in. Later, the news accounts in the Pittsburgh Post Gazette and other area newspapers reported that Sam was not angered by the betrayal of his son. Sam also showed no remorse for the crime. I can still recall the photograph of Sam in the newspaper after the indictment. The bright flash of the news photographer's cameras made the old man's face look almost white. His arms were stretched out with the palms face up. The caption, a quote of Sam's under the picture read "What else could a father do?" I cried when I saw the photograph. The old man who was so kind to me looked like a trapped animal in the picture.

The trial proceeded as expected. There was no serious defense for the aged Sicilian. Only that as a loving father who had warned Mario Genovese and pleaded often with his daughter, he finally decided he must risk sacrificing himself for the sake of his child. When Sam stood to face the judge for pronouncement of the verdict and sentence, he looked directly into the other man's face. As Judge Reinhardt passed the life sentence on Sam he added,

"I have great regret having to pass this sentence on you Mr. Trunzo. It is the regret that I am not passing sentence on the person who is most responsible for this tragedy."

Sam stood solid. He nodded and then looked toward his daughter Andria. She looked down and did not make eye contact with her father. Her brother Mike stood next to her weeping silently. One of the Trunzo family later told my father that Sam believed to the end of his life that he did the honorable thing in the interest of his daughter. He also believed that ultimately his daughter's soul would be spared though his own may be condemned. He would leave that matter up to God. In his mind, in his world, Sam had simply done what a respectable father must do under the circumstances.

Epilogue

Sam Trunzo was spared having to serve out his life sentence in prison at Western Penitentiary in Pittsburgh where most similar criminals were incarcerated. Instead, he was assigned for life to the Allegheny County Workhouse. There his regular job was to tend to the grounds and gardens around the facility. His children and relatives were able to visit him regularly. Sam passed away quietly in his sleep within three years of entering the facility. By his bed were the faded photographs of his children and their mother from earlier and happier days in Sicily.

The Tigers

I.

"Hey kid! What's your name?" inquired a voice from behind me. I pretended not to have heard him.

"Hey kid. Can't you hear?"

I was intimidated but knew I couldn't ignore the voice. I turned to look at the older boy and said, "Jim. What's yours?"

The dark haired boy in the tattered jeans and grey jacket responded, "Jackie Conflentti. I think my dad knows your dad."

Just aged nine, and at little league baseball tryouts only because my father mandated my attendance, I was to say the least, a little uncomfortable. Or better stated, I was just plain scared. I was scared I wouldn't do well. Or that a bully would decide to have some fun at my expense. And most ominously, I was scared my dad would be disappointed in whatever the outcome of it all might be.

The scent of moist spring grass on that early evening was mixed with the distinct odor of the leather of my new baseball glove held closely to my chest. The glove Dad had brought home for me earlier that day. As I stood around with the other boys waiting to be put through fielding or batting drills, I thought about what Dad told me before leaving.

"Jim, look alive out there tonight. You might become a ball player in time if you pay attention and learn."

Over the past year Dad had been taking my brother Totty and I out and throwing ball with us as well as giving us plenty of batting practice. Being three years younger and smaller than Totty at that time, I thought I looked pitiful next to him. And I did. Totty had already proven himself to be a good athlete. He was a natural. And I simply didn't like sports. I was reluctant to participate. My interests were more along the lines of building and flying model airplanes. Or climbing trees and exploring the woods. Or playing with my chemistry set. Anything but sports.

I lacked confidence. I was just "the little brother". The role I had learned as the youngest of three boys in our household. Whether it came to being pushed around, or left behind when the others went on their adventures, or just being considered a bit of a nuisance, I was not taken seriously. As a result, I didn't have much confidence in myself or what I was capable of. And that carried directly over into this first experience in organized sports.

Jackie Conflentti was a threat to me whether he meant to be or not. Any boy a little older or bigger or just appearing more confident was a threat. So, my first season in little league baseball was a chore more than anything. I had been assigned to tryout for the Cardinals that first year. The Cardinals manager knew I was Dr. Anderson's son and Totty Anderson's "little brother." My dad was a respected and important man in our town. I was going to get a chance. But it didn't matter to me. I didn't want it. But whether I wanted it or not I was overruled. So I would endure.

It was cool that April evening in 1955 at the stadium atop the hill over looking Coraopolis. I zipped up my red wind breaker jacket as there was a light breeze and I felt chilled. Soon I stood in a line waiting to field ground balls being hit to each of us during the tryout drills. One boy, Joey Cardeman was not doing real well when his turn came and a couple of the boys laughed at him. Joey was in my fourth grade class. Joey had a hare lip that affected his speech and he was smaller than most of the others. But he just glared at those laughing at him. I could see he was going to be OK. He was a fighter.

A few times I let some other boys cut in front of me in order to spare myself the humiliation of what I feared might happen when my turn came. One boy, Bo Bozetti cut in twice. Bo was a good athlete and I knew he'd make the team with no problem. When my turn finally did come I made my best effort and though not looking real sharp, I was able to keep from being laughed at by the others. Bo even said "Good job" one time to me when I caught a hard low grounder on the first bounce.

Later that night I was informed that I wasn't going to be cut and would remain a Cardinal. As a result I ended up struggling through my first baseball season and spent almost every minute of every game sitting on the bench in the dugout. Occasionally the coach would put me in the game. As a token of respect for Dr. Anderson. During that season I hoped that Dad would let me off the hook eventually and I wouldn't have to participate the following year. I was wrong.

II.

The next spring in 1956 when Dad took me out to practice with one of his friend's sons a discovery was made. It was that I could throw a baseball fast and with control. In fact I could pitch better than most boys my age. And I could also hit well. I had more athletic ability than I had realized. While I'd still prefer to fly model airplanes, I was becoming a little more comfortable with baseball. Though I only participated because my father wanted me to, baseball had become more bearable.

Dad's friend, Hiram Carpenter, had a son. The boy was in my class but was smaller than me. But "Hiram Carpenter the Third" as he often referred to himself was a good little ball player. He was also smart and competitive. And little Hiram had something I had not yet developed. He had confidence. Being an only son he had no bigger brothers to pick on him. And his father continuously encouraged him. Hiram had no issues with self esteem.

Hiram Carpenter the Third was also a pitcher. And as it turned out, the boy became a blessing to me. He ignited something in me that would help me gain more interest in wanting to play baseball well. It was competition. I didn't want to let Hiram best me when we were out practicing together with our dads. He tried. And during that second year of little league baseball, I definitely did not want Hiram to be recognized as a better pitcher than me.

That year at the age of ten, I had been placed on the "Pirates" managed by a man named Slim Brenhiesen. Slim was a lanky figure with thin disheveled hair that kind of jutted back. He had a wild look about him. His rimless glasses were always a little lopsided and he almost continuously looked displeased. I had overheard my parents discussing quietly that Slim had become too good a friend with "the bottle". But in those days a lot of folks in our little town did. Slim also had a temper. I was uncomfortable around him. I wished they'd left me on the Cardinals that year.

Slim and my dad went way back to their childhoods together in Coraopolis. For some reason that I never learned, Slim had an issue with my father. Not enough that they wouldn't speak. But there was something going on between them that I never discovered. While Slim's brother Babe was a good friend of Dad's, and they got along well, Slim and Dad just didn't get along very well.

For much of the season that year on Slim's team, I again rode the bench in the dugout. At one point I heard Dad question Slim, "How is Jim doing, Slim?"

"Well Doc", Slim replied, "He's OK and I'm planning on letting him get some time on the mound real soon."

However, I didn't get to pitch at all that year. The few times I was put in the game it was in the outfield. I don't believe I ever caught a fly ball in a game that year. Thankfully my dad didn't blame me. In fact he was supportive and told me I was capable of playing well if I got the chance. He didn't indict

Coach Brenhiesen overtly. But I knew he thought Slim should be playing me and for some reason, he wasn't. Regardless I sat in the dugout and dreamed about my airplanes, or the soap box racer I was building or just about anything but baseball.

III.

At the beginning of my third and last season in little league baseball, Dad pulled some strings. I don't know who he talked to or what he did, but I was no longer playing for Slim Brenhiesen on the Pirates. I had been traded to the Tigers managed by John DiCicco. I don't think Dad interceded in any way in respect to whether I'd get to play or not. Just that I was no longer on the Pirates. I was glad.

By the time the season got under way, Coach DiCicco had selected me as one of the three starting pitchers in the rotation. Hiram Carpenter was one as well. So, I had dependable little Hiram there to spur me on to do my best because I was still competing with him. I now had a coach that liked me and some small measure of confidence in my arm. When I didn't pitch, I played center field in every game as I could throw reliably to home plate from deep in the field. I finally felt OK about baseball and was actually having some fun.

One evening before a game early that season I overheard a conversation between my parents.

"Raymond, are you going to be home for dinner tonight?" my mother asked.

"No. I'm going to dinner with Vic Lamark at Riddle's. It's been awhile since he and I have seen one another."

Vic had been one of my dad's closest friends while at the University of Pittsburgh. They had both been star athletes in the Pittsburgh area and as a result had an unusually good bond from the "old days."

"You know, Jimmy has a game tonight Raymond. Do you think you and Vic will go?"

"I wouldn't miss this one."

My mother asked quizzically, "This sounds important. What is it?"

"I think Jim is going to Pitch against Slim Brenhiesen's team tonight. I don't want to miss this. And I want Vic there to see Jim as well."

I thought about what I just heard. I actually hoped Dad wouldn't show up that night. Though I believed I'd pitch OK, I knew I couldn't guarantee my team would play well and I sure didn't want to have Slims' team beat us in front of Dad and his good friend Vic. How I looked in front of my father had become a dominating theme for me. I desperately wanted his approval but I seemed to never earn it. Unfortunately that theme carried across into many other aspects of my life. It often stifled my potential because I became so anxious around Dad I often made mistakes. I hoped I could overcome it that night if he and Vic showed up.

IV.

While warming up my pitching arm with Rusty Tucker my catcher before the game with the Pirates, I looked in the stands and couldn't see Dad anywhere. I was a little relieved. Coach DiCicco came over to me and said. "How you feeling Jim? You ready to go?"

"Yep. I think I'd like to beat the Pirates more than just about anything tonight."

The coach gave a wry smile and asked "Why's that son?"

I couldn't think of anything to say. So, I just shrugged.

The Pirates took the field first that night. There was no score by us and I was soon walking out to the pitcher's mound to begin my work. When I still didn't see Dad, I thought, "This is gonna be OK. Regardless of what happens all I need to do is to pitch my best and then let things turn out they way they will." I was relaxed and confident.

The first inning went well as the Pirates were retired quickly without a hit. Neither team had scored by the fourth inning.

However, as I stepped on the mound to begin the fifth inning I noticed a large familiar form in the stands in the distance. Sure enough it was Dad. Apparently he and his friend Vic had slipped in sometime without my detection. I wondered how long he had been there. My reaction was predictable. I became anxious. In fact I became quite nervous. At that time I had a compulsive habit of blinking my eyes hard when I was worried or restless. The blinking went into overdrive at that point.

"C'mon Andy. Strike 'em out", called the loud flat voice of John Tussey, our short stop. John was a good infielder and I liked him but he had perhaps the most annoying voice I'd ever heard. Kind of like a squeaky steel wheel on an old wheel burrow. I wished he'd be quiet. He was distracting me.

However, my pitching stayed consistent. The Pirates were retired again without a score in the fifth inning.

Sitting in the dugout waiting for my turn at bat, I could hear Slim. He was beginning to get a little angry with the performance of his Pirates. I couldn't make out everything he said. Just the tone in his voice. I'd heard that tone before and it was not pleasant or encouraging. It made me thankful I was no longer on his team. Coach DiCicco while firm was always supportive and encouraging to us. I liked playing for him.

Then it became my turn at bat. As I walked out to the plate I heard something that angered my eleven year old psyche. It was Coach Brenhiesen yelling to his pitcher.

"Ritchie! Strike this guy out. He's can't hit. You can handle him."

"He can't hit?" I repeated to myself. A former coach of mine and a supposed life long acquaintance of my dad had just said I couldn't hit! And Dad and Coach DiCicco and my teammates all heard it. I could feel my face flush as anger consumed me. I stopped and took a deep breath before stepping up to the plate. I completely forgot about my father with his friend in the stands. I forgot everything but what I had just heard from

Slim. At that point I was not exhibiting the nervous blinking. Just a cold stare.

Their catcher was signaling to the pitcher as I saw him nodding back from the mound before winding up. His first pitch was definitely outside. But the umpire called it a strike. "A strike!" I thought to myself indignantly. But that errant call was good for me. It converted my anger to cool determination. I became completely focused upon the baseball in his hand. I rotated the bat a few times and crouched a little as the pitcher wound up again. I squinted my eyes and clenched my teeth. After fifty years I can still see that pitch coming. It was a beautiful throw right down the alley, just a little high as it flew directly in.

My left foot lifted automatically as I prepared to swing. Both arms and shoulders rotated so hard swinging the bat that my body followed almost as an afterthought. I heard a solid "crack" as the bat connected squarely slightly below the center of the ivory colored ball. The shock from the contact of the bat reverberated through my wrists. For an instant before I began to run for first base I caught sight of the ball. I knew immediately there was no need to run hard. As it cleared high above the centerfield fence flying toward the Ohio River a couple of kids took off to find it. Leisurely rounding the bases I noticed a gull above the field. For a moment I became detached from myself and even the game. I imagined how the field and fans and me trotting around the diamond below must look to the gull as he surveyed us.

My mind came back to the game as I crossed home plate. I lowered my head but glanced to the side toward Coach Brenhiesen. I saw that his faced was red. He was mumbling something softly and shook his head as he stood by his team's dugout. It was then that I remembered my dad was there. I shyly retired to the dugout. We got no other runs in that inning. Soon I was again headed out to the pitcher's mound.

Then I heard my antagonist prompting his team. Because

of the close proximity of the dugouts, it was easy to hear Slim. He called his first three hitters for the inning over to him. I heard him say in an angry tone, "Listen one of you is going to hit a homerun now. I want you to unload on everything he throws that is even close to a strike!"

Though I was just a boy of eleven, something in his tone of voice and the words he spoke made me feel much older. I realized I was getting to him. I also liked knowing that the batters would be swinging hard instead of smart. I had forgotten about Dad again. Determination filled me once more. Slim had managed to awaken a strong urge to prevail. Not only against the Pirates. But mostly against him.

That first batter was Jimmy Teamor, a "long ball" hitter. I decided to throw to him low and inside where he would not have a chance to loft one over the fence. I was surprised that he fanned the air on each pitch I threw. Three strikes in a row! Slim had scared him enough to just swing that bat with everything he had without measuring the flight of the ball. That bolstered my confidence. One down. "Who's next?" I wondered.

It was their pitcher Ritchie Adams's turn to bat. I knew he would do his best to even the score. The competitive nature in me was now raging and I wanted to stop him cold. However, as soon as that first pitch to Ritchie left my hand I knew it was bad. It was going to be high and outside. A perfect spot to either knock the cover off the sphere or let the umpire call it a "ball". In his zeal to slam it, he leaned across the plate and swung furiously. His bat was not even close to the ball as Rusty pulled it in. "Whew! Thank you!" I said silently to myself. He let me off the hook on that one.

My next pitch would be a curve low and to the inside. Amazingly it did just that and he fanned it again. Slim was now furious behind his dugout. "Ritchie! What are you doing?" he screamed. The umpire called a timeout and walked over to

Slim. He said something quietly to the skinny irate figure that just stood there and ignored him.

I was now enjoying myself. My next pitch was a fast ball. Ritchie swung hard again. This time he almost connected. In fact it appeared that he would. But the solid thump of the baseball in the catcher's mitt confirmed he was headed back to take his seat on the pines in their silent dugout.

This was all perplexing to me. I had never seen anyone throw six strikes in a row let alone with a swing on every one of them. Not even Harold Dickerson, the best pitcher and athlete in our league. I wondered if I was I dreaming. The ball park lights came on. I stared up at them for a moment. It was not even close to being dark. Why were those lights coming on? Then I realized I was losing my focus. The lights reminded me, *It's time to get back to pitching.*

The third batter stepped up to the plate. As soon as I saw him I thought "*Oh no. Slim changed the batting order*". It was their catcher Bo Bozetti. Bo was my age. He was also a superior athlete and their best hitter. He was the one who had cut in line at tryouts when I first began little league that night in April two years earlier. And he was left handed and batted left which made it harder to pitch to him. Again I realized I was losing focus.

As he stood in the batters box, Bo's face was all business as he looked me directly in the eye. His stare just made me feel defiant. There was a genuine grudge match going on now. But it was not between me and Bo. It was between me and Slim. Bo was incidental to the situation.

I stood still deliberately for a moment before the wind up. I looked into the eyes of my catcher Rusty Tucker. Rusty was black. Or actually dark copper colored. But his eyes were light green. I'd never seen a black person with light colored eyes. Those eyes were not the kind you forget. Though that night was long ago I can still see him looking directly at me smiling and signaling "fast ball". I wound up and let go with everything in my arm. Bo swung so hard that he spun completely around after missing the ball. He then stepped back from the plate for a moment. Slim was now quiet while rapidly passing a baseball back and forth between both hands.

Stepping back into the box Bo rotated his bat menacingly. I ignored Rusty's signal for another fast ball. I knew Bo would expect that. Instead I attempted a "slider" as we called it in those days. I mishandled the pitch and it "floated" in toward Bo. "*Uh oh*", I thought. "*This one's going for a ride!*" But no, Bo somehow swung low underneath it! "*How did that happen?*" I thought. I again wondered if I was dreaming.

Now Bo didn't budge from the box. He knew the next pitch might be his last chance. And by the look on his face, one of detachment, I guessed he would measure the pitch carefully and simply try to connect with it not caring whether it exited the park or not. I deliberated on what I should throw now that he had come to his senses. Then at that precise moment a familiar voice called out of the stands. It was calm and firm. It was the kind of voice that "carried" and did not need to attempt to yell above the crowd. Just about anywhere and anytime, when this man spoke everyone could hear him.

"OK Tamulkey. Just put it in there."

Dad's special name for me was "Tamulkey". How he ever came up with that, my brothers, mother and I never figured out. And when asked he never explained.

That calm voice was welcome. How I wished I had heard it much more in my childhood. For the moment it dispatched the "little brother" role that I carried. In that moment, I felt briefly that Dad believed in me.

Meanwhile Rusty was madly signaling curve ball. In my typically obstinate manner I overruled my catcher with a decision to throw fast and inside. That would force Bo to swing early and hard when he saw it coming.

I wound up slowly. Bo looked confident. I swung my arm high over my head so hard in the downward arc that I slipped slightly off the mound. Like being fired from a sling the ball shot out of my hand fast and high. I saw Bo lift his right foot to bring the bat around. The ball appeared to be heading level with his chest. At the last instant, the ball began to drop! Bo's bat completed the swing beautifully with almost picturesque form. The only thing that wasn't perfect about that swing was that it only slashed the air.

As the umpire dramatically thrust his hand out with three fingers extended and yelled "Steeerike!" in Slim's direction Rusty jumped to his feet with a loud "Alright" that rivaled the volume of the umpire. You would have thought we had won the World Series.

V.

I don't recall there being any more scoring in the game against the Pirates that June evening in 1957. I know that we won. But I can't remember any more details after the dreamlike inning.

Then ironically after the game something very important occurred. Something that impressed a lesson on me that shaped how I would try to conduct myself in sports and in life from then on. Slim walked over to me and congratulated me on my play.

That one gesture by the skinny wild eyed man changed my impression of him for the rest of my life. It taught me that regardless of former experience with a person, it was possible for a single statement or gesture to undo everything that came before. Whether for good or bad. It taught me about the value of good sportsmanship. I learned that the willingness to congratulate your opponent even in defeat places the trials of competition and life in perspective. If a man can rise above defeat whether in sports or any other endeavor and still congratulate his opponent, he has something in him that is never defeated regardless of outcomes. I'm thankful for Slim even today.

The Wonder Years

I.

The three story gray brick building had been constructed in the late 1940's. Its' modern looking 'L' shaped floor plan set it distinctly in the 20th century as opposed to Victorian Central Elementary School sitting immediately next to it but still residing in the 19th century. At the age of twelve in 1958 I entered Coraopolis Junior High School. Because the two buildings were adjacent to one another, there was no change in the walk to get to school each day after I finished Central to begin junior high. I could still run to the building in under five minutes in the fall, slide down the icy sidewalk in winter, and leisurely stroll home in the spring time. However, something about this new phase of my education was very different.

A boy could no longer feel like a child at CJHS as grades 7 through 9 take him from age twelve to fourteen. Much of what happened in those transition years would cause wonder about developing personal identity as well as open new and mysterious facets of life. These same issues were addressed in a television program from the late 1980's titled 'The Wonder Years'. In the program the main character, a boy entering his teens, struggles with his role with family and friends, puberty, as well as facing challenges of early manhood. So in seventh grade at CJHS the focus and roles of us boys became dramatically different as our teenage years unfolded.

And there were the girls. Already ahead of boys in maturation and gaining a distinct and mystifying advantage. Their sex in grade school had put them at a disadvantage.

Earlier ignored or often even scorned by boys, they now were gaining the upper hand in at least one respect. They had acquired a certain mystical power. They could not be ignored. In fact, they often became the center of focus of many boys. And because they were generally quicker to recognize this advantage in those years, a number of them knew how to manage us better than we could handle them.

Now, certain girls who were earlier overlooked, were in a position where they could dole out attention if they chose to any a number of eager boys. A beautiful little girl named Barbara Yarhes became in eighth grade one in this enviable position. By the time she reached age thirteen, as the line from the song 'Gigi' described, her sparkle had turned to fire. She had become very popular. Along with her there were the others such as Wendy Vance, Polly Ebbs and Nancy Heinlein that commanded attention by simply walking by a crowd of boys clutching their books to their chests without having to say a word. It was down right annoying if not intriguing.

I had no sisters and the dynamic between my father and mother was not positive so I had no frame of reference in respect to how to treat or relate to a member of the opposite sex. Not only was I completely in the dark in respect to communicating with them, but I was totally ill-equipped to attempt to understand or communicate with them. And this became a problem; because I liked them. In fact I liked one of them a lot. That was the girl whose older sister would eventually marry my brother. She was Wendy Vance.

I first took serious note of Wendy in the seventh grade. It began when she had to get up out of her seat and write a sentence on the chalkboard in Miss Jacob's English class. Wendy wore a plaid one piece sleeveless dress that extended to just below her knees. With her back to the class, reaching above shoulder level to write on the board this was the first time I took serious note of how girls were constructed differently than boys. The narrow waist, first indications of curves and

63

long blond hair swaying as she wrote made a strong impression upon me. And her unusually pretty face with sparkling bright blue eyes made her a knockout. Physically I can't say she aroused any feelings of manhood as I was still in the latency stage of development. But she definitely stirred something. I was simultaneously interested and intimidated.

If I passed Wendy in the hall on the way to any class I would pretend to not notice her. If I did she might have smiled and said "Hi". In the event that were to happen I was convinced that whatever I would do it would probably demonstrate to her what a klutz I was. Maybe I would trip or walk into someone else or who knows what. So while I secretly admired her and in fact thought much about her, I avoided her. Besides, she always had a boyfriend at least two years older and I knew I could not compete with any of them. So all during seventh grade I suffered in silence while attracted to Wendy but believing she'd never be attracted to me. Years later I would learn that she liked me more than I realized. But in seventh grade she was something I simply longed but didn't yet understand and couldn't have.

II.

Due to complete boredom with school I became susceptible to any diversion in any class. My grades reflected this fact and that eventually would result in me being shipped off to military school by the age of fifteen. But in the meantime, I was to endure three years of CJHS before Dad had finally decided to try something different with me. While I was slightly more serious than I had been in grade school, I was still uninterested enough to either daydream incessantly or participate in any manner of nonsense with other students if they were game.

One spring afternoon during the eighth grade in Mr. Wilfong's history class I was ripe for a few laughs. Just Mr. Wilfong himself was enough to make a person chuckle. We called him "Willie". He was a gaunt serious looking young man with a perpetual frown etched into his face. I can't blame him for frowning as he had to be frustrated with what he was doing with his life. Especially with kids like me and some of my buddies to contend with on a daily basis. He had a deep baritone voice that sounded like it should come from a man at least twice his weight and I suspect he weighed no more than 125 pounds fully clothed, fed and soaking wet.

As with almost all my classes, I sat in the back of the classroom. On my left was Alice Wells and immediately in front of me was Marjorie Brown. These two young ladies were always amusing and I could not resist having fun with them whenever I could. Alice had a natural comical look about her without even trying. She was perhaps 4'10" in height and seemed almost as wide. Her round face was ebony with a disproportionate large smile, puffy cheeks and unusually white teeth to offset her skin. Her hair went straight up and back. Kind of like dark brown straw. She had a wonderful sense of humor and was unusually skilled in making amusing faces. She was just pure fun and I liked her. Marjorie brown had a pretty and happy face. She and Alice often worked as a duo in evoking mischief with each other or me. Her deep brown skin and large brown eyes were almost continuously accented by a smile and dimples. She was just a great girl that I enjoyed kidding around with.

On this particular day we were responsible for written reports and were required to come to the front of the class to read them. Prior to being my turn to go before the class to read my report, Alice, Marjorie and I had been whispering one liners about other students as they gave their reports or poking fun at one another and even Willie. Of course we did this quietly but occasionally Willie would turn around to glare at us when our giggling reached his ears. By the time it was my turn to face the class and read my report, Alice and Marjorie had me firmly ensconced in a mood of complete silliness.

So just to be different, instead of carrying my report up

in my hand I had managed to fold it into a tight wad of approximately two inches by two inches and stuffed it in the pocket of my shirt under my sweater. I swaggered to the front of the class attempting to suppress laughter and at the same time stifle at least two natural urges that often attend thirteen-year old boys shortly after a large lunch. As I turned to face the class I made the grievous error of glancing back at Alice Wells before extracting the report from my pocket. Alice was ready for me. She mustered a loony face that immediately had its desired effect. I broke up laughing. I tried mightily to regain my composure as Willie stared at me in disbelief. But I just stood there laughing.

At the same time I attempted to pull out and unfold the wad of my report. As I fumbled with the paper, it tore in half. Upon witnessing the absurd spectacle, Mr. Wilfong uttered with complete disgust, "Sit down Anderson!" I stumbled back to my seat laughing without ever reading a word of the report. If I recall correctly, I pulled a solid "D" in Mr. Wilfong's class that year. Poor Mr. Wilfong. Later I would regret making a mockery of his class that afternoon. I often wonder how many years he lasted in teaching. He was only in his late twenties at the time of contending with me, Alice and Marjorie.

III.

Dad had a name for everyone. Many of those names were not flattering. In fact they were downright demeaning in some cases. However, they were usually well founded upon some characteristic or mannerism of the person he tagged. In the case of Jimmy Miller, or "Cement Head" as christened by Dad, the name did seem to fit. Jimmy was a good kid and always meant well. But unfortunately he seemed to be accident prone, as well as a purveyor of accidents that happened to others in close proximity to him. While still in the eighth grade at CJHS I became one of those unlucky victims. And unfortunately the accident had a lifelong detrimental impact upon me.

It was a snowy evening in February 1960. Jimmy and I had decided to take our sleds up to the road leading to the high school football stadium and ride some in the late afternoon. The sun had just gone down but there would still be enough light to get in some sledding on the long road down the hill. We were having fun; for awhile. That was up until the fateful event occurred that literally changed my life. In fact the event still affects me fifty years later as I write this account.

"Hey Jim, do you want to race down the hill?" he asked me.

"No, it's OK. I'm sure you're probably faster. You're heavier than me and your sled is newer, so we'll leave it at that."

"Aw, c'mon. This can be our last run and then we'll go home."

Not wanting to be a spoil sport and recognizing that it would have to be our last run as it was getting dark, I agreed. So we trudged the quarter mile up the road to the top, stood beside each other and got ready to go. I said I'd start us and yelled "Ready, set, go!" We ran a few yards and jumped on our sleds and right away I was ahead of Jimmy. As we swerved down the twisting road I left him behind. In fact I was so far ahead I got up off my sled and waited at the bottom for him to catch up.

As I stood at the side of the road I saw him coming. In an attempt at humor, he was steering directly toward me to throw a scare into me. At the last moment before he would hit me, I jumped to my left. Unfortunately he steered to his right. As the front of his sled knocked my feet out from under me I slammed down hard on my left knee. My face pitched forward into the freezing wet snow. The wind was knocked out of me. I saw stars. I knew I was hurt badly.

"Jim. Are you OK? I'm really sorry. Are you OK?" he pleaded as he tried to help me to my feet.

"Jimmy, let me stay down here for now. I'll get up in a few minutes, but I can't right now", I responded.

I felt sorry for him and didn't want him to know the level of pain I was feeling but I just was not able to get to my feet at that point. I was dizzy and my knee hurt badly.

Soon I struggled to my feet and I told him I'd be OK and we started home. About halfway home as I limped along it began to snow and a freezing wind came directly at our faces. All of a sudden I felt terribly cold and in worse pain than when we started home. The knee was already beginning to swell. And by the time I got home it was so stiff I could barely bend it. The following day x-rays would reveal that the knee was broken. The prescription was three months in a walking cast that earned me the nickname "Chester" after the stiff legged character played by Dennis Weaver in the popular 'Gun Smoke' series on TV at that time.

If it had been a simple matter of a broken bone set in a cast, the entire event would have been forgotten. However, the cartilage in the knee was affected and the leg atrophied in the cast and the muscles of the leg would never be rehabilitated properly. A chronic condition would develop that would hinder my performance in athletics which would ultimately change where I went to college and plague me lifelong.

IV.

By the beginning of the ninth grade I had made the physical transition through puberty but in no way was behaving like a young man. Had it not been for the fact that I was still nursing a bum knee and leg I might have begun football by that time as I wanted to follow in my brother Totty's footsteps and become an athlete like him. Still without a constructive focus which sports may have provided I was just a boy who was a poor student and unsure of himself and relatively uninterested in anything school had to offer. So along with my friends Craig Maratta and Bob Stone, who like me were more interested in aimless mischief than school, I began the final leg of CJHS preparing to push Dad into deciding something radical would be in order for me.

By this time Wendy Vance was now dating seniors in high school and I still had never even been on a real date with her or anyone else. That was probably a good thing as I wouldn't have known how to behave if I had. So with newly acquired testosterone surging through my veins and no safe place to channel the resulting energy, such as on the athletic field, I was as restless as I could be. The direct result was that Craig and Bob and I began looking for new and even more creative ways to amuse ourselves. We became what my father would term "The Unholy Three". While he knew we were up to no good, I made sure he never caught me. But the threat of that made it all the more tempting to break rules; or anything else for that matter.

Craig, Bob and I created our own excitement in any number of unique and even dangerous activities. We especially loved anything that made loud noises accompanied by bright flashes and devices that involved projectiles. Whether bullets, arrows or rockets, we experimented with all. Bob had somehow even acquired a .22 caliber revolver that he often brought along just for fun. It came in handy for picking off street lights or birds or any of a number of other targets we felt worthy of its attention. The fact that this was an extremely dangerous practice as well as an incredibly dim-witted endeavor never touched our awareness. One of Bob's favorite amusements was to walk into the Coraopolis branch of the Pittsburgh National Bank with the loaded revolver under his shirt and make deposits or withdrawals from his savings account.

More interesting than guns for me were rockets and explosive devices. We did not want to harm anyone. We simply were looking for something exciting and dangerous to do that would provide thrills. A few years later, many kids in their teens would experiment with drugs for the same reason. Just looking for "kicks". However, thankfully drugs with the exception of alcohol, were for the most part an unknown at that point. So our kicks, at least before we had our drivers licenses, came from making bombs, rockets and even a functioning bazooka.

While Bob had the intellect, and Craig the wreck less abandon, I usually had the ideas. I would design the devices. Bob would ensure they worked properly and Craig would help. We had loads of fun. Admittedly, it was not wholesome fun that could possibly yield any constructive end, but it gave us something to do other than become addicts to television, studies related to school, or attempting to socialize with girls.

In the meantime around Thanksgiving that year Dad had telephoned Herb Snell, the Principal of CJHS at Herb's office.

"Herb, this is 'Doc' Anderson. Have you got a few minutes I can talk with you?"

"Sure Doc. What can I do for you?"

"It's about Jim. We need to get him on track at school so he'll be ready for college in a few years. I know he's not doing well. What do you think we can do differently?"

"Well Doc, to be completely frank with you, he's not college material. I think the best thing you can do is to encourage him to enter a trade school where he can learn a good skill. Or maybe he should consider entering the military. He just doesn't have the ability to do college level work."

Thankfully my father was not prepared to accept that assessment. Not only was he too proud to think that one of his boys was not bright enough to attend college, he was just too stubborn to accept defeat with me. After calling Herb, he had a talk with me about the fact that I was headed no where as things were going. He told me if my grades didn't show a significant improvement by the end of ninth grade, he would have to take me out of the Coraopolis school system and send me away from home to the same military school my brother George had attended.

I briefly attempted to spend more time with the books.

But not only did the subject matter and the way it was taught bore me, I had a very poor attention span. I simply could not concentrate on anything unless I had great interest in it. And I did not have interest in school work and couldn't force myself to. I did have an interest in science, as proven by the design of the rockets and other devices using chemicals and mechanics demonstrated. But our science class was purely academic and the teacher did nothing to stimulate much interest from me. So I went on focusing my time outside school on pyrotechnics and playing pranks with Bob and Craig.

But then there came a decisive event that made me realize it was time to quit playing with explosives. In fact I had nothing to do with the event. It occurred on a peaceful Saturday afternoon. Apparently Bob and Craig had acquired an empty artillery shell casing from a World War II cannon. Since I had been away for a few days immediately before their experiment with the shell, and they didn't know I had returned, I was not a party in the episode.

My mother and I were having lunch. Unexpectedly there came a huge roar off in the distance. This being the Cold War era, at first we wondered if perhaps the Russians had scored a hit on Pittsburgh 15 miles up the Ohio River. When we realized it was not a nuclear blast we speculated upon what had caused the commotion.

"Mom, maybe it was someone's furnace blowing up."

"Jimmy it's summer and it came in the direction of Bob Stone's house. Do you know anything you're not telling me?"

"No Mom. Honestly. But whatever it was, that was a serious explosion. I don't think even Bob could have pulled that off."

But in fact Bob had pulled it off. He and Craig had filled the artillery shell with powered zinc and sulfur, the same material we used as rocket fuel on various occasions. But in addition they had added saltpeter and charcoal which in essence produced a substance with similar properties to old fashioned gun powder used in the Revolutionary War. The shell had been buried deep in a pit the two boys dug in an empty lot near Bob's house. They expected that burying the bomb would negate any chance that there might be serious danger from detonating it. They were wrong.

When the shell detonated it had so much explosive force it propelled rocks around the pit in all directions. Some windows were broken but luckily neither boy nor anyone else for that matter had been injured. Mayhem caused by the blast scared neighbors and the police did indeed arrive shortly there after. The boys were eventually found out. When I later learned of the trouble they were in, realizing that by all rights I should have been in on the affair, I decided it was time to find a new focus for my restless energy. By that point, Dad had announced the fateful decision to ship me off to military school and I decided that I'd try out for football when I got there. With that decision I transitioned from experimenting with pyrotechnics to lifting weights to begin to build myself up physically for a new potential interest.

As I left junior high school, Wendy Vance, Jimmy Miller, Bob and Craig, as well as the town of Coraopolis behind, I had no idea what was in store for me. But at that point, I didn't much care. It had to offer more potential than what I'd been experiencing. In fact, something good was about to happen. I owe a debt of gratitude to my father for it. The lack of direction and identity during my "wonder years" was about to come to a close.

The Coach

I.

"We can't send a greenhorn like him off to football camp without help. He doesn't know what he's doing. He may get hurt. I want you to show him some things."

"Aw Dad, they're going to teach him what to do when he gets there. Besides, without putting on the pads, it won't do much good. It'll probably be just a waste of time."

"I don't care. He needs instruction. Take him out and show him the basics of blocking and tackling. Teach him about playing defense."

This exchange between my older brother Totty and father in the summer of '61' wasn't encouraging. I felt like an imposition on my brother. Yet again. The youngest brother of three boys carries some unique challenges. One is attempting to earn respect. Especially from our dad. Overhearing their discussion stirred more than a little resentment in me.

The idea of going out for the football team at Greenbrier Military School in Lewisburg, West Virginia was not entirely mine. Yes, I had resolved that I had to do it. But it was in some respects an obligation. I had to try football because I had something to prove. I had to prove I was capable of doing as well as my big brother. I had to prove I could hold my own and develop an identity other than "the baby" of 'Doc' Anderson's three sons. It had been three years since I'd participated in any kind of organized sport and that had only been little league baseball. But I felt drawn back to sports even if it was only because it was expected of me.

"Dad, if he doesn't want to show me anything it's OK. I'll be alright. I can take care of myself", I chimed in. I wasn't real sure I believed that but at the time it sounded good.

But I was overruled. Totty, though begrudged, took me outside. We walked out into a hot August afternoon. I squinted in the sun while trying to look confident.

"Now look. You're going to have to learn a three point stance first. Get down like this", he said as he demonstrated how lineman position themselves before each play began. He and Dad had decided I would be a lineman.

I felt awkward. My tail bone was too high and I was tilted to one side and off balance. While trying to grasp every bit of his instruction he knocked me around a little to get me used to the intense physical contact of football. It was his way of attempting to toughen me up some and get me ready.

Totty also drew some diagrams on paper and explained. "Here are the hash marks. They're important not only because they help in placement of the football, but they give you an idea of where the next play might be going." I pretended I understood. I attempted to absorb it all. But in one hour confined to one afternoon, I simply didn't learn enough to make much difference. But he satisfied his requirement so he could tell Dad he tried.

I wanted very much to do well. I wanted Totty to see that his little brother was capable of getting along on his own. Most importantly I wanted to make my dad proud of me. Everyone knew that Doctor Anderson had been a star athlete at the University of Pittsburgh. Not only had he played football there, but although only a sophomore, he had been a starting center on the basketball team. A two sport letterman in a major university. I dreamed of earning his respect and credibility. Maybe this could be it.

The new challenges I faced would be daunting. I was about to be sent away to a military school because my academic performance had been so poor in the Coraopolis public schools. In fact the high school principal made a statement to Dad that I was not "college material" and should consider a trade school instead of college. Dad was determined to prove him wrong. He wanted the best for me and hoped Greenbrier would help.

So, at age fifteen I'd be away from home at Lewisburg, West Virginia. I'd be facing a tough academic test as well as the challenge of going out for football. And I had a knee problem from an injury suffered two years earlier in a sledding accident. My left thigh had atrophied and as a result the hip and knee were weak. But none of that mattered. I believed whether I would do well or not was going to be a direct result of my effort to fight against nagging doubts about self worth

II.

Mom's black 1960 Plymouth Fury eased slowly up the entry drive beneath tall overarching elms before the huge red brick building. Two large brass cannons sat imposingly across an asphalt drive in front of the main entrance. The September sun glittered on their polished barrels. The architecture of the building reminded me of a citadel poised on a mountain. The front of the building with its archways and staggered corners was impressive. This first view of Greenbrier made me a little uneasy. Once I entered that building, I would not be able to leave its grounds. It was a stark realization that my life had just changed dramatically. What that change would mean I could only wonder.

Before I knew it, we had unpacked my possessions and had me settled in my third floor room in the top of the "quadrangle". The quadrangle was a structure of four walls arranged with an open court in the middle. Within those walls were the rooms of hundreds of cadets. Outside students doors on the inner walls of the quadrangle on each of the three floors were grey concrete walkways that allowed us to travel from room to room and ultimately out of the quadrangle.

Mother offered some last minute counsel and was saying 'goodbye' within an hour after we had arrived. "Jim, please pay attention to the faculty and coaches. Remember to listen to what they tell you and don't be resistant to taking direction from them. And make sure to eat well. Telephone this weekend to tell me how you're doing. I love you."

And with a hug, she was gone. I went to the window and watched her car pull slowly down the drive and away. I felt alone and abandoned. Her words, " . . don't be resistant to taking directions" rung in my ears. In time those words of hers would prove prophetic.

Over the next few days we new cadets were issued uniforms. We became subject to the commands of other students with "rank". We learned to march in unison with other boys. Experiencing so many new changes and rules I wondered how I could endure the detention like setting. And I missed home. I began to write letters to family right away and to look in my mailbox for confirmation that my friends and loved ones had not completely forgotten about me.

III.

"Hey. Wanna race to the gym to see who is fastest?" asked Kenny Kamees to me and my new roommate Jimmy Hubbard. Kenny, a short swarthy complexioned boy of Lebanese descent wanted to prove himself too. We were all headed over to the old gym to sign up for junior varsity football. Kenny wanted to show off.

"You go ahead and run and we'll see you there", I suggested to Kenny.

He took off. We watched his little legs and arms pump madly as he raced no one.

"Guess he wants us to be impressed. Are you impressed?" asked Jimmy jokingly.

Having arrived at Greenbrier just four days earlier I was too preoccupied with other things including what would be coming up that afternoon and in the next few days to actually care how fast Kenny could run. I was also considering why Jimmy was going out for football with me. This was his first time away from home too. He had latched onto me like a security blanket. Jimmy was going out for football because he wanted to stick close to his roommate. It was one more thing to be concerned about. I felt a protective urge to look out for Jimmy though I wasn't even certain I could look out for myself.

Greenbrier Military School had a strong athletic program. In fact everything about GMS in those years was strong. The academic program. The military training. The marching band. The school was all about excellence. As a result I knew the competition to make the junior varsity football team would be just as tough as making a varsity football team in many high schools back home in Western Pennsylvania.

And above the junior varsity was the varsity. The varsity was for the post graduate students at GMS. These athletes would come to Greenbrier after graduating from high school for an academic preparatory year before going to college. The varsity actually had a couple of colleges on their schedule as well as the powerful teams in the Virginias Military School League. In fact the majority of the athletes on the varsity at GMS had been outstanding players who were also being "seasoned" a year to better prepare them for going on to play at the college level.

Arriving at the gym and waiting to be fitted for equipment Jimmy and I spotted one of the toughest looking guys I'd ever seen. The large man with the lopsided jaw and crew cut hair just looked like a former marine with hand to hand combat experience. And in fact he had fought Japanese hand to hand in Iwo Jima and suffered from a permanent deformation of his jaw. Bill Seachrist was one of the coaches working with the JV's. While still handsome in a rugged way, he looked tough as nails. Of course there were many older and experienced team members there that looked pretty rugged to us as well. It all made me wonder if going out for football was a good decision. On the other hand, I was resolved to do my best and see if I could make the team. I wanted badly to prove I could do it.

The Head Coach of the JV's was Dick Mohn. Dick was also a former Marine with battle experience and even had his picture in Life Magazine in a feature story on the United States role in the Korean War. He was one of a kind. Though not a big man he instilled respect. He demonstrated a soft spoken and confident demeanor. And it seemed he always had a load of chewing tobacco in his mouth. While he and Bill Seachrist both looked as though they'd just as soon chew you up as talk to you, they shared a common characteristic I'd discover in many faculty and coaches at Greenbrier. While tough on the outside, they were kind and devoted mentors who cared about the cadets at GMS. They were good for us. Dad had made a smart decision in respect to Greenbrier for me.

IV.

It was hot and muggy the first day we trudged out onto the practice field for JV tryouts. A fly keep buzzing around my head as I walked carrying my helmet. Already sweating I felt a little like a clown in my uniform. The oversized shoes and shoulder pads didn't fit. The hip pads wouldn't stay unless I kept pulling up on them. I was small for the position my dad and brother had told me to try out for. I was to be a lineman. An end. I should have been assigned to the backfield. However, because I was just a sophomore, Totty and Dad had told me I'd still grow quite a bit over the next two years and should play on the line. They said that maybe by the time I was a senior I might be able to earn a letter on the JV team.

"OK lineman, form a circle over here around me" ordered Coach Seachrist. "We're going to do some hitting and see what you're made of".

The coach had laid two large cylindrical canvas filled bags

with heavy stuffing on the ground about four feet apart. I wasn't sure what was about to happen but it didn't sound like much fun to me. It was a "one on one" drill in which two linemen would get down in their three point stance between the two blocking dummies and on the whistle attempt to block one another out of the channel formed by the bags. As I watched the mayhem that ensued I hoped that whoever they teamed me up against would be around my size and age. But that wasn't to be. When my turn came I was dismayed to see that Coach Seachrist had matched me against Steve Fusco. Not only was Steve a returning senior and letterman, he was eighteen years old and was definitely bigger than me.

"Anderson, where did you learn to get into a three point stance?" yelled Coach Seachrist as I prepared to go head to head with Fusco. I didn't respond. I just submitted to the large firm hands of the coach jamming me down lower and into what he considered a more appropriate position to begin the drill. I held the position as Fusco got down.

Almost as quickly as the whistle blew the upward arc of Fusco's right forearm slammed into my face so quick and hard that I was half standing just as his helmet drove into my stomach. I reeled over backward and landed hard on my tail bone. Seeing stars it took me a few moments to come to my senses. I heard a couple of guys chuckle as I got to my feet thinking, "OK, well now that's over I can let the next two go at it and try to regain my senses." I was wrong.

Coach Seachrist decided to use me and Fusco to illustrate good blocking technique versus no blocking technique. The next few minutes were effective in not only making me wonder how I was going to get out of this whole asinine idea of playing football but how I might also escape from Greenbrier all together. I wiped the blood from a split lip. At that point I was dazed and beginning to wander off in the wrong direction. Mercifully, Seachrist ordered two new contestants to step up for their turn at the drill.

The beating I endured in front of the rest of the lineman that early September afternoon did accomplish at least one good end. After that debacle I decided nothing could be worse and it should only get better if I could hang on. So the next day instead of quitting the team as some seemingly wiser cadets had done after the first day, I became resolute to even the score with Fusco. Besides, if I quit what would I tell my father? I'd stick it out till they cut me from the team or the end of the season came.

V.

As it turned out, that season on the Greenbrier JV football team wasn't so bad. Coaches Mohn and Seachrist put me in the games some to give me experience. Dick Mohn was actually one of the most positive influences on me as he was for many of the cadets. And not just football players. Appearing to be a man of steel, yet with a warm heart, he was a role model. Perhaps he and Coach Seachrist let me in the games out of compassion or maybe they thought I might be worth something the following year. I don't know. Regardless, I was placed on the traveling squad and I even played in some games.

During that fall I discovered there was a big difference between the talents of the junior varsity and varsity players. The varsity didn't practice with us and the only time we saw them in action was at home games. When I first saw them play, I was in awe. As I watched the varsity play against their opponents I could see that the strength and skill level of those players was beyond what we had on the JV team. And they definitely earned their name the 'Fighting Cadets'. Schools like West Virginia University, Georgia Tech, Maryland and Tennessee regularly considered Greenbrier varsity talent as possible recruits.

So when the JV team was at home and the varsity was playing at home, we got to watch the "big boys" do their thing on Saturday afternoons after our early games finished.

I was highly impressed. I can recall thinking that even after I graduated from high school, I probably would never be able to make the varsity.

VI.

By the fall of '62' I had added 15 pounds and another inch of height. My dad decided that I should be sent to attend the early football camp for the varsity and returning junior varsity players. The camp began two weeks before the fall session and was designed to help the varsity begin to prepare for their grueling schedule. Of course the fact that guys from the JV could also go to the camp was a real plus for us who wanted to be better prepared for the upcoming season.

At the Greenbrier football camp, there was no varsity or junior varsity. Everyone was treated the same. In essence all had an opportunity to make the "big league" team. As it turned out very few high school guys ever made the varsity. There might be three or four a year that did. I wondered who might make it this year.

However in the fall of '62' an unusual number of players recruited to GMS for the varsity either did not show up or became injured at football camp. In fact, there were at least seven or eight key players lost. As a result, I learned that the coaches might take as many as five or six players from the JV level group to play for the varsity. I didn't give it much thought though as it was a moot point for me. I was just concerned about being able to make the JV team. And at 160 pounds I was still small for a lineman but hoped I could do well enough to earn a letter for the JV's that fall.

But in that football camp someone was about to change everything for me. And even my opinion of myself. He was to have a great positive affect upon my life. Varsity assistant coach Dave Ritchie was young. Possibly age 25 at that time. About 6'5" and 225 pounds of solid muscle, he looked more like he ought to be playing professional football than coaching at Greenbrier. This was his first year as a coach at GMS. He had been an excellent fullback at Greenbrier a few years earlier and went on to play at the University of Cincinnati. It's an understatement to say that Dave was intense. He was also an excellent student of football psychology and knew how to bring out strong performance in his players. And there was something about him that connected with me, though I couldn't quite identify what it was at that time.

VII.

Early in the football camp Coach Ritchie singled me out. We had begun the first day of practice with the old familiar "one on one" drills that had introduced me to Steve Fusco a year earlier.

"OK, were going to see how each of you are blocking. Fisher, come up on this side. Mason, you get on the other", called Coach Ritchie.

Both young men were big strong athletes. Jim Fisher would go on to star at West Virginia University and then be drafted by the Cincinnati Bengals. The following year John Mason would play for Furman University. As the two linemen collided and fought to knock each other out of the blocking lane, I stood with my arms folded watching their technique. Each stayed low and kept their balance. The contact of their helmets and pads sounded like thunder. I took note of their technique and determined to stay low when my turn came.

Soon it was my turn. I decided whoever they put me up against, I couldn't let happen again what occurred the first day of football tryouts a year earlier with Steve Fusco. Especially the split lip. As it turned out I was matched up against Aaron Wood who was at least 40 pounds heavier than me. However, I knew that if I could stay low enough he'd be unlikely to knock me back. And I determined I'd hit him first.

When Coach Ritchie blew the whistle, I instantly threw a

forearm to Aaron's head. His helmet snapped to his right side. I exploded off my stance and hit him with the full weight of my body through my shoulder and forearm. But he didn't move. He was too big and strong for me. We slugged it out for a moment until the whistle signaled us to stop. We lined up and had it again. Another stalemate. At least I had kept my dignity this time around. We got up and walked back to watch the next combatants. The dirt and sweat in my eyes stung. I noticed some blood dripping from my right elbow. I decided from then on out I'd be wearing a forearm pad. Aaron looked like he hadn't even been in a drill yet. Great! It was going to be a long two weeks. But I had held my own against a bigger man.

I'm sure Coach Ritchie considered that I was smaller than most if not all of the other lineman. I think because of that he did something that was a good coaching strategy that helped me gain confidence as well as toughen me up. In drills and scrimmages he seemed to pay special attention to encouraging me as I was always competing with larger men. But because I was small, I learned to become quicker and more combative than anyone else at camp. In fact the combativeness earned me a little respect, though my skill level left something to be desired. To survive I developed a fierce and aggressive style. Coach Ritchie began referring to me as either "Andy" or "Hard Rock" depending upon his mood. Both names made me feel like he took a genuine interest in me. While the head coach Dave Taylor was reserved and detached, Dave Ritchie was passionate and involved.

During scrimmages coach Ritchie seemed right in the middle of the action. He drilled us on technique as well as attitude. And then there was a statement he often repeated that stuck with me.

"When you're on defense and you see blockers coming toward you, don't stand there waiting from them to come to you! You go after them. Lay 'em low!"

At that time in my life I had been influenced by issues that served as sources of a passionate desire to excel. The truth is that I was carrying anger. The sources of the anger stemmed back to experiences from early in childhood up to being sent away to Greenbrier. Always being cast in the role of the underdog and having to deal with being picked on almost continuously was one thing; but deeper issues stemmed from the constant discord between my parents as well as a history of abuse. While I eventually learned that anger was not healthy, it did have some utility for an undersized and younger kid competing with larger and older athletes. It fed unrelenting determination which became a compulsion.

Apparently Coach Ritchie appreciated my aggressive nature on the field. I knew that. Later Dad told me that at the end of football camp he asked the coach how I was doing. Dave responded, "He's mean, Doc. He's mean". I never heard the end of that statement. Especially when I was being obstinate with Dad. He would refer back to Coach Ritchie's description of me and then use it to illustrate to me how contentious I was.

The "mean" adjective did describe my style of play. But I wasn't dirty. In fact I was a good sport, at times complimenting my opponent after the action had ended. I had learned something about good sportsmanship from an influential little league baseball coach years before that stayed with me. However, whether at practice or in a game, I played with every bit of ferocity my undersized frame could muster. And I worked even harder just for Coach Ritchie. I wanted to earn his approval. He seemed to care about me. While I was obstinate and not easy to coach, I was learning to become a much better football player due to him.

At the end of football camp when we were all to return to the Greenbrier campus to begin the new academic year, I was confident I would probably play much more on the JV team because of my experience at the camp. As I was packing my gear to leave on the bus Coach Ritchie motioned me over to speak with him.

"Andy, would you like to be on the varsity?"

Stunned by his question I stood staring at him for a moment then responded, "Sure. Do you think I can?"

He simply responded, "You're a varsity football player now. I have plans for you, Hard Rock."

I was more than surprised. It had caught me completely off guard. I knew he appreciated how hard I tried. But bringing me to the varsity at this stage? I decided it had to be a function of the loss of so many of the guys they had been counting on that either did not show up or were injured. In fact that was a large part of my selection. But still, there were a number of guys that were more experienced that weren't selected. So I knew there was something else the coach saw in me. I attributed it to him wanting to develop me.

VIII.

That fall, a couple of days before the first game we were taken to the equipment room to be issued our uniforms and jerseys. I told Coach Ritchie I wanted number '89'. That was the number of the University of Pittsburgh All American Mike Ditka. Ditka demonstrated a ferocious style of football that I wanted to emulate. Coach Ritchie chuckled and encouraged me by telling me he thought the number would be appropriate. I was so proud of that Jersey I wanted to sleep in it.

The fall of '62' was not a good season for the Greenbrier varsity. Normally GMS was one of the best teams in the conference. That year without the usual high level of talent we enjoyed in other years, we struggled. Our first game of the season was an away game against a strong Hargrave Military School team. We were crushed 30 to 0. I rode the bench during the entire game not expecting to play. As I sat there watching Fisher, Mason and the others getting beaten up I was frustrated by what appeared to be a lack luster effort by our guys. That style of play might have become a hallmark for the GMS varsity that year. But it was not something Coach Ritchie was about to tolerate.

The second game of the season was against an unimpressive Augusta Military Academy at their field. Somehow we squeaked out a 7 to 6 win. However, our play was not inspired. The only reason we won was that Augusta was even less inspired. I rode the bench again.

We limped into our third contest at home against Emory and Henry College. It was a night game. Shortly before half time a brawl erupted and both benches cleared to join the chaos at mid field. I ran out into the battle as well. But I didn't join in the fisticuffs. The good sportsmanship learned earlier prevailed in me. I actually tried to help the officials and coaches from both sides break the fight up. Dave Ritchie saw me pulling two guys apart. He smiled and winked at me.

I'm not sure why, but after the half time, Dave decided to put me in the game. It was my first time to actually play for the Greenbrier varsity. I found myself as an undersized high school junior playing football head to head with college players. I don't think I did anything particularly memorable in that game. But I played at my most intense level to keep from getting crushed by the bigger and more experienced foes we faced. No matter. When that game ended the score was Emory and Henry 23 and GMS 6.

It was during the week after the Emory and Henry loss in which an event occurred that would have a significant influence on me for the rest of my life. And our team as well.

We were having a practice scrimmage on a cold cloudy afternoon. The scrimmage was full contact football but with time between each play to assess and diagnose the action. I was playing defense as the first team offense ran plays against us. No one seemed to be into the practice. Except me. The players were demoralized by the poor showing in our first three games. And it showed in their sluggish performance in this practice. However, as the plays were being run, my habit of always hitting and running as hard as I could continued. I was furious that no one else seemed to want to work hard to prepare for our next game. At one point I collided directly with a running back and connected with so much force the sound of the collision caused everyone to look in our direction.

At that point suddenly coach Ritchie blew the whistle and commanded everyone to get in a circle around him. He was mad!

"You guys are slacking!" he shouted. "The way you're running these plays, we might as well not even travel down to Fork Union this weekend. You won't be ready."

A number of the team members looked down afraid to make eye contact with the irate young man quaking with fury. I was standing directly behind him thankful I was not in his line of sight. His outburst was so severe I feared he might grab someone and slam them to the ground. Then incredibly he wheeled around and grabbed me! His hand grasped the back of my shoulder pads just under my helmet. He hauled me around beside him to face the team and shook me like a ragdoll in front of them. As he jostled me before my teammates he yelled, "See this guy? Here is one kind of football player we need more of! Andy has one speed, full speed. If the rest of you were like him, we'd be undefeated!"

Then as he released me the coach's voice became measured and deliberate. His eyes like slits. Extending his fist and index finger outward he stated, "I want to see every one of you work like he always does. Line up and run it again like you mean it!"

In that moment, the coach accomplished something for me no one else ever had. He changed my identity that quickly. He made me feel like I could be a winner. More significantly, I realized that there was at least one man who believed in me. I was no longer a boy desperately attempting to prove myself. And the team had been shamed into facing the reality of their losing attitude as demonstrated that afternoon. During the rest of that practice the hitting was intense. By all.

IX.

As we went through warm up drills on the field at Fork Union, Virginia that Saturday, I looked forward to the game. Even though Fork Union was a powerhouse and we were limited by the injuries and other events that hurt our team, we had new life. Coach Ritchie had shaken up the team enough during the week, that even if we did not win, I expected we would play like our namesake. The 'Fighting Cadets'.

Our players fought a continuous uphill battle against a much stronger team that afternoon. Our 5'8" running back Daniel Iezzi, who was named all conference after the season ended, exemplified the change in what our team was now about. Every yard the little man gained that afternoon was through sheer force of will. Occasionally he would burst free on inspiring jaunts only to be stopped short of the goal line. The other players demonstrated the same fierce spirit. By the end of the first half and only behind by one touchdown we were definitely in the game. In the locker room Coach Ritchie cited the valiant effort.

"Now you guys are playing like winners! Take it to them in the second half. Lay 'em low!" he yelled as we left the locker room to take the field again.

From my seat on the bench I watched our fullback Skip Murdoch along with Iezzi moving the ball steadily. But in the second half our reserve players had to be pressed into action to spell our first string teammates. I was one of the reserves put in to play left end on defense. I was surprised to be going in, but I was eager to play against the larger Fork Union players. I had a point to prove. It was that I could hold my own against anyone.

Though over matched I doggedly collided with their men without letting any yards be gained around my end. On one play a running back from Fork Union streaked outside my territory to turn up field for a potential big gain on us. Somehow I skirted by his blocker attempting to clear the way for him. I caught him right in front of Coach Ritchie on the sidelines. We tumbled end over end near the feet of the coach.

"That's it Andy! That's the way to hit!" cheered the young coach.

His encouragement fed a tenacious desire to prevail. I jumped up and ran back to join my teammates savoring the passion of battle. On each play I hit anyone near me with an opposite color uniform as hard as I could as long as play was in progress. And the times I was knocked down by them I jumped up quickly to show I was unfazed.

At one point a big Fork Union lineman barreled toward my end with their fullback carrying the ball behind him. Seeing the oncoming freight train the words "lay 'em low" sprung to mind. Instead of bracing myself in an attempt to hold my ground I lowered my head and rushed directly toward the blocker staying as low as I could. As we met I swung both forearms up into the blockers chest with every bit of strength in my economy sized body. The sound of the collision made my ears ring. He and the ball carrier behind him only hesitated. That was just enough time for Fisher to shed his blocker and then slam directly into the ball carrier. The four of us tumbled under a deluge of players from both teams piling on. Under the mass of bodies I heard Fisher say, "Good job Andy!"

I never felt tired in that game. The ferocity of the action caused me to forget completely that my foes were bigger, stronger and more experienced. I was as alive that afternoon as I ever have been. Or ever would be. All of my senses were as keenly aware of the smell of the autumn grass and the crisp fall winds as where the football was and the runners carrying it. I took a beating but liked to think I did my job.

When the game ended we had been outscored. But we had not been outplayed. Dan Iezzi, Jim Fisher, John Mason, Skip

Murdoch and the rest of the team had never given in. They had fought like wild cats through the entire contest. But there was simply too much talent and depth on the Fork Union team for us to keep pace with their scoring that day.

The balance of the season was grueling. We did not have enough depth to overcome our opponents. But we played with heart and character. And with the guidance and encouragement of my coach I became more seasoned and confident. I was undersized and young and my team was not going to win much that year. But I worked as hard as ever at practice as well as the little I played in each game. I gave everything I had for coach, my team and the hope that I might eventually earn the respect of my dad.

That year Dad traveled to Portsmouth, Virginia to see us play Columbia Prep. I played a little in the game. We lost again. But I got to show Dad that I was playing football in the big leagues. He didn't comment on my play other than telling me I needed to keep better visibility of the action outside my territory when the ball was run to the opposite side of the field. That was Dad. The focus was always on what you needed to do better.

After the end of the '62' season I spent almost all of my free time at Greenbrier with the men who were going off to college to play football. We worked out regularly and lifted weights. We even played football outside in the winter months without pads when we could. I joined the track team in the spring to further my conditioning. The JV football coach Dick Mohn was also the track coach. He drove me hard. He chose me against my will to be the anchor man on the mile relay. It was the toughest event. A 440 yard sprint in which your legs turned to clay by the end of the race. He pushed me every way he knew how. Though I had a weak left leg and it did not allow me to perform as I should have he succeeded in strengthening my competitive character as well as my physical strength.

Over the summer months I went regularly to the weight

room at the YMCA back home in Coraopolis. I gained much more muscle mass and another inch of height. I didn't know what the fall at GMS would hold but I was driven to show up at football camp ready to earn a starting position if at all possible. The sacrifices I had made to that point included the pain of long hours of lifting, running, and attempting to learn everything I could to give me an advantage once the hitting started again at football camp. I did regular extra weight conditioning for the left knee trying to strengthen the weak leg as much as possible. And the physical conditioning was paying off. In a no pads pick up game during July with the Coraopolis varsity players, who had won their conference championship the year before, I had no trouble excelling. Most important, I believed I was on the verge of finally earning respect from Dad. If I could just keep it up and do well enough, maybe he'd recognize that I was good at something.

X.

As I drove the black '63' Chrysler Saratoga through the winding roads of rural West Virginia, my brother Totty and his friend Richard talked about their former high school football experience back in Coraopolis a few years earlier. They had been assigned to take me back to Greenbrier that fall for football camp of my senior year at GMS. Totty wanted me to drive. The beauty of the West Virginia hills and farms beckoned me back to Lewisburg for the year that I was now looking forward to more than ever.

At the age of seventeen and in the best physical condition of my life to that point, I was anxious to get to our destination to see who the coaches had recruited for the '63' team. Since the majority of our varsity was composed of new players each season just graduated from high school for a post graduate year before going onto college, the coaches would start from scratch again to build an offense and defense. Basically a brand new team.

Arriving late that afternoon I walked past some of the

footlockers of the new recruits. A few had their names and addresses attached to the lockers as they'd been shipped. I read some. Dick Luzzi from Belleview, New Jersey. Doug Macy of Rockville, Maryland. Powell Smith, Temple Kessinger, and more. I was curious about each. Who would I compete with for a starting position? Would I have a chance?

Heading toward the equipment room I ran into Jim Fisher who was back for another year. At age eighteen Jim would probably be one of the captains as he was the only returning man who had been a first team player the year before. I asked him if he knew much about any of the new talent. He did. He told me that Dick Luzzi had been selected as a high school All American by Scholastic Coach Magazine. But when I saw how small Dick was I wondered if he was as good as his reputation. Doug Macy had been All State in Maryland. And there were a number of others that had equally impressive credentials. My hopes of being a starter wavered. But I was glad to see we had the talent we missed a year before.

After visiting the locker room and being fitted for pads, shoes and uniforms, Jim and I headed over to dinner. Entering the hall the smell of fried chicken and biscuits made my mouth water. As I studied some of the new men I was especially impressed by a guy from Quaker Valley High School in Sewickley just across the Ohio River from my hometown of Coraopolis. Other than his crew cut hair Brian Rader looked like a modern day Adonis. And he would soon prove he could play even better than he looked. Like a pro. Dave Ritchie and the other coaches were sitting at the coaches table discussing who had arrived and planning an address to the new players after dinner. There was a mood of optimism in the air. Jim, the coaches and I felt that it promised to be a much better season than the year before. I was more hopeful than ever to accomplish something to please my father.

The following morning we began the day running through various drills and had times taken in the forty yard dash.

Though my left leg did slow me a little, I still turned in the best time in the forty for the lineman. Being an end that was important as we would be expected to function as pass receivers on a number of plays and speed was essential. Though now 6 feet and 173 pounds, I was still small for my position. But I had some experience and confidence and was as now as motivated as ever.

The two weeks at camp would establish who was to be the starting offense and defense. We learned much about one another, as well as ourselves. I drove myself relentlessly. I was almost always first in line at drills and for wind sprints. In a drill with tackling machines I can recall hitting the two man sled so hard I almost turned it over while Coach Ritchie was standing on it to serve as extra ballast to make it harder to push. He recognized how driven I was. Just being around him brought out the best in me.

In the drills and scrimmages no one demonstrated more passion and desire to excel than I. And that paid off. At the end of camp Jim Fisher and I were chosen as co-captains. It was also decided I would be the first team left end on both offense and defense. Everyone else on the line was well over 200 pounds except me. But what I lacked in size I knew I'd make up for in desire. I had worked continually from the year before to get to this position and I had high goals in my mind. Not only did I plan to serve as a worthy captain because of the trust Coach Ritchie and the others had placed in me but I wanted to prove that worth more than ever on a winning team.

XI.

Our first game would be at home against Hargrave. They had humiliated us the year before. None of our new players had been there for that and it was not a big point to most of them. But to Jim Fisher and me, our coaches and the three others that returned from the previous year, the memory of that day burned within each of us.

The night before that first game I lay in my bunk in the quadrangle staring up at the ceiling which reflected the lights from outside. One persistent thought consumed my mind. I was intensely prepared to give every ounce of energy and effort for the sixty minutes I would play the next day. Because I was on all special teams as well as offense and defense, I would most likely play every minute unless we built up a big lead. Fully focused, I fell into a deep sleep and woke the next morning feeling anxious to go.

That afternoon, wearing our new green, white and gold uniforms and burgeoning confidence Jim Fisher and I walked out to mid-field for the coin toss before the game. I looked beyond the playing field up the hill where my first practices on the JV as a sophomore had been held just two years before. I remembered the shaky beginning and felt appreciation as well as wonder that I had been fortunate to come this far in such a short time. I was more than a little happy to be in this position.

Hargrave won the toss and we kicked off to them. On the kickoff they returned the ball to near our thirty yard line. As I and the others lined up on the first play on defense I noticed the offensive end directly across from me was very large and the tackle next to him was even larger. I looked like a runt and my teammate next to me, Mark Ferris from Allison Park, Pennsylvania was definitely smaller than his opponent. I wondered how we would fare. But my conditioned attitude of confidence mixed with aggression took over.

As soon as the ball was snapped and the first play began my concerns were dissolved. After the whistle blew at the end of the play I saw Ferris's opponent lying on his back with Mark standing over him. And I had sidestepped my opponents attempt to block me and wound up in their backfield as one of three GMS men hitting their runner simultaneously before he got anywhere. We held them on the next two plays and they had to punt to us.

The solid thump of their punters foot propelled a high spiraling kick that arched beautifully in the deep blue autumn sky. It floated down into the waiting arms of Dick Luzzi. He did not "fair catch" the ball as he planned to return it up field. This was the signal for the rest of us to begin to block Hargrave players so Dick could get a decent return and put our offense in a good position to begin our attempts at moving the ball.

Once Luzzi had the ball, Fisher, Ferris and I could see he'd be running up the left side of the field behind our blocking. Fisher immediately floored one Hargrave man without going down himself and then quickly nailed another. I was able to take out a Hargrave player with a "roll block". Apparently a number of other GMS players were hitting their blocking assignments as well. Luzzi snaked his way up the field behind us and somehow found an opening at mid field. Then Dick turned on the speed. I was amazed at how fast that guy could move as he left the few remaining standing Hargrave players behind him streaking the rest of the way down the field for a touchdown. That ended any concern I might have had about Dick because of his size. That reminded me that I also was a "little" guy.

The extra point kick, also by Luzzi was good. We led 7 to 0 only four minutes into the first quarter. Dick had ignited our team like a fuse to a sky rocket.

But Hargrave was not deterred. When they got the ball again, they began moving it. The balance of the rest of the first quarter was rugged action with evenly matched play by both teams. I felt good and thought I was playing well both on offense and defense. But at the end of the first quarter I welcomed the time out. Playing both ways as well as on special teams in the hot September sun was draining. The manager ran out onto the field with a box of oranges for us. The sweet cool juice from those slices rejuvenated me and the rest of the team standing at midfield. Fisher and I both encouraged the others to step it up in the next quarter.

As we began the second quarter Hargrave managed to score a touchdown. However their extra point attempt was wide and we held onto a one point lead. We knew we'd have to use our passing attack to balance the capable running of Luzzi, Rader and the others.

Our quarterback Bob Frame and I had proven in football camp that we were a good passing combination. So the coaches decided we should begin to capitalize on that to increase our offensive production. About halfway through the second quarter when we realized that Hargrave was doing a decent job of holding our ground game to minimal production, we called a pass to my side. It was "sideline" pattern where Frame would drop back and fake a throw to a receiver out of the backfield but then pivot and pass to me as I went down and out toward the left sideline.

Upon the snap of the ball I drove inward toward the linebacker as though I was blocking him. But that was a fake and I turned downfield. Their defensive back picked me up to guard me. I feigned a step toward the center of the field to cause him to break in that direction. He did. I then sprinted to the outside looking over my left shoulder to see if Frame had thrown the ball to me. Bob had but it was high and slightly behind me. I had to leap up and extend my arms while twisting backward in an unnatural position to pull the ball in. I snagged the ball and prepared to land and head for the end zone. I didn't see the Hargrave linebacker who had pulled off the line to help my defender cover me. Just before I landed to take off the linebacker drove his helmet hard into my left leg. The weak leg.

As we both crashed to the ground I held the ball tightly to insure the first down. After we untangled I went to stand up to hand the ball to the official. I did but something was wrong. My left leg was not responding well to my attempt to jog back to the huddle. I hobbled to the huddle trying to shake off the problem. But something was wrong. As we broke from the huddle to get back up to the line and run another play the coach could see I was hurt and he yelled for Fisher to signal a timeout. I was assisted from the field.

"What's wrong, Andy?" asked coach Ritchie.

"Not sure Coach. Something feels out of place."

"Well, sit there for awhile. We'll get someone to look at it" he said.

A physician attending the game was called. After he asked some questions and examined me, I was taken inside the locker room. Later I was driven to the hospital for an x-ray. While I was gone GMS won the game. But I was out of action for awhile. Maybe for good.

That night as I reclined in bed in the infirmary staring out the window with ice and pain killers clouding my mind a mixture of confusion and disappointment consumed me. In just 24 hours from the night before my high hopes and expectations had been crushed. How could I overcome this? Because I was having trouble just standing let alone walking, this injury was something that pure desire could not overcome quickly. Was the season completely over for me? Why did this have to happen? What would Dad think?

XII.

The next day the doctor prescribed rest and regular icing. They told me it should be alright in only four to six weeks if I took it easy. My reaction to this was one of complete rejection by me. The verdict was something my mind simply could not accept. Later talking with the coaches, I insisted I'd be ready to go the next week against Augusta. They didn't buy it. And come that Saturday against Augusta the only time I was on the field was the coin toss before the action began. GMS won the game with an unexciting performance as I watched from the bench, when I could bring myself to watch. I was slipping into depression.

The following week we faced Frederick Military Academy.

I lied about how I felt and managed to convince the coaches to let me in the game a little to test my leg. Frederick was outside the Virginia Military School league so that non-conference game didn't count in the standings. I played a few minutes on offense to determine my recovery status. However Dick Kallock had taken over my position on defense. My play on offense was not near what I had been capable of before the injury. I tried to show more spirit, but I was clearly hindered. It seemed everything I had accomplished up until the injury had been wiped out. Though Rader ran wild that afternoon scoring two long touchdown runs, Frederick was the strongest team to visit GMS in years and they won.

I was struggling emotionally even more than physically. Because I was not able to do well at the thing that was most important to my identity at that point in my life I became negative. Depression evolved into resentment and cynicism. I was too immature to take the event in stride and maintain a positive attitude.

My eroded state of mind promoted a lack of focus that set the stage the following week for an event that I have attempted to blot from memory for the forty five years since it occurred. While time and experience have taught me that it's what we do in the present and look forward to doing in the future that counts far more than the past, still some moments always haunt us. Rationally we know they don't matter. But emotionally no matter how hard we try, some things just stay with us.

Arch rival Fork Union was coming to GMS for our homecoming. Dad and Mom traveled the 350 miles from Coraopolis by car to see the game with a couple of their friends. They would stay overnight and leave the following day. As usual, Fork Union had a strong team. However, GMS had a good team as well although I and a couple of other starters were hampered by injuries. I tried to hide how much the leg was hindering me and the coaches let me play first team on offense for the entire game. But not on defense. Kallock now had taken over my position in that regard.

I played mediocre that afternoon. And not one pass was thrown in my direction. But our team had played pretty well. As it turned out when we got down to the last two minutes, we were leading Fork Union by one point. Whoever won this game would take over first place in our conference. Then a strange turn of events happened that seemed like a bad dream.

After GMS had just scored for the go ahead touchdown by Rader with less than two minutes to go we had to kick off and simply hold them for a minute and a half to win the game. As our kicker advanced to kick the ball he stumbled slightly and his foot hit the side of the football. Instead of it lofting downfield it was a "squib" kick tumbling off to my side of the field. I could not tell whether the ball had passed the ten yard point to qualify as a valid "on side kick" meaning we could recover it. It had. Technically all I had to do was jump on the ball as it was considered fair game for whoever recovered it. Somewhere in the distance Coach Ritchie was yelling, "Andy jump on it! Jump on it!" I didn't hear him. Instead I stood over the ball looking on as a FUMA player recovered it. In the stands Dad watched my error dumbfounded.

Fork Union got the ball with a little over a minute to go instead of us. Their offense kicked into high gear and shortly they scored the winning touchdown with a few seconds to play. The GMS Homecoming was spoiled. And instead of us being in first place in the league standing, they were.

After the game Coach Ritchie called me over. "Andy, what happened? You remember we discussed onside kicks this week at practice. What were you thinking?"

"Coach, I was confused. I'm sorry", I mumbled as tears welled up in my eyes.

"OK. Well, listen. Put this behind you. The next time you'll know what to do. But don't dwell on this Andy. We all make mistakes. Forget about it and move on."

I tried to embrace what the coach was encouraging me to do. But I couldn't. I had to face Dad and my teammates. Now things seemed even worse than the setback from the injury.

The rest of that season I never got back up to my former ability level. Either physically or mentally. I tried, but I had lost my edge. My leg hampered me. And I didn't serve effectively as a co-captain. I was there for the coin toss before each game but not as an alert leader on the field.

And because of yet another blunder on my part, Coach Ritchie had one final lesson he would be forced to impart to me. It occurred in the last game of the season at North Carolina Military Academy.

At dinner the night before the game in the NCMA dining hall I had no appetite. But later I was starving and snuck out after curfew to a local restaurant. Ironically Coach Ritchie stopped in the restaurant as I was there. He saw me but didn't say a word or acknowledge my presence. But the next day he told me why I would not play in that final game of my senior year. I spent the entire afternoon during the game on the bench thinking of how I had disappointed the man who had earlier placed so much faith in me. And I could do nothing to make things right. That event impressed upon me the fact that the consequences I faced were a direct result of my own unthinking actions. Though I knew he cared about me, he would not compromise standards in respect to breaking curfew.

There was no way to know it at the time but something very positive would eventually come from the set of circumstances of that afternoon as well as the disastrous football season of my senior year. The seeds of important lessons had been planted. But it would be many years until I would appreciate the lessons and reap the ultimate rewards from those bleak moments in my youth.

I left GMS with hopes that I would realize my potential in football in college. I had originally hoped to attend Ohio University in Athens Ohio for my undergraduate degree and had met with Dave Hess their head football coach to discuss the possibility of a football scholarship. However, because of the chronic knee and related atrophied condition in my left leg, and no real proof of my abilities during my senior year, OU as well as a number of other schools were not willing to offer me any scholarship. And ultimately they were proven right as to my disappointment I was even unable to contribute to the football team of the small college I was admitted to after GMS. I even did poorly at an attempt at track in college. The knee and leg condition had not only changed where I attended college, they would serve to challenge me all the way through my life.

XIII.

Thirty one years came and passed between the fall of 1963 and late 1994. In those years countless tests would befall me. In fact many challenges would make the fall of my senior year at GMS look inconsequential by comparison. And thankfully a lot of good events would make all the difficult times and set backs more than worth it. But over time I came to realize that coach Ritchie's influence had served to toughen me for far more trying moments I would face along life's road. He had taught me that we all ultimately face the consequences of our actions and that it's how we handle the hardships that determine our character. Thanks to him, I believe I achieved far more in life than if I had not learned that lesson at an early age.

Dave Ritchie was still coaching in 1994. He had become the Head Coach of the Canadian football league British Columbia Lions. And that year his Lions had overcome a series of hardships and while considered underdogs all the way along, won the Canadian professional football championship. With his triumph as a championship head coach he had become highly respected in the Canadian football league. Upon learning of his victory I had telephoned the British Columbia head office to leave a message to tell Dave one of his former players from many years ago at Greenbrier called to say "congratulations". I didn't expect to reach him or even for him to remember me. I did not ask to have him return my call. But the receptionist insisted on my telephone number just the same. I just wanted him to know that there were those of us who still appreciated his influence in our youth. So I left a congratulatory message.

Later that afternoon at work my secretary stuck her head in my office.

"Jim, there's a call for you. It's someone named Dave Ritchie. He said you'd know him."

I was stunned. Somehow the busy coach in Canada had not only received my message, doubtlessly one of many, but made the time to call me back. I told her to put him through.

"Hello?" I said.

"Hi Andy! Thanks for the call today. I was out when it came. I'm happy to hear from you."

"Coach, I can't tell you how much it means to me to be able to speak with you after all these years. Thank you for calling me back. Congratulations on your championship."

"It was a tough season and we were a surprise to get into the playoffs. The guys overcame adversity all year long. I don't know where they got the inspiration to overcome all they did to win the Grey Cup."

"I know where they got it Coach. I think I can speak for a lot of us who were your players. I'm sure your current team as well as hundreds of us coached by you over the years feel the same about you."

Dave went silent for a moment. Apparently what I had just said had a powerful effect upon the battle hardened coach. After some silence he said, "Thanks Andy. Tell me about what you're doing now."

We talked for awhile about my work, our families and other interests. I told Dave how I was also making a living as a coach. But instead of athletes, my charges were executives and professional managers as I provided leadership programs and coaching for a living. I told him how I had learned so much about leadership directly from him. And I told him how he had done more than anyone in my youth to encourage and strengthen me. And of course we briefly revisited the "old days" of Greenbrier. I didn't want to remind him of my last year. I was still trying to forget it. But I had an unresolved ache that tied directly to him from so many years earlier. I felt a powerful need to somehow attempt to reconcile it with him.

"Coach, there's something I've wanted to tell you for a long time. And now that I have the chance, I don't know what to say."

He remained silent, waiting patiently for me to go on.

"It was a long time ago and I don't want to remind you of the details", I began. "But I'll just say that you deserved better from me than I delivered my last season at Greenbrier for you."

"Andy, I just remember you as someone I was thankful to coach. You know, we've all had times when we made mistakes or didn't perform our best. I can tell you I've had plenty of those times over the years."

"Well Coach that's a good point. But more importantly I'd like you to know that you are the man who had the most positive influence on me in my youth. That's the truth and I'm forever grateful for what you did for me."

Once again the tough coach became quiet. I did as well. I think we were both overcome by emotion. Possibly him from hearing a heartfelt expression of gratitude from one of his players and I from years of emotion bottled up in respect to that season. Strangely I felt like I was still one of his players. However, he never made me feel I needed to apologize for anything. He just encouraged me again.

As we talked I was reminded that if we allow the past to define us, we are lost. Living is only in the present and what matters more is what we are determined yet to do. And the greatest highs as well as the worst lows are brief moments that are never what they seem. And then they are only memories and nothing can be built upon them for long. Whether they were good or bad. I felt honored to speak with him. And I felt a connection with my coach as though there had only been a moment since last being under his charge. Not thirty one years.

After we said 'Goodbye' and hung up I sat staring out my office window. As I looked at the grey leaden sky that November an image came to mind. In it I could see a fervent young coach in one moment changing the life of a boy in front of his teammates. And in that one action he turned the direction of that boy's life for the better.

Epilogue

The audience was a couple of hundred of alumni from Greenbrier Military School, some wives, children and a few others. Looking down from the stage with microphone in hand I paused and let silence overcome the hall. I had been invited to speak to the group as they attended the induction of Dave Ritchie into the Greenbrier Hall of Fame. With all focused upon me, I began.

"In the sports world, whether you're a successful coach or a star athlete, people tend to see you only in that role. Often they never have the opportunity to see the real person beyond the surface. Today we have the opportunity to pay tribute to a man who while an outstanding coach is much more than that. I'm speaking of the man beyond the coach."

Again I paused to evoke attention. The audience appeared eager to hear what I was about to say.

"It was 46 years ago when I first met Dave Ritchie, in the fall of 1962. I was coached by him for two years. Since that time I had just one telephone conversation with him in 1994, and only this Thursday night talked with him again. But I believe I now know enough to tell you more about the man beyond his role of coach."

Over the next 10 minutes I spoke from the heart in a manner as passionate yet deliberate as I ever have. With a portable microphone I had the freedom to move out from behind the podium and use body language to supplement the words. I did not follow a script but instead knew exactly what they needed to hear about the large gentleman sitting in the front row with Sharon his wife of fifty years, children and grand children.

As I spoke I made direct eye contact with many in the audience including Sharon, his children, old friends, and Dave. The only challenge I had in the monologue was to not become choked with emotion. I succeeded but as I saw the tears in Sharon's eyes as I not only spoke of the character of her husband, but about her role in his and their children's lives, I had to concentrate to keep myself together. The audience was completely attentive as I spoke. They laughed or smiled in response as appropriate.

Revisiting the congratulatory telephone call I made to him in 1994 when his team won the Canadian football league championship, I related part of the conversation. I told the group how, Dave had stated, "Andy, I don't know where they got the inspiration to overcome all they did to win the Grey Cup". Then I told the audience, "Well, let me tell you. I know where they got the inspiration. And so does everyone else that ever played for him. If he asked me to step back out there on that field this afternoon, I would."

I saw more than a few whose eyes welled up. It seemed as though something in me guided my words. All I had to do was let it come out. It did and it was perfect. Coming to the end of what I had to say, I paused again for a long moment. Then looking at my coach I finished. He stared back at me with a warm smile on his face.

"Finally, on behalf of all the students you taught, the

athletes you inspired, and all that you and Sharon did for your family and friends, thanks Coach. God bless you."

The applause was well beyond what I had hoped for. All in the audience stood and I turned toward Sharon and smiled. There were embraces with her and others as I left the stage. And then my coach, still tall and strong at age 70 put his arms around me and spoke words that made everything worthwhile. He removed any doubts I had about letting him down. Finally I felt that I had honored his choice to believe in me forty five years earlier.

Later at the end of the event, I watched the coach and his wife and their children walk out together with well wishers surrounding them. I stood off to the side by myself saying a silent prayer of thanks for having been afforded the opportunity to stand and speak about a man who played such an important role in my life for the better. And I silently thanked my father for having made the decision to send me to Lewisburg many years earlier.

Ocean Breeze

Dream and watch the shadows come and go,
The lamp is low.
While you linger in my arms,
My lips will sigh I love you so
Dream the sweetest dream we'll ever know,
Tonight the moon is high,
The lamp is low.

— *Mitchell Parrish*

I.

The old white two story frame perches on the bluff facing east toward the blue Atlantic. When the tide is in, spray from waves crashing below on granite boulders is visible from the weathered porch. This evening a few gray and purple clouds drift above the ocean horizon as the setting sun twinges them with mauve and gold hues. Gulls hold steady against the breeze, occasionally circling down to the water where the salty fragrance fills the air. On the beach, a lone figure stands staring out at distant whitecaps. She's motionless for a few moments before proceeding on her way down the sandy beach.

Eventually she turns to stroll uphill from the shore to the trail toward the porch of the old house. Bare foot and in a cotton dress her youthful form is silhouetted as the wind presses the ivory colored fabric against her. Long brown hair swirls gently around and across her face. She swings her arm with a beach hat trailing in her hand. The other hand carries a few colorful shells. A ray of the setting sun casts a warm tone across her face. Suddenly she twirls on a heel and stops, laying down the hat and shells she places both palms upon her hips. The ocean breeze caresses her shoulders and neck as she tilts her head back looking upward toward the shadowy form of a sand piper circling above.

She closes her eyes and a vision fills her mind. Swaying gently back and forth from one side to the other she smiles. The vision is a memory carrying her back to a moment she revisits often; never tiring of it. Slowly she lowers herself to the long grass next to the path. Sitting facing the ocean with both feet pulled up and her arms wrapped around her knees she continues to sway slowly while she softly hums a few bars of 'Moon Glow'. In her mind she's again seated on the same bluff facing the sea as she was that evening. But then she had watched a full low moon's reflection sparkle across the water. And she was leaning back against him. His arms cradled around and over hers as he held her gently; neither of them speaking.

The gull calling just above brings her back to the present. The sun is now down and the sky is turning dark grey above the ocean. She rises and places the shells in the hat while continuing up the path toward the darkened empty house. Taking her time she walks up the few steps onto the porch enjoying the scent of the fresh air. Somewhere in the distance she hears the bell of a rusty buoy rocking on the water. Turning to face north she looks out across the bay to the lighthouse barely visible in the distance. Long since deserted it still stands fast against time and tide. She admires its noble presence. Somehow she feels akin to it.

As she touches the door knob she fades again into her memory and he's walking behind her entering the old house. It has been five years already. How quickly that time passed. Stepping in she gently shuts the door behind her. Standing in the dim hall she closes her eyes leaning back against the wall in the silence. Her head tilts slightly as the old floor creaks for no apparent reason. Then her head bows forward her eyes still closed. She is overcome by the memory that today is the anniversary of the telephone call from his mother changing her young world forever.

Her memory recalls the unforgettable phone call as if it were yesterday.

"Hello?"

"Hello, Valerie. This is Ruth Ann."

The tone of his mother's voice caused a sudden chill to pierce the heart of the twenty two year old woman. In that moment she became both paralyzed and completely aware of what the call is about. Still not wanting to believe what her intuition was telling her, she responded hopefully, "Hi Ruth Ann. What is it?"

The quiet deliberate voice of his mother replies, "I'm sorry. We've just received news about Craig."

There's silence between the two women. It seems an eternity to both as each waits for the other to speak. Finally, Valerie breaks the silence.

"Oh no! No! What can I do?"

"I suppose there's nothing really that any of us can do other than be close during this time. And if you want . . . ."

But Ruth Ann is silenced as she hears the young woman on the other end of the line begin to sob softly. And then Ruth Ann, ever strong waits for a moment while holding herself together. After a moment she resumes, "He'll be returned tomorrow. And then we're planning the funeral for Friday. Would you like to go to the airport with me when his plane arrives?"

Valerie is quiet and then regaining her composure offers, "Yes. I want to go with you. What time should I come over?"

"Please come over to the house around noon. I'll tell you more then."

"You know Ruth Ann, I love you."

Ruth Ann becomes quiet for a moment. Then she replies, "I'm so sorry this happened to you Valerie. Goodnight."

Hanging up the phone, the young woman suddenly felt dizzy and nauseous. She slid down into the chair beside the phone and doubled over with her crossed arms wrapped around her. While crying she rocked gently to and fro wondering what happened and what she will do.

Snapping out of the memory of the telephone call, she opens her eyes in the dark of the hallway and is back in the present. Five years. And she feels the same about him. Nothing has changed except that she's five years older. She needs him as much as when he left that evening she last saw him. And she clings to the memory of him. In fact he lives in her mind. He does not speak to her. But she speaks to him sometimes. And she hopes that somehow perhaps he can hear her.

She moves through the quiet old house toward the porch. Laying her hat and the shells on the stand near the living room entry she stops to turn on the lamp. There is no one there but her. When she comes to the house this time each year, it is always alone. Just for a weekend. It has become a ritual. While the owners rent it out some each summer they are friends of her family and they continue to offer the house to her without cost. Though she attempts to pay they insist on her visiting for free. They know this is a time of reflection and renewal for her. But each visit she remains in the same cycle of thought about him. There is no renewal. There is simply a resolution to steel her self to go forward in another year without him. She wonders.

Is this what he would want? Or would he want me to build a life with someone else? Surely he would want me to go on and make a life without him. Why don't I?

She opens the door to the side porch and walks out. Staring eastward across the water she feels some small contentment. Content that her career is proceeding well. Glad that she has her friends and her art. And content that the love she carries still lives. Turning, she steps over to the porch swing. The old rusty chains creak softly as the music from 'Deep Purple', one of his favorites, fills her mind.

Lord, how much longer will I carry this yearning?

On the swing she ponders the fact that her parents, friends and Ruth Ann speak often about moving on. But she knows they don't understand. He was not just the young man she loved. None of them really understood him. He was a deep soulful young man that wouldn't reveal himself to anyone; but her. A handsome true life James Dean character. Troubled yet with more charisma and unpretentious charm than most Hollywood actors. And he loved her. He could not or did not try to tell her in words. He was not an orally expressive man. But he was passionate about life and those who cared about him. And she loved him and nothing would ever change that. She believed that he would be the last thing in her mind at the end of her life.

They had connected in a way that was unlike any other couple Valerie was aware of. In part because of his trials he was a vulnerable young man. But he kept up a tough exterior. However, he was deeply sensitive. He had opened himself to her and believed in her. She was confident that no one else had gained that position with him. And as a result, no one knew him as she did. She resolved that she would always go on loving him.

II.

My friendship with Craig began in the summer of 1960. I had accompanied my brother Totty over to the Maratta's home to visit Craig's older brother Jan. Totty and Jan were teammates on the Coraopolis High School football team and were a couple of the most popular guys in their class. I'm not sure why I was along but since they were friends perhaps they thought Craig and I should meet. I at fourteen and Craig at thirteen were close enough in years to possibly become friends.

Craig's childhood and young adulthood was lived under

the constant shadow of Jan. Jan had excelled at everything including academics, sports, and positions of leadership. He eventually became a highly respected surgeon in the Pittsburgh area. And their father Dr. John Maratta was one of the most well known and successful surgeons in Western Pennsylvania. But Craig was mediocre as a student. And though he would prove himself a fine athlete he continuously faced the disapproval of his father. In fact, John Maratta demonstrated cruelty to Craig that defied explanation. From a very early age the boy developed deep seated self-doubt and a feeling of inferiority. Though he had unusual charisma and was by no means unintelligent, he felt much like a misfit by his early teens.

That day I met Craig, he and I went to the Maratta's basement to try out our shooting skills with his BB gun. Right away we had a natural connection. And we had similar interests. Also, the influence of our fathers must have been part of an unspoken alliance. The mistreatment we both endured fed anger and restless rebellion in each of us. Additionally, we had in common the fact that neither of us was able to match the academic or social skills of our older brothers. And being the youngest in each household, we were both in the role of "baby" brothers.

There were other similarities. We were both intense young men with sensitive natures compelled to play the role of tough guys. This restlessness and our sense of adventure led us to pranks and various acts of minor vandalism that while not serious were the kind of behavior that often drew the attention of Coraopolis law enforcement officials. Actually, we enjoyed jousting with the cops. However, because our fathers were both strict and also held in high esteem in the community, our greatest concern was not the police. It was our dads finding out about any of our shenanigans. That risk made the tomfoolery even more tempting and exciting.

Our vocabulary while not profane was that of aimless young punks. Mom once observed to both of us, "Jim and

Craig. The majority of your vocabulary consists of three words. Man, bad, and blast." And with that she laughed while walking away. We did use those words often. "Blast" meant either "to go" or to "bomb" something. We were highly into devices that would make loud noises accompanied by smoke in those days. "Bad" meant "good" or "awesome". And "man" was what we called one another or it replaced exclamations such as "damn" or "hell". A typical exchange might go something like, "Man, let's blast to Pittsburgh tonight." "Bad" accompanied by a slow nodding of the head would then be a logical response indicating agreement.

In the very beginning of our partnership, which soon included Bob Stone, a boy genius of thirteen with an equal interest in mischief and explosives, we stuck pretty much to neighborhood pranks. Often the targets of our misplaced energy would be people around town that we perceived as impediments to our activities. One person in particular, who took objection to our launches of homemade rockets and routine use of fireworks, was a teacher in the junior high school. With a PhD. in mathematics from the University of Pittsburgh she insisted on being called "Dr. Jones". Emily Jones was an overweight spinster in her late fifties who lived with her eighty something mother in a large yellow brick house straight out of a gothic novel on Highland Avenue, about a block from Bob Stone's house on the same street.

One hot July night in 1960 we three boys were bored. Sitting under the old fashioned globe streetlight on McCabe Avenue watching moths circle the light we grew tired of pretending we were actually inhaling the 'Lucky Strike' we passed around as it burned down. The conversation was about much of nothing. Finally, it was Bob who first directed our attention toward Dr. Jones that evening when he said, "I know what would be cool."

"Yeah? What?" I replied.

"Well, Dr. Jones gave me a dirty look when I was out in front of her house today."

"What were you doing?" I inquired.

"Me and Cellenti were just kicking a can in the street. I didn't like the way she stood on her porch with her hands on her hips giving us the evil eye", he said.

Bob then asked, "Do you still have some cherry bombs?"

"I have a few", I said.

Craig got Bob's idea without any more explanation and simply nodded his head slowly and uttered "Baaaad" while staring off at nothing.

I laughed and said, "OK. We need another cigarette to put on the fuse so I'll have time to get up on her porch and lay it against her screen door. Then we'll have a few minutes to get down the street and lay low."

Still with the far away look in his eye Craig just bobbed his head a few times.

Within a few minutes I had the cherry bomb with the fuse poked into a glowing cigarette in hand and was crawling on my belly across Dr. Jones front yard. Bob and Craig were on the outside of her yard fence keeping a watch out. Unfortunately, they were not watching well enough.

Regardless, after I stealthily crept up onto the old fuddy duddy's porch and gently laid the bomb in place, I rejoined them and we strolled causally down to the corner and got out of sight. A strategic error in this move was that we could not see the front of her house, or the Walzachs across the street from her house on their porch sitting quietly in the dark observing the entire farce. Apparently they telephoned both Dr. Jones and the law.

We should have known after some time when nothing happened it would be wise to simply scratch the plan and move on. However, my bullish nature got the best of me. When Bob said, "Maybe we ought to forget it for tonight" my monumental stupidity prevailed.

"No. We're going to blast. Tonight." I asserted.

We crept back down the street. Not willing to use the cigarette delay fuse this time, I had Craig light a match and touch the green stem of another blood red little ball of fury. As its lit fuse brightly sparkled I tossed it perfectly up onto our nemesis's porch. It rolled up to the door and went off like a miniature stick of dynamite. Craig exclaimed "Bad!" yet again. However, just then the two patrolmen who were concealed on each side of the street flicked on their flash lights. "All right boys. Hold it right there!"

Though we hadn't planned it, our instincts took over and the three of us sprinted in different directions simultaneously. Bob down Highland Avenue in the opposite direction of his house. Craig up Highland Avenue and me circling behind Dr. Jones' residence. Rather than continue running, for some odd reason I spotted a large bush in her back yard that appeared to be a safe cover. I dove in and hugged the ground. But shortly one of the patrolmen began nosing around in that same backyard with his flashlight. As the beam passed slowly just above me a couple of times, I held my breath. My face was pressed into damp dirt and I thought I could smell a mixture of night crawlers and dog urine in that soil.

How could he not see me?

I expected at any moment for the cop to reach in and take hold of my shirt.

What is Dad going to do when he gets a call from the police?

I held on and froze like a rock. Thankfully it was only a matter of time until the young officer gave up and returned to the front of the house to take a report. I slithered out of the bushes and crawled slowly across the alley behind Dr. Jones' house. Once I got into a clear area I took off for the woods. I ran long and hard toward a safe haven. It was a place where Bob and Craig and I often met after committing random acts of asinine behavior. But this evening only Craig and I showed up.

"Man. That was close", Craig said.

"Man! I wonder if anyone recognized any of us", I responded.

"Maybe. But it was worth it. That was really bad", said Craig.

"It was pretty dark. I wonder if we were recognized", I observed.

"I wonder if they got Stone. He ought to have been here by now."

"Well, there's nothing we can do about it now", I said.

We talked a little more and decided to call it an evening. After we split up I headed home in mortal fear. I was not at all concerned about the authorities. I was concerned about what would happen if Dad found out.

The following morning as I lay on the living room carpet watching Saturday cartoons with Dad lazing in an over stuffed easy chair behind me I received one of the most memorable frights of my young life. Though it was only a little after 9:00 AM I spotted Chief of Police John Brush striding up the front walk toward our front door. The Chief had his hat pushed back and carried something that looked like a report of some kind. The sunlight gleamed off the polished handle of this service revolver bouncing in the holster on his hip. I was quaking with fright.

Uh oh! What should I do?

I stifled the desire to blurt out, "Dad, last night I did something that I shouldn't have and I have to talk with you about it!" The utter lunacy of the urge to offer up such a remark convinced me to just pray and wait for the inevitable. The door bell rang. A sweet melodic tone that mocked the stark terror of the moment. As always, the floor groaned as Dad headed to answer the door.

"Good morning, Doc. Sorry to impose upon you so early", said the Chief.

"That's OK 'Brushy'. What can I do for you?

Here it comes!

"Well Doc, Mrs. Dithridge called a little bit ago. She says she saw a large brown dog with distemper roving the neighborhood. We're asking everyone to stay indoors until we find him", responded the big cop. I felt the tension in my body dissolve almost immediately and only then realized my heart was pounding. And I had come so close to blowing this reprieve by spilling my guts when I saw the Chief coming up the walk!

Thank you, God. I'm going to be good from now on.

As it turned out, Bob had made it home safely undetected and somehow we got away with the assault the night before. I quickly forgot the promise I made to God and we proceeded through the summer unscathed by the authorities through similar ludicrous acts. But after that summer and for the next three years, mostly because of my abysmal performance in school, and because Dad was smart enough to figure out what the 'Unholy Three', as he called us, were up to though never caught, I was shipped off to military school. Then it was just Craig and Bob without their compatriot who was being held hostage in the mountains of West Virginia behind the fortress like walls of Greenbrier Military School during each academic year. I still hung out with Craig and Bob in the summers and when coming home for holidays, but things changed in the dynamic between the three of us with me being out of action with them so much.

III.

Then in the fall of '62', a year after I began at Greenbrier an event occurred that sealed the pattern of tragedy in Craig's life. He was only fifteen. It involved Bob Stone. The seemingly innocuous incident occurred in the front yard of Bob's home. The two boys were playing with golf clubs. As Craig swung a club back to practice a stroke he didn't see Bob standing so close. Bob was not paying attention. The club struck Bob between his legs. He immediately fell to the ground doubled up in agony. Bob's father rushed him to the emergency entrance of Sewickley Valley Hospital. Initially it appeared that the wound would heal. However, unknown until it was too late a malignant cancerous growth began in the center of the injury site.

Before the cancer was discovered and over the next two years Craig began to change from a boy to young man and channel his raw passion from pranks in the dark alleys of Coraopolis to outstanding performance in the basketball gyms in the Ohio River Valley. By the age of sixteen he was becoming a star athlete for Coraopolis' rival Moon High School. And on the sidelines in her red and white MHS colors, Valerie Welch and the other cheerleaders led the crowd in chants for Craig and their heroes. While the fateful event with Bob Stone had occurred before his junior year, it appeared all would be well and Craig was focusing his energy into playing ball.

The only serious distraction for Craig from basketball at that time was the score of high school girls that pursued him. With thick dark hair, deep brown eyes and dimples, it appeared the handsome young man was bound for glory of some kind, even if only on his good looks alone. Combined with a brooding and mysterious presence that could be suddenly pierced by a disarming smile, Craig was like an aphrodisiac to women. Of all ages. There were rumors about one attractive young English teacher's interest in Craig. But nothing was ever confirmed or denied by him. When questioned by his buddies about her or any other female, he would simply shake his head and utter "Man" while walking away.

When I would come home from Greenbrier for vacations, Bob and Craig and I would team up. But something was becoming different. My disciplined orientation from military school made me seem a little different to the two of them. Ironically I was also beginning to achieve unexpected success in athletics on the Greenbrier football team. At the same time Bob was excelling at science and his superior intellect divided him from me and Craig. The chemistry between the three of us was changing. By the summer before my senior year at GMS I didn't see Bob but a couple of times. Craig and I would still spend time together because we both were athletes which created a common bond. But then instead of bombing old ladies homes, we were cruising spots at night where the girls and guys frequented or working out together to prepare for our upcoming sports. And of course we'd attend parties at various girls' homes around the area. Young ladies were always inviting Craig to something.

In the summer of '63', the last we would spend together regularly, we actually began to strike up serious discussions from time to time. They might have to do with what we wanted to do after high school or sometimes we'd exchange views about national events or even our families. But we always avoided talking specifically about our fathers. Kind of like ignoring the 'elephant in the living room'. I liked being with Craig. Though I never did get a sense for how deep he actually was; there was something about him that connected with me.

After the cancer surfaced in Bob and then spread resulting in his death at the age of eighteen, Craig was to put it mildly, crushed. And it seemed there was nothing he could ever do to make things right. He struggled mentally and emotionally. His father had him seeing a therapist as his behavior became more problematic. I had heard about him getting into drugs and encounters with the law. I knew I didn't fit in with his new friends or their interests. After I graduated from Greenbrier and was attending college Craig and I no longer spent time together. The brooding self doubt had seeped into the young man's identity so deeply that no amount of therapy could undo it. It would take something far more powerful than counseling therapy to lift him out of the depths of depression he had fallen into.

IV.

It was in the late fall of 1965 that I first met Valerie. She was eighteen and I nineteen. At that time the legal age for consuming alcoholic beverages in Pennsylvania was twenty one but only eighteen in West Virginia. My hometown of Coraopolis was only 45 minutes east of the state line and there were some night clubs just across the state border in West Virginia that many of us would frequent. One evening around Thanksgiving when I was home from college the telephone rang. Mom answered it and called, "Jimmy. Henry Kretchmar is on the phone."

"OK, Mom. I'll be right there."

After picking it up on the upstairs line, Henry spoke. "Hey man. What are you doing tomorrow tonight?"

"Not much. You got any ideas?"

"I'm thinking of going down to the Terrace Lanes. Any interest in going along?"

The Terrace Lanes was a bar and restaurant in Chester, West Virginia about 20 minutes from Henry's house near Beaver Falls, Pennsylvania. It was an easy drive and lots of kids we knew from our area liked to go there to dance and of course consume beer. We were no exception. So it was agreed that I would head west and stop to meet Henry at his house. Then we'd go on in his '64' GTO to see what kind of adventure we might find in West Virginia.

The following evening as Henry and I drove along, we talked about our summer jobs, what our buddies were up to, sports and the typical things nineteen year old males focus upon. I asked him if he knew anyone else going over that night to 'The Lanes'. He said he thought a couple of "fine" girls from Beaver Falls might show up. I didn't pay much mind to that prospect as it sounded pretty speculative. But I always held out the hope that I might be lucky enough to meet someone of the opposite sex that I'd like and who might actually be willing to talk to me.

After parking the car we agreed to stay just long enough to decide whether or not there was a good reason for remaining or moving on somewhere else. Entering the dimly lit bar we sauntered in a semi-circle around the large dance floor slowly checking out the evenings prospects. The song 'Let's Dance' by Chris Montez accompanied by a pounding organ backup was blaring over the sound system.

We'll do the twist - the stomp - the mashed potato too - any old dance you wanna do - let's dance!

At that time of my young life I walked with a swagger and carried a persona that just seemed to encourage some guys to want to test their fisticuff skills on me. I'm still not sure why. While I was not looking for trouble, it often came looking for me. After stepping up to the bar, Henry encountered a guy he knew from his town by the name of Mike. After being introduced to me Mike wasted no time informing Henry and me that some guy he knew from Beaver didn't like my looks.

So what else is new?

Mike said, "Jim, there's a guy here who says he's gonna kick your ass. He thinks you eyed his girl funny when you came in and he's says he'll be looking for you outside later."

"Yeah? Can you point him out to me?" I asked.

"He's that guy over there talking to those two dudes at the end of the bar."

Eyeing my potential antagonist, I made an assessment of whether or not I ought to be concerned. He kind of looked like Gomer Pyle with long sideburns and greasy hair combed straight back. He was tall and thin which would make his belly an easy target and his beak like nose just begged to be reshaped. He was obviously drunk and probably couldn't have defended himself from the bar maid he was ogling. I shrugged, immediately forgot about him and went back to my business of surveying the scene while nursing my beer.

Henry then spoke up. "Hey. I believe I see one of the girls

I thought might be here. I'll check back with you in a little bit."

Henry ambled off into the crowd. I just stood there next to Mike leaning back against the bar wondering what I would do to keep from getting bored. I was not much of a dancer and had next to no socials skills. I guessed I'd just hang on for awhile and hope that Henry would come back soon enough with some girls in tow or that maybe I'd find someone to talk with. About that time Mike saw another buddy of his and left me to go talk with him.

As I leaned against the bar glancing around and attempting to look cool in my jeans and madras shirt while sipping my Budweiser, a girl caught my eye. At first I thought she was looking in my direction but then I decided she was just too pretty to take note of me. She sat with a couple of other girls at a table in the corner. They kind of looked like college sorority types. She was absolutely lovely. With long brown hair and large blue eyes along with a clingy white cotton button down she was drawing attention from more than just me.

Whoever she is, she looks outstanding!

While I had little confidence she'd give me much of a response, I deliberated on whether or not I should go over and ask her to dance. As I vacillated back and forth on what to do she finally looked directly at me and smiled. I stupidly looked behind me to see if she was smiling at someone else that was beyond me. Nope. No one there.

OK Pal. You've got nothing else to do but go over there. Besides if she blows you off, Henry and Mike are no where in sight to see you get shot down. Get moving.

The Skyliners came on singing 'Since I Don't Have You'. I casually walked in the general direction of her table pretending like I was going to walk past. I didn't look directly at her but kept her in sight to see if she'd perk up when I headed by them. She cast a slight sideways glance at me just as I neared their table. That's all I needed. I strolled directly up to her Budweiser in one hand and the other hand jammed in my pocket.

"Hi. Would you like to dance?" I asked.

She tilted her head to the side, giggled at one of her girl friends and said, "Sure."

Following her out onto the dance floor I purposefully gave a firm bump to good old Gomer who was by that time clumsily stumbling around being held up by a Janet Reno look alike who I'm sure must have been his insurance in case his big mouth got him in trouble. Now if it had been her that threatened me, I might have been concerned.

"So, where are you from?" I asked the vision in my arms.

"The Pittsburgh area. Have you ever been to Moon Township?" she responded with a disarming smile that almost made me forget what she had just asked me.

Regaining my cool composure I responded, "Yep. I'm from Coraopolis. In fact I have a friend that lives in Moon. Maybe you know him."

"Who's that", she said.

"His name is Craig Maratta. He was a captain on the Moon basketball team."

"You're kidding!"

"No. Do you know him?"

"Well, we dated during our senior year. But I haven't seen him for awhile. What's he doing?"

"I haven't seen him in awhile either but I heard that he's got a job at a mill in Ambridge and is hoping he doesn't get drafted."

As we slowly swayed around the dance floor I decided to redirect discussion away from Craig. By that time I remembered that I had heard about her from him. But because he was a former best buddy and though I hadn't seen him for some time I was not comfortable talking about him.

But I was definitely interested in talking with her about

anything else. As the song ended I asked who her friends were and she took me over to introduce me.

Man, don't blow this.

The two girls at the table were now talking to a couple of guys that had pulled up chairs by them. This left Valerie and I free to engage in learning more about each other. I found out that she had been a cheerleader at Moon which didn't surprise me. With her great looks and All American charm she would have been a logical choice for that activity. Once she learned I was Craig's friend who had been at Greenbrier she told me she remembered who I was.

The rest of the evening Valerie and I talked and danced. I was temporarily in heaven. She was a lovely young woman in every way. Beautiful and smart but with humility. And she had an innocent charm that indicated genuine grace. I felt like I was completely out of my league with her but hoped I might see her again. Around 11:00 her friends decided they'd better get home. I was fortunate enough to get her phone number and she invited me to call her sometime.

Yeah, like you have to tell me to do that!

I said 'Goodbye' to Valerie and just about that time Henry came up.

"Hey man. Who was Miss America?" he inquired.

"Oh just some girl that went to Moon and is now attending Penn State."

"Just some girl? Right. You looked like she had hypnotized you."

"C'mon man. I didn't look that overwhelmed. Did I?"

Henry and I bantered a little about it some more and then I asked him about the girls he had gone looking for earlier. He told me they were still there and he wanted to introduce me to them. So, we spent some time with them but I could not get my mind off Valerie. Finally around midnight we decided to head for home. The evening had definitely been a good one.

I called Valerie about a week later and arranged a date

with her during the Christmas holiday. In the meantime I had learned that the break up between her and Craig was not something he was happy about. That made me a little uneasy. However, I figured if she would go out with me, I ought to try it to see if here might be some potential.

The evening in December I went to her home to take her out, her father answered the door. He gave me the once over as I stood uncomfortably in the living room talking with him waiting for her to come down. Shortly she walked down the stairs and I tried not to stare. She was wearing form fitting chocolate brown slacks, an ivory sweater accented by her sorority pin and a disarming smile. I knew her father was watching me as I looked at her so I tried to look cheerful and not at all mesmerized by my angelic date. After helping with her coat she and I walked out into the snowy December evening with me holding her hand so she wouldn't slip on the icy sidewalk. We went out to eat at a local spot and then to see 'Goldfinger' starring Sean Connery.

I don't know what I could have possibly done that evening to be more of a flop with Valerie. In addition to being a little uncomfortable about the fact that I knew she had been Craig's girl I was just not able to engage her in any smooth conversation. While my interactive skills were not terrific, normally I could at least carry on a decent conversation with most ladies. Not that night. Many uncomfortable silences were broken by halting conversation about nothing of interest to either of us. I was certain I must have been the biggest dud she had gone out with to that point in her life. It was apparent she was uncomfortable and try as I might to save the evening; it just wasn't going to happen.

Over the next few weeks I made a couple of unsuccessful attempts to arrange another date with her. I wanted a chance to resurrect myself. All to no avail. I decided it was no use and elected to leave her alone. Not long after that I discovered that she and Craig were dating again. The only solace I gained was that if my former buddy liked her and she was back with him, then that was for the best. However, I decided that maybe I never should have asked her out to begin with.

V.

Around the same time I learned that Craig and Valerie were dating again, I became aware that Craig was hanging out with some guys who I knew were trouble. One in particular, Danny Crenelli had been brought up on drug related charges but was out on parole. I just couldn't understand what Craig would find of value in being friends with a guy like CrenellI.

Valerie dated Craig off and on for a year or two from that point. But by the time I graduated from college in 1968 they were dating steady. She refused to tolerate or have anything to do with the trouble makers he'd become involved with. Eventually she was successful in getting him to disengage completely from them.

Valerie became a shining ray of hope in Craig's life. She was good for him. She was able to accomplish something that no one else could. She recognized the outstanding qualities of the young man and made him begin to believe he was worthwhile. The right woman can do great things for a man. In her case, she was building his self-esteem and bringing out the better qualities in him. He began to believe that he was OK and worthy of love by someone who he thought was the most wonderful person he had ever known. Under her influence his behavior began to turn around. He had hope.

He even entered junior college and began to look forward to making something of his life. He could never undo his role in the death of Bob Stone or gain the approval of his father. But he had a beautiful woman with outstanding character who loved him. He began to look forward to an encouraging future.

But the pattern of tragedy was about to rear its head again

in Craig's life. Later she reported that early in 1970 they had a conversation that turned out to be eerily prophetic.

"Valerie, I think I better go to Canada" Craig had said to her.

"Well, what will you do there?" asked Valerie, now aged 22.

"Don't know. But I just have this strong feeling I'm going to be drafted and killed in Viet Nam."

"Craig, don't say things like that!"

"I wish I didn't feel that way. But I better get out of here before I hear from the draft board."

Craig's intuition couldn't have been more accurate. However his father counseled him to stay in the U.S. and his fathers' will prevailed. When the draft notice came, John Maratta over rode Craig's inclination to high tail it for Canada. He lectured Craig on how he ought to do as well as he could for the short stint in the service. Deep down inside Craig wanted very much to please and earn respect from his father. So he went into the army with the best of intentions. After finishing basic training with the highest scores in his company and coming home briefly on leave, Craig was bound for Viet Nam. The beginning of his tour of duty was August 6, 1970.

After only two months 'In Country' Craig was beginning to accept the tough and unforgiving conditions. He wrote regularly to Valerie. While he occasionally referred to missing her, strangely his letters did not talk about the future or coming home.

It was early the morning of September 7, 1970 when Craig and some others in his squad were collecting Claymore mines that it happened. The Claymores were often used on defensive perimeters to keep the Viet Cong outside of American camps. However, the wily Cong would occasionally rig the mines so that when the Americans would collect them as they broke camp to move on, the mines would detonate on the very troops that employed them. Unfortunately this was not an uncommon occurrence. The Viet Cong had no where near the equipment or resources of the American forces. So they came up with ingenious ways to turn the Americans own force back on themselves.

As a young American private in Craig's squad attempted to gingerly uncover and lift a Claymore, the mine exploded. The shattering blast killed or wounded the few soldiers in the immediate vicinity. Craig Maratta, serial number 159384097, was one of the fatalities. What was left of him was packed in a rubber bag and shipped home to America.

Sadly, it appeared to Valerie, his family and all of us who knew him that Craig's death was senseless and he died in vain. Because of the reluctance of the American administration during Viet Nam, overly focused upon politics and re-elections, our military was stifled from doing what was necessary to win that war. And as the anti-war protesting and negative coverage in our news media increased at home, the Viet Cong simply held on until America lost the will to remain in the struggle. America pulled out with the fall of Saigon in April of 1975. An estimated 58,000 American lives were lost in Southeast Asia. In that number, Craig Marratta was one more statistic with his name being eventually placed on panel 07W - Row 118 of the Vietnam Memorial in Washington, DC.

VI.

On the porch swing Valerie moves slowly as the moon rises higher over the serene ocean. The low light from the oil lamp on the glass top of the table casts a faint orange glow upon her face. The tune 'The Lamp is Low' plays in her mind.

Dream beside me in the midnight glow, the lamp is low. Dream and watch the shadows come and go. . .

The wind is beginning to die down. By now the gulls have taken to their perches for the night. It is a lovely and haunting evening. A few stars become visible high overhead, struggling to make their presence known against the bright light of the moon. She is happy here. And she is thankful for all that she has. She is moved to a prayer of gratitude.

Lord, thank you for all that you've blessed me with. For my family. For my work. Thank you for this place of peace that I visit each year.

After a while she begins to feel like going up to the bedroom. She isn't sleepy. She's just ready to return to the room where she finds great comfort. She rises. Proceeding to the table, she gently blows out the lamp. Hesitating, she walks back to the porch fence. Placing her hands upon the rail she leans slightly forward. The fragrance of the rambling rose is in the air. She closes her eyes and smiles enjoying the pleasant fragrance.

Entering the house Valerie turns off the light on the living room table. After locking the front door she ascends the stairs in the dark to the upper level. She visits the bathroom to prepare to go to bed and then remembers she left her suitcase downstairs. Quickly she scampers down and back up the stairs. The slight exertion makes her feel even less like sleep.

She finishes in the bathroom and enters the bedroom. There she takes his picture out of her suitcase and places it on the night stand next to the bed. After removing and hanging her dress she turns out the light and reclines on top of the covers. Valerie does not feel alone. She believes her lover is somehow near to her in spirit there in the quiet room.

Lying in the dark she watches the old ceiling fan revolving slowly above. The moon's light streams in to illuminate the wall opposing the window facing the ocean. The Victorian era house has no air conditioning. But the ocean breeze and the abundance of windows keeps it comfortable. Listening to the steady rhythm of the surf upon the shore she is comforted. She is in harmony and thinks of nothing in particular. There is just the awareness of what she feels. The soft breeze occasionally touches her. The lace curtain by the window stirs. Somewhere in the distance she hears the tolling of the buoy as it rocks in the water.

Her eyes turn from the ceiling to gaze out the window. Above the ocean a few clouds are lighted by the moon. Their silvery outlines conjure images. They remind her of her childhood playing in the meadow near their home in spring. She remembers that one time she and her friend Natalie were watching clouds and discussing what they imagined the shapes to represent. Lying on their backs they told each other what they saw. Castles; the face of a princess; dragons.

He loved the song 'Puff, the Magic Dragon'.

Her mind lets go of the memories of the meadow, the clouds, and those early days of childhood. She lets go of all thoughts; but him. She wonders to herself.

Is his presence a figment of my imagination? Or is he really here close to me? Is he watching over me the way I feel that he is?

Eventually a single tear rolls down her cheek.

Five years. How long will it be until we're together again?

Eventually the sound of the far off waves on the shore becomes her focus. Rolling on her side Valerie embraces one of the pillows. Her hair streams across the other pillow. She relaxes completely. Soon sleep overcomes her. Just after she drifts off the room grows deathly still. The curtains hang motionless. Then in the dark, her hair is brushed back gently from her forehead by the ghost of the ocean breeze through the open window.

Epilogue

Completing the finishing touches before the mirror, she contemplated the preceding twenty three years since Craig had been taken from her. Life must go on. And she must as well. Valerie understood that living for the past isn't living. She speaks to him before she steps out into the hall.

I believe you would want me to go through with this today.

He isn't you. But he loves me. And I have learned to love him. I hope you accept this.

She walks down the hall with her mother at her side. Valerie sees Ruth Ann about to enter the sanctuary. Their eyes meet. Ruth Ann smiles brightly toward her. Valerie is lifted by the grace of the older lady's presence. She closes her eyes for a moment. Then she steps forward and walks to take her place before the alter.

The Mentor

If you can keep your head when all about you are losing theirs
And blaming it on you
If you can trust yourself when all men doubt you
And yet make allowance for their doubting too

— Kipling

There are people who come into our lives occasionally that change our future. Sometimes they do this for the better. Other times for worse. The choice upon which course can be determined by us if we are astute enough to recognize the potential influence of that person. Many influence our choices such as where we attend school or where we live or work and that also changes the direction of our lives. But beyond just influencing choices some people have a continuous long term effect that can even change us and as a result the future. And those are the ones that count the most.

I.

The initial view of the campus in early May of 1969 was stirring. White and pink blossoms seemed to be everywhere. Driving through the west entry I was immediately impressed by the spectacle and the fragrance of the flowers that graced the terraced campus. Michigan State University was the first land grant college in the United States. Originally established in 1855, Michigan Agricultural College as it was known then has always been one of the most beautifully landscaped and maintained colleges in the country. There were rhododendrons, azaleas, roses, orchids of all colors and more. In addition maples, elms, oaks and other stately trees with buds or new iridescent green leaves complimented stately red brick and stone buildings representing various styles of architecture. And then there were the coeds. On that May afternoon the young ladies were as appropriate to the setting as everything else on the beautiful campus. My mind was made up. I would attend Michigan State.

On that first exposure to MSU, my head crowded with frivolous thoughts having nothing to do with enhancing my academic education, I could not have imagined the enormous role that university would play in my life. Or the influence I would eventually be fortunate enough to have upon persons who worked for or attended MSU over the next twenty two years. While I don't consider Michigan State my alma mater, because of the roles I played there it would ultimately become central to much of what I gave some of the best years of my life to.

Having graduated with my Bachelor's degree from Thiel College in Greenville, Pennsylvania in 1968 I hoped an additional Masters degree from a 'Big Ten' school might bolster my long term opportunities. While attending Thiel I had joined the Marine Corps Officer Candidate program and was accepted to attend their Flight Officer program at Pensacola, Florida to enter upon graduation. However, a Pars defect in my spine detected before graduation from college led to being honorably discharged from the Marine Corp before being commissioned. Unexpectedly I had no career plan or direction as I left Thiel. So after graduation I took a job with Travelers Insurance Company in Pittsburgh to buy some time to figure out what I wanted to do. One year of experience at Travelers convinced me I should consider earning a graduate degree that might open more career options other than the insurance industry.

My visit to Michigan State was a direct result of being

invited over by a friend named Jim Ummer. Jim was attending graduate school at MSU and he had suggested I consider it as a prospective place for me to earn my graduate degree. Jim had arranged for me to meet and talk with some of the faculty in his academic program. He also introduced me to the Director of the residence hall system in the hope I might obtain employment as a residence hall student advisor to help pay for the cost of the degree as well as gain a place to live at no cost. I had held a similar position in a student residence hall at Thiel College as a senior.

And in fact I did gain a position as a hall advisor for the fall of 1969 when I began my graduate degree at Michigan State. The first year was a difficult adjustment. Both as a hall advisor and as a graduate student. I was never a good student either in college or at the graduate level. And babysitting the students in the residence hall was not something I was particularly excited to do though I had such experience at Thiel and welcomed the position. By the second year of the program I became the Head Resident in charge of Williams Hall, one of three coed residence halls established that year. The first coed halls in the history of Michigan State. It was not only an unexpected honor, but that position more than paid for tuition, room and board as well as extra cash for incidentals.

II.

It was during the second year of my Masters program when I began a practicum in the Placement Office at Michigan State that I met the man that would change my life direction more positively than anyone. Jack Shingleton was the Director of the Michigan State Placement Office. By that time he was known informally as the Dean of College Placement nationally because of his reputation and influence. Many universities modeled their placement operations after Jack's operation which assisted thousands of graduates in finding careers each year. In 1968 Jack had been thrust into the national spotlight as the central figure in a 90 minute special feature prepared by CBS News on the role of higher education in America. During that program CBS had interviewed him much on the subject of what colleges should do to best prepare young men and women for careers as well as life.

Part of the CBS program also included Jack in a debate in the Michigan State board room with a group of academicians about the place of a college education in preparing people for responsible roles in our culture. I had by coincidence watched the program when it was originally broadcast. In the debate the academicians had rallied against Jack maintaining that higher education should stay with a more traditional academic focus than emphasizing career preparation. Jack's position was that higher education should play a more practical role in preparing graduates for productive and useful positions in society beyond just academic interests.

One of the most memorable vignettes in the debate was spurred by Dr. Milton Muelder, a Dean at Michigan State. At one point after Jack stated that higher education had a responsibility to prepare students to lead useful lives in the professions as well as other applied career paths Dr. Muelder spoke up. The Dean stated, "We all know Jack Shingleton is a fine placement officer and Michigan State is fortunate to have him. But frankly his sophomoric view of what academic institutions should do in education is uninformed and misses the point of why people attend universities. They should attend principally to become enlightened, not to pursue vocational interests."

Jack responded immediately but in a measured and deliberate manner. He said, "I think Dr. Muelder has just illustrated the essence of an attitude that's all too prevalent at many of our academic institutions. If institutions of higher learning ignore the realities of the world beyond their ivy covered walls, they fall far short of what real education for the future should address. Universities that ignore the importance of preparing youth for productive roles in society will suffer not only decreasing enrollments but the respect and value that they need to continue to be an important part of America's future."

Dr. Muelder and the others in his camp had no viable response. As the CBS program ended, Jack had clearly won the day. He made the point that higher education must be in touch with the outside world and future to attract youth seeking purpose and meaning in their lives. The highly watched and acclaimed program enhanced his position as one of the most well known and respected educators in America during those years.

Jack also managed to achieve national fame not only because of his influence on policies governing higher education but because of his unusual talents in speaking, writing, and even national senior division tennis. Having been a World War II pilot and accomplished athlete during his early years, he was about as well rounded a man as I've seen. Later he served as the Director of Athletics at Michigan State and eventually became Chairman of the Board of Michigan State. Jack was a true 'Renaissance Man'.

When first introduced to Jack as I began the practicum in his office, I immediately noticed that he looked one directly in the eyes when speaking. Rocking back and forth slightly on his heels with hands crossed in front or clasped behind his back and standing close he would listen thoughtfully. Standing 6'1" he still seemed taller because of his intense presence. When he spoke he did so with authority but few enough words to hold others interest. His steely blue eyes would squint to emphasize a point or he'd raise one eye brow to indicate thoughtful consideration. Jack was never one for casual conversation. Most of the exchanges with him were either profound, informative or focused upon a specific topic. And he was always fascinating.

In addition to his good fortune in life beyond his talents

and intelligence, Jack had been blessed with something very rare in most men's lives. His wife Helen, who he had known since the age of fifteen had a huge positive effect upon him. Helen herself was highly intelligent, lovely and as positive a woman as I've ever known. In many ways she would encourage, buffer, or redirect Jack for the better. They had three children together and stayed married until her untimely death from cancer in her early seventies. The two of them continued to stay genuinely romantic over all the years. After her death he elected to avoid developing a relationship with any other woman though they were quite available to him. He explained to me that was because she was the only partner he would ever need and he believed she still lived in his heart. He was to say the least, an incurable romantic with a keen sentimental side.

III.

Ultimately I did manage to skim by and satisfy the requirements for the two year Masters Degree awarded to me in 1971 at MSU though my academic performance left much to be desired. Immediately after graduation I accepted a position at Oakland University in Rochester, Michigan as the Assistant Director of the Career Planning and Placement Center. I was employed there until the fall of 1972 until I evoked the ire of the Dean of Engineering over a comment I made in the media about limited opportunities for graduates at that time. But by that fall I was invited to return to Michigan State to direct a brand new student employment program at the university and begin one of the most unusual and rewarding odysseys of my career. I was to head the Student Employment Office which had just been designed by Jack Shingleton and agreed to by the Human Resources Department at MSU. My office and staff reporting to me had a dotted line reporting relationship under Jack's authority. I was responsible for directing the administration of the new program that employed over 15,000 enrolled employees at the university.

"Jim, this isn't going to be just a job. It's going to be much more. Probably one of the greatest challenges and opportunities you'll ever experience", Jack told me on my first day of employment as the Director of the Student Employment Office. Neither he nor I could know how prophetic that statement would be.

He went on, "There're over fifteen thousand employees on the student payroll in 275 departments in each twelve month period on campus. A big part of what you and your staff will have to do is ensure that everyone employed is paid correctly and treated fairly in respect to the employment policies. This won't be easy. Not only because it's such a large workforce, but there'll be some departments that may try to get around the pay scales and policies we've established." That was an understatement. I had to watch many of the departments closely. At times I felt like an IRS auditor and was occasionally treated with as much disdain. I don't blame them.

In the first year I spent much time communicating with both department heads as well as students working out difficulties in attempting to have the entire campus adjust to the new program. Our pay scales were the highest in the Big Ten and our employment policies were the best. But because it was all new and centralized through my office, there were a number of snags and resistance that I and my staff had to work out. We did. It was going well. At least for awhile.

It was in the second year of the program that an unanticipated challenge occurred. It had nothing to do with the policies, pay scales, procedures or any of the departments on campus. It was due to an ad hock group on campus that called itself the "Student Workers Union". This group wanted to organize the enrolled employees under its banner and win recognition as a formal union with full collective bargaining power. Headed by two enrolled employees by the names of Tim Cain and Doyle O'Connor, it had the behind the scenes support of some liberal faculty at MSU as well as the AFSCME union on campus. The American Federation of School College and Municipal Employees knew that if the Student Workers Union could win recognition, the effect would eventually result in a drastic cut in jobs offered to students and a swelling of AFSCME ranks. So while AFSCME would not come out publically in support of the SWU, they helped support and encourage it for their own interests.

The tactics employed by the SWU were classic strategies employed by predatory unions that endeavor to seize power. They were behind numerous attempts to stir unrest, bogus claims of unfair labor practices, efforts to demonize the employer in the press, and characterizing themselves as the solution to a problem that did not exist. Similar to many political types that want power. And in fact some of their members even went so far as to beat up an outspoken student employee by the name of Phil Lange. Phil had taken it upon himself to become an opponent to them by mounting a truth campaign about the SWU. He knew what they were all about and felt it unjust that the University could not point out the hypocrisy of the SWU because of the potential of unfair labor charges if we did. Of course even if the charges were eventually proven unsubstantiated, in the meantime they would earn much press and attention that would work to the advantage of the SWU.

So while Michigan State had actually taken a major step forward in improving employment opportunities and pay for enrolled employees, the SWU tired to make the case that the program was simply a ploy to exploit student workers. Being in the central and most visible position in the program, I became a primary target of their slanderous claims. As a result, the next three years I held the position, I with Jack's counsel and support was squarely in the role of battling a union attempt.

During those years Jack was a confidant and my mainstay in fighting the battle. I was in the frontline position but Jack was behind me advising often along the way. A better mentor

I can't imagine. That's not to say it was always smooth between us. In fact Jack and I both were highly emotional and volatile personalities. Because of the stresses and sometimes differing views on how to handle issues we occasionally got into strong disagreements that resulted in shouting as well as other less than professional behaviors. At times this occurred in front of staff members who would run for cover if things got testy. In later years he and I would look back on those bouts in recollection and laugh about them.

But behind it all, there was great loyalty and appreciation for each other. We always ended up shaking hands and returning to mutual support. I felt he and I were actually closer than many family members. Even to the time of this writing, thirty five years later, I feel the same way about him.

During the ongoing battle with the union organizers Jack coached me to not give the credibility of a perceived response to their accusations or lies but instead work hard on a continuous positive information campaign in support of the student employment program. One of the most important lessons he imparted to me was to commit to memory the lines of 'If' by Rudyard Kipling and attempt to practice them daily during the battle. While that may seem a bit banal the wisdom in those words guided me often in difficult and trying times. And I saw them modeled by him at every turn.

I appeared often in the news and at various speaking functions discussing the merits of the program. In all of those cases I avoided being tripped up by trick questions or ploys to lash out at the organizers. However, occasionally Jack would jump into the action and lash out. Because he was not perceived as the primary representative of the university in the struggle, he could get away with that much easier than me.

As is often the case in any political or power struggle, the news media played an important role. The Michigan State News, which printed over 100,000 copies daily of their paper for over 45,000 students, 20,000 employees including faculty and staff and other readers in the East Lansing community, was the primary media player. On a memorable occasion with them Jack had walked into his office one morning to see a headline in the State News trumpeting "Student Workers Largely Encouraged by SWU". He and I knew that was not true. It was just an attention grabbing headline by a liberal editor. Jack grabbed the newspaper and we took a trip to the Editors office. I went with Jack to make sure things didn't get too far out of hand. I knew what his temper was like. Jack barged into the Editors office unannounced and lifted the paper high over his head. He then slammed it down hard in front of the editor and exclaimed "Do you want to print the truth?" The frightened editor choked out, "Of course."

With his face red and his eyes squinting Jacks immediate response was, "Well, that's not the truth. What would make you print something like this?"

It was all I could do to keep a straight face as the editors hands began shaking as he skimmed the story. Eventually after Jack cooled down we did have a rational discussion with the editor and the writer who had written the cover story. During that discussion it became apparent to the State News staff that they were not dealing with characters that were intimidated by the power of the press. I played the role of the calm head, a stretch by any standard, to balance Jack's role as the volatile landmine waiting for the next time they made such an egregious error.

In fact my own dealings with the State News were helped somewhat by an unplanned and fortuitous occurrence. A writer by the name of Peggy Gossett and I developed a relationship during 1975 and 76. Through her I got to know the editors of the paper and some of the writers personally. The fact that I had this inside connection with the paper did help us gain more balanced coverage of the stories written over the last two years of the battle. I didn't attempt anything inappropriate with them to gain an advantage. But simply the fact that they knew me in a social context I know influenced how they approached their fact finding as well as writing. Eventually Peggy gained national prominence covering women's professional tennis and professional football. She was one of the first female reporters to become well known nationally in sports circuits.

In addition to the State News, WJIM television as well as radio stations in Lansing and Detroit and two other local NBC and CBS affiliate television stations often got into the action. So a large part of my responsibility was to become the university spokesperson in respect to the issue in the media for three years. Additionally we had some court appearances having to do with the legal issues related to the unionization attempt and ultimately the certification of the group for an election. I was the central witness representing the university. There again with Jack's coaching I learned how to handle myself on the witness stand. That skill would eventually pay dividends in my professional life later serving as an expert witness for clients as well as at a trial in which I was the primary litigant much later in life.

While I had originally signed up for the position with Jack and MSU in the fall of 1972 simply expecting to run a strong employment program for the students and the university, in addition to that role, I had unexpectedly taken on the challenge of becoming a union buster. This was ironic as I felt strongly that some unions were essential in protecting workers interests. But it was this experience that demonstrated to me that there are many unions that are principally in power for the sake of their officers own ends and the workers interest were incidental. I term them "predatory unions" and their presence has been well documented in American history.

An increasing and stressful part of my role was to settle labor disputes. Though there was no union yet, the SWU spurred many issues between employees and university departments in the hopes of gaining credibility as well as news coverage to the effect there was a legitimate reason for a union. It became such that I could never rest. But as always, my mentor provided excellent guidance behind the scenes. I juggled the press, employment issues, administering a large employment program and tried to continue to referee issues within departments across the campus while they were still adjusting to the system. The efforts became exhausting.

IV.

"Mr. Anderson. This is Will Murphy of WJIM news. We know there is soon to be an election in respect to the union attempt going on at Michigan State and I'd like to know if I can come over and interview you."

It was early 1976 and Will Murphy was at that time the anchor man for the 6:00 evening news for WJIM, the major television news station in mid-Michigan. I had been interviewed often by WJIM and other television stations and newspapers over the preceding three years, but this story might become most significant. It was about to be aired shortly before the election in which the SWU would either be accepted or rejected. This interview would be the lead story on the news that evening.

When Will and his camera crew showed up a little later that day, he and I chatted as the make up person put something on my face to reduce the glare from the camera lights.

"How long has this unionization attempt been going on?" asked Will before the camera was turned on.

"It began in 1973 Will."

"Why are you fighting this? What's wrong with the students having their own union?"

"Will, our strategy hasn't been to fight with union organizers. We've simply put together the best employment program for students in the 'Big Ten' and made sure the persons eligible to vote understand the advantages of the program."

"Well, don't you have to discuss what would be wrong about certification of the union if they win?" Will asked.

"We're not going to do that Will. We know if the employees are well informed about the facts of what they currently benefit from, they'll know how to vote."

A few minutes later my office was lit by bright lights and with the camera rolling, Will began his interview of me.

Will opened with, "We are here talking with Jim Anderson, the Director of Student Employment at Michigan State University where an election will soon be held to rule upon certification of a union to represent the student employees."

Then placing the microphone in front of me and facing me squarely, Will asked, "Jim why are you and MSU telling employees to vote against the Student Workers Union?"

Having become experienced in staying focused and speaking in sound bytes from many previous on the air interviews, I responded. "Will, as I stated just before you turned on your camera, we've not been telling employees to vote against the unionization attempt but have simply been providing facts about the advantages of the existing employment program at Michigan State, which pays the highest rates in the 'Big Ten'."

Over the next few minutes Will attempted to bait me with a number of other leading questions that would encourage me to express negative views about the SWU organization. I stayed positive. In the news program that evening which included disparaging remarks about our program by SWU representatives, Will had nothing negative from me. Of course if I had said anything negative, the SWU could have claimed unfair labor practice charges against MSU. As it turned out, they looked bad in that news spot because of their obvious negative style versus our positive approach.

On the morning of the election, I was encouraged by a seemingly inconsequential statement of a student I encountered on the campus. One of the polling places was the old gymnasium on the west campus. There were a number of pro union characters parading around with signs promoting the SWU. But most of the students on campus that passed them ignored or looked at them with obvious disdain. One student in particular spotted me and walked over possibly recognizing who I was. "Sir, is this where we vote on this unionization thing?" he asked.

"It is if you're an employee of the university and also a student", I replied.

He looked at me and smiled responding, "Sounds good. I can't wait" as he turned to walk into the building with a couple of other friends.

That evening when all the results were in and tabulated the vote was 10 to 1 against the union. This was an unprecedented occurrence in union elections in Michigan history. It was a huge win for the university and me personally. Jack called me on the phone that evening and we talked it all over. He flattered me for the work I had done in the program over the four years. But I felt the real credit went to him as without his guidance I'm confident the outcome would have been different. I told him that in no uncertain terms.

Shortly after the victory, I decided to leave Michigan State. The four years in the position had been draining and I couldn't see how anything else I could do in that role would top what had occurred. And we had crushed them so soundly we knew they wouldn't be back for a long time, if ever. Most importantly by defeating that group, we protected part time jobs for thousands of students that would have been removed through attrition and replaced by AFSCME members over the next few years had the student workers become unionized. So at the age of 29, being single and financially solid, I decided to retire from the Michigan State role and tour Europe for a few months. I definitely needed a change of scene.

V.

While I had no plans to return to Michigan State, it wasn't long, 1980 to be exact, that I was drawn back into the affairs of the university. It happened unexpectedly. Almost as though providence was guiding me. And my mentor again came back into my life.

After returning from Europe in 1977 I took a position with a 'Big Eight' consulting firm in Detroit as an organization development consultant. We performed audits and reviews of the management and human resource systems of client companies. Actually I worked for two such companies in the space of four years. Arthur Young and Company in Detroit and Touche Ross in Atlanta. I learned specific skills that had to do with review and upgrading hiring programs, employee assessment systems, reward and compensation, and other organization development requirements. However, being highly independent and not fitting well in any position where I had a boss, by 1980 I decided to start my own consulting business and possibly earn a Ph.D. in business.

Due to a large number of business contacts in Michigan I returned there from Atlanta because I expected more opportunity to develop consulting business on my own. Additionally I considered earning the Ph.D. in business at Michigan State. However, after taking a couple of trial courses at MSU in the fall of 1980 it was obvious I was not cut out to continue any more advanced academic path. But by coincidence I met the Associate Dean of the Graduate School of Business during my ill fated experiment with courses in the doctoral program. His name was Phil Carter.

When Phil learned about my 'Big Eight' consulting experience he asked if I would be interested in teaching a course in Organization Behavior in the Graduate School. I was surprised he would entertain such as a notion as I had only a Masters degree and no Ph.D. like the other faculty in the MBA program. But he thought that would be an advantage as he figured I would teach the course as a practitioner instead of an academician. And he remembered me from the battle with the union organizers a few years earlier. He was impressed by what I had been involved in at the University as well as the 'Big Eight' consulting firms. He was willing to take a chance on me though there were many others with more traditional academic credentials. I agreed and accepted an adjunct faculty position in the spring of 1981 teaching one course at night.

In December of 1980 I had filed the paperwork to incorporate my consulting business in Michigan. Ultimately that consulting business, named MSR for Management Services and Resources, would span thirty years. During the day I handled client work of MSR and during the evening I taught in the MBA program. In fact both of these endeavors became far more successful than I had envisioned when I began them. I soon earned a fulltime position teaching at night in the Graduate School with a good salary and insurance benefits and the autonomy I required as I was not responsible for research or reporting to anyone. I held the teaching position for eleven years until I left Michigan for Colorado in 1991. Simultaneously, MSR grew. Slowly at first. Jack continued to stay close and encourage me with both the teaching and consulting.

VI.

It was while I held the faculty position at MSU that some of the most rewarding and productive times of my career occurred. Because I was not responsible for research and used a practitioners approach as suggested by Jack in my courses, I enjoyed teaching immensely. Additionally I cared very much about the students and seeing them gain practical value from my courses. I didn't teach like most of the academicians with a straight lecture approach and multiple choice exams. Influenced by Jack about how classes should not just study a subject but include how to apply the learning in practical settings I used creative approaches that promoted discussion, debate, presentations, cases studies and much involvement between me and my students. And Jack's influence prompted me to set the standards high for my own teaching excellence. Additionally I would bring in experts from time to time to bolster course content beyond just my expertise.

By 1983 Phil Carter informed me that I had become the most popular faculty member in the School of Business as demonstrated by the ratings the students completed on the faculty of each course they took and the demand for enrollment in my classes. After the student ratings were turned into the College of Business and reviewed they were given to the faculty to read and keep. I was so proud of the ratings I continue to keep them and am willing to share them with anyone interested to this day. In the eleven years I taught at Michigan State I computed that I had the opportunity to teach over 2,100 students in my classes. There were many I remember well and who kept in touch with me over the years. The intrinsic rewards to me of that experience rivaled the victory over the union years earlier as well as the chance to have a positive affect upon many young people.

All during my years of teaching Jack and I stayed close. While he was no longer a person I reported to, he had become more than a mentor as a close friend. By 1989 we collaborated on a book written to guide professionals in career change. The book titled 'Mid-Career Change; Strategies for Success' was published by a company in California and helped a large number of corporate and business types refocus into positions and career paths that would improve their lives. Simultaneously while teaching, writing the book and consulting, Jack and I also set up an office at Michigan State to assist faculty who left the university to find employment outside academic settings.

Jack and I would spend time together dining, talking, fishing, or at social functions. He was kind enough to invite me, my father, my friends and children to his cottage on Platt Lake in Northern Michigan on more than one occasion. I remember well him encouraging my son Eric trout fishing. Or taking my father out on the river to fish together. Jack was an accomplished trout fisherman and published a couple of books on the subject. In fact he was a prolific author and had published a dozen books on a variety of subjects including fishing, tennis, career success, and related subjects.

Stemming directly from my experience at MSU my consulting business MSR Corporation became my primary vocation from 1980 all the way through to 2010. My professional services included assessing and coaching executives and sales professionals; developing hiring, appraisal and training systems; and conducting a few hundred executive seminars over the thirty years of the business. I had the opportunity to coach and train thousands of professionals in those years. The coaching skills I applied had been learned directly from my experience with Jack. In essence I built a business and career upon what he taught me.

In the years from 1980 until 1991 Michigan State, the first eleven of MSR, teaching at MSU gave me more opportunity to make contributions to others lives than I ever imagined. Additionally my lifestyle was enhanced by being afforded all of the benefits any fulltime faculty member could enjoy at a great university. Cultural and educational opportunities were unlimited.

And of great importance, athletic opportunities were availed to me at Michigan State. Not as a spectator; but as a participant. I was able to play as much basketball at the men's intramural facility as I could possible fit into my schedule. All the way through into my mid-forties I played against young men. While a problem knee and leg continued to challenge me, they were far less an issue in basketball than in playing football or running track as I had attempted unsuccessfully in high school and college. In essence I was given a second chance to play sports. And though I was significantly older than my opponents and team mates, I managed to play well into my mid-forties and finally enjoyed the opportunity to excel in athletics that I had lost as a young man.

Michigan State was good for me in so many ways that I'll always appreciate my involvement there. And it was Jack and Phil Carter who made it possible. They had believed in me and placed me in positions which others had far greater formal credentials for. Principally I am most thankful to Jack as he was the person who brought me back to MSU in 1972 to head the program which ultimately opened all of the other doors in teaching and consulting over the years. I am indebted to him as I and my family have been greatly enriched by his influence.

The Prayer

I.

"Someday you're going to grow up to be a fine man. And we're going to be buddies. I'll be very proud of you. Now hold the basket with me while your mother takes the picture of us. Smile Jimmy."

What is it that would indelibly impress those words from Easter of 1952 in the mind of a five year old boy? Was it just one of those moments that represented childhood? Or was it because I had on my first Easter outfit with the coat that Mom got special for me? Or was there something else? Perhaps it was the first awareness that my dad had high expectations for me. Even at that early age, a little boy can form dreams and hopes. It was expected that I grow into someone he would be proud of. And we'd be buddies.

It seemed that Dad played a larger role in our lives than most fathers in my circle of friends as long as I could remember. His influence on us was overwhelming. Even his influence in our town was large. Almost all knew Dr. Anderson as an important man. As his son, I was expected to become something special. By him and others.

All three of us boys wanted to please Dad and earn his respect. But even more, we wanted to be loved by him though we didn't discuss or even think consciously about it. As long as he lived, whether we admitted it or not, we were seeking some demonstration from him that he loved us. We searched for things we could do that would connect us to him. But for the most part, particularly after I left early childhood behind,

151

he was not the kind of man that could make us feel that he was pleased with us. Or that he loved us. It wasn't that he didn't want to. I believe it was simply not something he was capable of.

II.

"Jim, this is Tot. I'm at Parkview Hospital. Dad was brought in this afternoon diagnosed with a heart attack. He collapsed shortly after arriving by ambulance and quit breathing. He's on a respirator now and isn't expected to last through the night."

"I'll be right there", I responded while at dinner with a friend.

It was the fall of 1995. Mother passed away two years earlier in Florida where she and Dad had resided since 1970. We just moved Dad out to Colorado a few months before because he was not doing well on his own at the retirement center in Florida. Here we had him located at an excellent assisted living facility. And my brother Totty and the rest of us visited him one at a time or sometimes together almost every day. We often took him to our homes, for walks or out to eat. He did not suffer from neglect. However, he did suffer from dementia.

"That nice young man came to take me to dinner last night." Dad would sometimes say to my older brother Totty.

"Do you mean Jim? Your son, Dad?"

"Oh yes. That was Jim. He takes me for walks too."

That dialog, probably repeated a number of times over the last few months of Dad's life with us in Colorado was replayed with me as well on occasion. Except in those cases Totty was the young man he could not identify. The last couple of weeks I spent with him another conversation was also repeated more than once.

The large sad blue eyes would gaze at me for a few moments.

If he could remember my name, he would say, "Jim, what do you think I should do?"

I would respond, "About what Dad?"

"Well, I don't know. Is there anything you think I should do?"

"Yes, Dad. I think you should pray as much as you can. And let me take you to church."

"You know, I gave the church a lot of money over the years. Pastor Brown told me more than once how much they appreciated my support."

"Well Dad, that's good. But that's not relevant to here and now. I think more than anything you should pray about what you're thankful for, and for guidance in the here and now."

"When we were children, our mother often led us in prayers at our besides before we went to sleep."

"That was over eighty years ago Dad. Why don't we pray some now?"

However, I just could not seem to get him to either join me in prayer or go to church. Still, every time he'd ask me "What should I do?" I would continue to encourage him to join me in speaking to our Creator.

During all the years we knew him until close to the end, Dad was unusually bright. His memory was superior to anyone I have known. Often he would launch into recitation of countless lines of poetry memorized in his youth and retained for practically his whole life. I heard 'Elegy in a Country Church Yard' and stanzas of 'The Rime of the Ancient Mariner' often. We did not recognize Alzheimer's in him until perhaps the age of 85. Then it progressed quickly. We watched the impressive and highly intelligent figure fade quickly over those last couple of years after Mom died. Also, until the end, we knew that he was physically a strong man. However, we had no idea how tough he really was. That was to be displayed dramatically in the last few hours of his life.

III.

Saturday morning two days before collapsing in the hospital, Dad had spoken to Totty on the phone. He reported that he didn't feel well and believed he had a bad case of indigestion.

"Dad, what did you have to eat and when did it start?" Totty had asked.

"Well, we had fish last night in the dining room. I think I just ate too much."

"Did you report this to the nurse at the center?" asked Totty.

"Naw. I don't think they can do anything."

"Well how do you feel today?" his son queried.

"Not good. I think I'll just stay down today and watch television."

Totty called Dad again on Sunday and was told he'd just like to rest that day watching golf on television. Monday, when Totty telephoned Dad to determine what time one of us would go over to visit with him, Dad reported he still felt poorly. Totty then decided to call the nurse on duty at the center and have her look in on him.

In the afternoon she visited Dad. She was shocked to see that his blood pressure was sky high. In fact he had suffered a heart attack sometime Saturday night or early Sunday morning. And no one knew it. Not even Dr. Anderson himself. She called for an ambulance immediately and alerted the hospital that he would soon arrive.

The admitting physician reported later that when the defiant old man got out of the ambulance, he refused to be carted into the hospital in a wheel chair. Instead he walked into the emergency entrance under his own power. The admitting physician told us later in detail how the conversation proceeded. Dad's last statement before collapsing in front of the physician was. "You know, I led a good life." And at that point a stroke caused Dad to lose consciousness and tumble to the linoleum floor. He ceased breathing. Immediately a respirator was inserted into Dad to force air in and out of his lungs.

IV.

Arriving at the hospital that evening after the phone call from Totty, I was directed up to the critical care section where Dad was. As I walked down the hall to his room, the smell of antiseptic and the musty odor so common in hospitals filled my nostrils. It signified an ominous atmosphere that I was not comfortable in. Coming up to the door of his room, I wondered what I would encounter. The door was ajar and I quietly stepped in behind my brother sitting next to Dad's bed.

The contorted figure of Dad was lying tilted to his right side. The left knee was drawn up a bit because the stroke had hit the right side of his brain which affected left side motor functions. His head was turned up toward the ceiling; both eyes were dilated and wide open staring blankly at nothing. The right eye protruded out of the socket due to the pressure from the ruptured ventricle in the brain behind it. Both eyes were unblinking. The face was a pasty grey color. His mussed up hair gave him the appearance of a slain wild man concocted by a Hollywood make up artist.

"How long have you been here Tot?" I asked.

"Since about six o'clock."

"So, what's the story?"

"Well, the only reason his heart is still beating is because of the respirator. They told me if they take him off that, his heart will stop beating from lack of oxygen. They also told me his brain is dead. There's no activity."

"And if they don't take him off the respirator?"

"He's not supposed to make it through tonight regardless."

"OK. I guess I'll just pull up a chair and wait it out. What do you plan to do?"

"I'll stay", he replied.

I pulled a chair on the other side of Dad. The room was quiet except for the whirring noise of the machine that was pumping oxygen into Dad. We sat quietly for a few minutes. Looking at Dad a number of memories and visions of him began to come to mind. I remembered him dancing comically in front of the television to the rock and roll music of the Dick Clark Show. Teaching me how to hit a baseball. Standing up for me when my brothers were poking fun of my attempts to make a bow from a tree branch. Taking me for long evening drives in the country listening to the station that played movie theme music on the car radio. And more.

Most of what played over in my mind that night was the good about him. But he had been a tormented man. His behavior, especially from our teens on, alienated him from us and Mother. Sadly, those stormy dark times overshadowed all. And yet, there was still something in me that loved him regardless of everything. Looking at the broken figure on that bed I felt compassion. I moved in closer. Taking the damp cloth off the stand, I carefully dabbed his forehead and cheeks. I brushed his hair back. I even lifted his limp palm for a few moments to see if there was any flicker of life in him. There was nothing but a still cold lifeless hand in mine.

"Are you able to stay all night?" Totty asked.

"I can't imagine leaving here under the circumstances. I want to stay. What about you?"

"I agree. We should stay", he responded.

Totty called our oldest brother George in California and told him what was going on. George decided to stay there and be kept posted on developments.

V.

Through the night the minutes ticked by slowly. We took turns dabbing his face with the damp cloth. Occasionally we would gently pull down each eye lid as the nurse instructed so that the eyes would stay moist. And we talked softly.

Our conversation that night was mostly about him. It remained focused on events that were positive or humorous. I knew that sometimes persons considered deceased or in catatonic states for weeks had later come back to consciousness and reported conversations overheard in hospital rooms such as this. If he could hear us, I didn't want him to hear either grim reports on his prognosis or anything that bothered us about him.

But that night it was impossible to imagine he could hear anything. Looking deep into those blank dilated eyes they appeared like dull lifeless glass. Their color had changed from blue in life to a muddy grey hue. The eye protruding from the socket looked like a light bulb with no shade and no current. The sallow complexion and cold feel of the skin covering his cheeks was that of a mannequin. And the medical staff had told us that there was nothing left but a heart beating only because a respirator forced oxygen through the lungs and into the blood stream. The tests had been conclusive about no brain activity.

So, we waited. And we talked.

""When we took the fishing trip to Canada with Dad in '59', did you think Mom was sorry we didn't take her?" I asked.

"Are you kidding? She was elated she didn't have to go", Totty responded.

"Yeah? Why?"

"Well let's be honest. About all she ever knew in that house was waiting on us boys and Dad with no time for herself. I have to believe us going away for a week to Perry Sound was the closest thing she knew to a real vacation probably all the years we lived there."

"It was thirty six years ago but I remember most of it like yesterday", I offered.

"Me too. Remember the bear?"

"Man do I. But you know what the most vivid memory of the whole trip was for me?"

Totty responded, "Dad. I dropped my rod."

"You got it! When Mr. McCormick let us borrow his prize rod that night before we left; I decided I'd never touch it. And then two days later the first evening we were trolling and Dad had me using it, I was really nervous. How I let it slip overboard and disappear into that lake I'll never understand."

"Well, maybe because you were so nervous", Totty retorted.

"Boy I thought I was in big trouble. I figured I'd wrecked the whole trip because I heard Dad tell McCormick we'd take such good care of it. I think that was the first time I'd cried in a couple of years. I knew I'd disappointed Dad. But do you remember what he did?" I said.

"No. I don't."

I responded, "Well he hugged me right away and told me it would be alright and he knew where he could purchase one exactly the same to replace it. Boy, I thought I was going to get it and then he completely caught me off guard with that response."

"Yeah. He could do that sometimes."

I went on. "And then on the last day as we were trolling the lake that afternoon the one in a million chance that I would spot the rod lying on the sandy bottom as we went right over it!"

"You didn't even say anything Jim. We just saw you go overboard and disappear beneath the surface in an instant with no words and for no apparent reason. Man that scared the hell out of us. Why'd you do that?"

"Tot, I didn't have time to discuss things. The boat was moving. If I had tried to tell him to turn around I figured we wouldn't get back to exactly where it was."

"I never saw Dad so relieved as when you popped back up with that rod in your hand."

"And McCormick never knew the difference. What were the odds of that happening? That was definitely the best memory of the whole trip for me", I responded.

We went on. Over the small still hours of the night we kept vigil with more and more stories and memories of adventures and events with our colorful father. If he could hear us, it had to be heart warming to him even in his dire condition. But neither of us thought he could hear us.

At one point, maybe between 3:00 and 4:00 AM we both lapsed into semi-sleep. But not for long. I kept opening my eyes slightly looking at Dad to see if anything would happen or change. It didn't. He never moved. And that was consistent with the doctors telling us he no longer had the ability to move. Or even blink his eyes. He was a lifeless form. The slight rising in the chest driven only by the respirator forcing his lungs to function.

By around 5:00 I asked my brother to step out of the room. We crept out into the hall quietly. "What do you want to do?" I queried.

"Well, they say he can't last so I guess we just wait until sun up and then decide what to do if his heart is still beating", he offered.

"Yeah. But let's consider the alternative. If his heart continues to beat, what do you think?"

"I'm not sure. If he's kept breathing in a vegetative state on the life support this may go on a long time. That's going to be very costly and he had told me more than once he didn't want that."

I pondered things carefully for a moment or two. I knew that I was the one who had less issues with Dad than my brothers. I couldn't blame them considering all that had happened over their lives having to do with him. But I realized that if anyone of the three of us would make the decision to pull life support, it had to be me. Either of the others would likely be tormented for the balance of their lives by the possibility of guilt that may attend them making such a decision.

With complete deference to my older brother Totty who had been fiscally as well as generally most responsible for Dad in his decline, I said, "OK Tot. Here's what I propose. Leave the decision up to me if and when it has to be made. I don't want you or George to be burdened with it. I still love the old bastard and if anyone must send him on his way, I think it has to be me."

"Hey. You get no argument from me."

I added, "Let's just see what happens over the next few hours. If he's hanging on by mid morning, I'm going to ask for another opinion. Then we'll go from there."

VI.

"What time is it?" I asked.

"It's a little after seven. I think I need to go home and get cleaned up. What about you?" Totty responded.

"I agree. He's already proven the doctors wrong. I'd say this could go on for quite awhile. I also want to know what other tests may be appropriate and if they'll do them."

Shortly after that a specialist in brain scanning entered. We talked a little bit and I asked her if they would do another scan. She responded they would and they'd soon hook Dad up to see if anything had changed. They would also analyze his urine and blood as well as do other tests. She told me they'd have results by late morning and I could call in. However, Totty and I wanted to return after getting cleaned up. I wanted to meet with the attending physician in person after we got updated results from tests. And then I wanted to talk with my brother in person as I felt there was an important decision coming up for me.

Before leaving I went back over to examine Dad. He had not moved in all the hours we'd been there. Still the same blank stare on the pallid face. Still the contortion of the leg and left side of his broken body. Still looking like a prop from a Hollywood horror flick.

As Totty and I rode down in the elevator we discussed the financials. Dad's insurance as well as the assets set aside for an emergency like this were substantial. Financial consideration should not likely become an issue in the near term. Additionally I told my brother that if somehow Dad held on through this, I'd take him to my house for as long as necessary. He responded, "I can't imagine that being necessary. OK if you want to."

VII.

"This line represents brain waves of automatic functions. These other ones in the center represent conscious and subconscious activity", explained the doctor holding a sheet that reminded me of a financial chart.

He traced his finger along a line representing Dad's prefrontal cortex activity. It was an absolute flat line. It indicated nothing was active in his brain. In essence the test demonstrated that he was brain dead. Additionally other tests discovered that Dad had a major infection in his blood stream. It was pneumonia. Furthermore his kidneys had quit functioning. And to make matters worse on top of the heart attack and the stroke, Dad had two leaking aneurisms close to his heart. Surgery was simply not an option.

"So, doctor, what are the chances Dad may ever regain consciousness?" I asked.

"Well, I've never seen anyone in a condition like this regain consciousness", was the response. Then, "The only reason his heart is beating is because he's on life support. Once he's disconnected his heart will cease to beat. In the meantime, his brain is gone and I'd suggest the odds of there ever being brain activity again are astronomical. I'm not saying it's impossible. But I have to be honest with you and tell you that in my opinion, I don't think there's anything to look forward to for your father."

Shortly after the doctor left the room Totty and I stepped back out into the hall. I began.

"Totty, this looks bleak. I want to sleep on it tonight and make a decision tomorrow morning about discontinuing life support. I'm just not ready to let him go today".

"Jim, you do whatever you feel you need to do. We heard what three different physicians have had to say. But in a circumstance like this, I know there are other considerations that you must having going on in your mind. I spoke with George by phone and he agrees. The decision is yours."

With that, we both decided we'd leave. We asked the nurse to keep us apprised if anything changed and we left. I headed directly for my office in the Tech Center. There were things I needed to attend to there before the end of the day. After that I planned to go home, try to sleep and then return tomorrow morning if his heart was still beating.

VIII.

By the time I pulled into the parking lot at my office, the sky had become dark and a light grey mist filled the air. After turning off the motor I sat for a moment looking at rain drops trickling down the windshield. I tried to recollect all I had to do in the next few hours. It was hard to focus on work. Because it was cold I pulled my collar up around my neck and hurried into the building. I had no umbrella and shuddered with a quick chill as I entered. Trying to remember everything I had to do that afternoon was not easy. The picture of Dad's body lying in that bed in the critical care wing still filled my mind.

Soon I was sitting at my desk catching up on things that had to be handled before I left. Around 4:00 I laid down my pen. A vision of Dad from my early childhood unexpectedly popped into my mind. What the significance of the vision was, I couldn't identify at that moment. But I remembered it vividly.

In the vision Dad was carrying me up to bed as a small boy on a Halloween evening. I was too small to go out for Halloween. I had been watching Mom pass out candy to kids in our front entry. I was sleepy and Mom decided it was time for me to turn in and asked Dad to carry me up and get me ready. As Dad was taking me up the stairs, a couple of kids standing in the hallway saw me in my dad's arms. I distinctly remembered one of them asking me, "Did you get to go out trick or treating tonight?"

I replied, "No, but my Mom is going to take me to a Halloween party yesterday."

The boys looked quizzically at one another after hearing this response. Then Dad quickly corrected me by saying, "He means tomorrow." Obviously I had not mastered much of the English language yet. And I was so small that it was still a ritual that Dad would carry me up to bed. Then a realization struck me. In the early years before the tumultuous times began Dad had been affectionate and tender with me. Those memories had been buried by the occurrences of the later years. But under it all, in the beginning and while I was a small boy, he had been a warm tender father. Awareness of love that still remained within me for him moved me to stand and walk to the window of my office to offer something.

Staring out into they heavy grey mist I couldn't see much. Except memories of the big man who in the early years would come and look in on us as we pretended to be asleep in our beds at night. Looking out the window I was moved to pray silently.

"Lord I come today with a request. Dad is close to facing you now. And you know what he'll have to answer for. Lord, I ask you to bring him back to consciousness in my presence so that he may hear what he needs to hear before he faces you. Lord, you are his father as well as mine. I ask you with all my heart to let him hear

what he needs to hear one more time before he's gone from here. I ask this in the name of Jesus."

That Tuesday evening after work I drove home slowly. I prayed some more in the car about the decision I would have to make concerning the life support. In short I simply asked that I be guided to make the best decision that would follow His will above all.

IX.

Wednesday morning dawned with a crystal clear blue sky. To my surprise under the circumstances and a choice with eternal consequences I had slept peacefully. I decided to take Melissa and Eric with me to the hospital to see their grandfather. I knew what I must tell the doctors on that day. Because of the kidney failure, the pneumonia, aneurisms and everything else, there was no sense in attempting to force him to breathe. If he could on his own now, then he would. If he could not, that would be left up to natural forces.

We arrived at the hospital before 9:00 AM. Riding up in the elevator I prepared the kids for what they were likely to see.

"Melissa, Granddaddy doesn't look very good. He's in pretty rough shape. Do you think you can handle that?"

"It's OK Dad. I think it's important that we see him anyway", replied my sixteen year old daughter. Eric agreed.

After departing the elevator we first went down to the nurses station to check his status. Immediately one of the nurses attending him was called over to speak with me.

"Mr. Anderson, his condition has changed."

"How so?" I inquired.

She responded, "Rather than me trying to explain let's go over and see him."

I was puzzled but understood she didn't want any more questions. We followed her to his room. She slowly opened the door and I and the children stepped inside and moved toward his bed. It's an understatement to say I was surprised by what I saw. The blinds were still closed but not completely. A ray of sunlight illuminated a swath across the sheet covering the form. Dad was lying straight on his back, no longer contorted. The eye that had been protruding from the socket was back in place and both lids were closed. His left knee was straight. And he seemed to emit small coughing noises intermittently. I asked the nurse, "Why does he seem to be coughing?"

She replied, "Well, that means he's fighting the ventilator."

"Why?"

"When someone is doing that it means they are trying to breathe on their own", she said.

"But, I thought he was incapable of breathing."

She didn't answer my query. But she went on to say, "I've been doing this kind of work for over twenty years and I've seen a lot of things we never expected."

Stepping up close to him, I leaned down and carefully examined his face. It now had a pinkish hue and the skin on his cheeks was warm to the touch. I was in wonder as I contemplated the change.

Then the nurse said, "I want to make a suggestion. Why don't you talk to him?"

After everything I'd seen and heard from the doctors over the past two days I was confident it would be a waste of time to speak to Dad. And I had forgotten my prayer the day before asking that he be brought to consciousness so I could speak with him. But I wanted to be respectful to the nurse and considering that Dad looked so different than the last time I saw him, I complied.

Leaning back over him, I touched the left side of his head and spoke softly.

"Good morning, Dad. I brought Melissa and Eric to see you today."

Nothing. Then a little closer to his left ear, I spoke a little louder, "Dad. Open your eyes."

Unexpectedly the most shocking and memorable sight I have ever seen occurred. His lids actually lifted! Blue eyes no longer dilated or blank looked directly up at the ceiling. I almost reeled back but held my ground. At first I couldn't speak. I didn't know what to say. Then I said, "Dad, look at me." Slowly his eyes turned to focus directly toward me. Not believing what I was seeing I actually stopped and attempted to wake myself from what seemed to be a dream. Then realizing I was fully awake, I turned to the children. They just stood quietly looking back and forth from me to Dad.

The term "Doubting Thomas" came to my mind. Not accepting that the lifeless and contorted body I left the day before could now be so different, I continued. I took his left hand in mine. It now felt warm.

For a few moments I simply stood there holding his hand. Then an image flashed into my mind. It was the remembrance of him speaking to me at Easter so many years earlier. *"Someday you're going to grow up to be a fine man. And we're going to be buddies."* Once again I saw Dad with that same hand I was now holding on the basket with me. I was back there on that morning with him. The grey brick and concrete of the house and the old brown mat in front of the door surrounded us. The reflection of his rimless glasses shone brightly again.

Still not accepting that he was back conscious, I continued.

"Dad, if you can understand me, squeeze my hand three times."

Faintly and slowly, almost like a twitch, the thumb and forefinger of his hand moved. Once, twice, and then a third time. Then it was still. And yet I remained skeptical.

"Dad, I want you to lift your left knee."

This was the leg that had been contorted by the stroke. I knew that the left side of his body was supposed to be paralyzed. I watched the knee carefully. At first there was no movement. I continued to stare where his knee bulged under the sheet.

Then there was a slight movement! He could not lift the knee. But he was trying and there was definite movement. I was dumfounded by the realization that he could actually hear me. And he could understand! It was only then that I remembered the prayer from the day before.

X.

We looked into each other's eyes. That connection was without words. I don't know what was going on in his mind. For me there was just the simple awareness that he was brought back to me for the moment. Looking at him with the ventilator stifling any opportunity for his speech, I thought carefully about what the moment demanded of me. Then a calm reassuring peace consumed me. The right corner of my lips tuned up and I felt my gaze softening as I looked at Dad. I knew what he needed to hear.

"Melissa and Eric come over and say 'Hi' to Granddaddy."

"Hi Granddaddy. I love you" said Melissa. Then Eric. "Hi Granddad."

Melissa took his hand. Eric placed his hand on Dad's other arm. I stood and watched as the kids spoke softly to their grandfather. I was moved by the natural compassion and gentle loving manner of my children. I collected my thoughts and said a silent prayer.

"Lord, thank you for bringing him back. Please guide me in speaking with him now."

I stepped up close to him again and began to talk quietly.

"Dad, you've been asking me lately what you should do. I've told you that you should pray. So, we're going to take some time now to do that. I'll pray for both of us".

Reaching down I took his hand again with both my hands and lifted it to my chest.

"You know Dad, you told me how your mother used to have you kids pray at bedtime each night. Well, you know when I was a little boy Mom and you had me say my prayers. That's a habit I've continued all through life. I think it's still necessary Dad and I'm grateful for the chance to pray with you now."

I began. "Our father in heaven. Hallowed is your name. Your kingdom come, your will be done on earth as it is in heaven. Give us this day our daily bread. And forgive us our sins, as we forgive those who sin against us. Lead us not into temptation, but deliver us from evil. For yours is the kingdom, the power and the glory for ever. Amen"

Gently placing his hand back down at his side, I stepped back slightly.

His eyes were looking back toward the ceiling. I decided to talk to him about things I hoped he should hear. I knew his mother was a woman of great faith. She was gone before I arrived but I heard much good about her from my mother and aunts. And I actually still possessed Grandmother Mary's handwritten poetry and prose. So I told him about things she had written about her children. I suggested he remember how she looked when he was small. His eyebrows furrowed slightly.

The nurse who had asked me to speak to him had left shortly after the moment he opened his eyes. But she had now returned. She stood smiling at him. He gazed at her then back to the children. Then again at me.

"Dad, you know what? I want to tell you about a place I think you'll like. It's a small mountain lake not far away. And when you're out of here I'm going to take you with me up there. We can fish. Or we can just sit in the boat and watch the sunset like we did on Sparrow Lake when I was small. We'll be buddies Dad."

Then hugging him I smiled and told him that I loved him. To my surprise his eyes welled up with tears which began to flow down his cheeks. I gently brushed them away with the palm of my hand.

"Dad. Listen to me carefully now. You must pray on your own and I can't tell you what to say. But whatever is on your heart now, please give it to Him Dad. He loves you and wants you to reach out to Him in prayer."

His eyes closed. I sat quietly wondering what may be going through his mind. Silently I prayed. *"Lord please hear your son Raymond and accept his prayer."*

There was no way for me to know what he was thinking or if he was even praying. I hoped he was and that somehow there would be reconciliation for him. Knowing I could never know in this life and maybe not beyond what would happen between him and God I could only pray that somehow he was asking for forgiveness and acceptance.

We stayed by Dad until Totty showed up. After awhile Totty spoke with him. Neither he or I mentioned to Dad that George would not be coming to see him. Then later Dad drifted off to sleep. He would not return to consciousness again. He held on into the evening and through another night even though the ventilator was removed. That strong heart continued to beat on and his lungs breathed unassisted. He simply would not give up though there was no more conscious capability in him.

Finally the following day one of the aneurisms burst. After weathering the fury against his body like a ship caught in a hurricane storm being dashed against rocks, the extraordinary strength of the tough old man was no longer tested. He was finally released from the trials of this world.

XI.

Stepping into his empty apartment at the retirement center I was immediately struck by how barren it looked. The last of Dad's possessions had been removed the day before. I was there this morning to check around and make sure nothing had been overlooked before turning the keys in on his place. Though he had only been there a couple of months, I detected a familiar smell that reminded me of him. The scent of his favorite after shave still lingered.

Walking around I picked up a few remaining things. The bright sunlight illuminated the ivory walls making everything appear even more empty and stark. A discarded handkerchief; an offer for a free meal at a local restaurant; a few coins lying on a shelf in his clothes closet. I stopped and listened. There was silence. I was struck by the finality of it all. I hung my head overwhelmed by the emotions I had held in for the past few days. And it was then that I fully grasped that he was now only a memory. His ashes would be taken to Florida to rest in the plot chosen years earlier. Everything in respect to him and his life seemed finished.

Looking out the window across the city toward the Rocky Mountains, I considered that there was yet still a decision to make about him. It was to either let his memory be dominated by things best forgotten or to focus upon things worth remembering. It occurred to me that the same is true of almost all the departed. We have a choice in respect to how they will be remembered and spoken of. If we're realistic we don't attempt to color or change the truth about them. But we do choose what memories we will embrace. I reflected upon the fact that ultimately the same applies to our own lives. We can either look back and dwell upon our mistakes and regrets. Or we can focus on what went well and more importantly look forward to what we can do better.

The drama of Dad's passing illustrated something important to me. He did not go quietly into eternity. He fought to hang on and I know the Lord led him back to fulfil his youngest son's prayer request. Though at the time it seemed impossible that there would be answer to that prayer, it came. The fulfilment of that prayer changed my life. I wondered what it might have done for Dad's life. I have been lifted by the fact that against all the odds, my father had been given a brief respite to hear that his creator still loved him and wanted him to turn to him after all. The realization of that grace lifts my memories of Dad as long as I remember him. And I am now a man of much stronger faith as result of what I experienced with him.

Alameda

"It is not the critic who counts; not the man who points out
how the strong man stumbles, or where the doer of deeds
could have done them better. The credit belongs to the man
who is actually in the arena, whose face is marred by dust
and sweat and blood; who strives valiantly; who errs, who
comes short again and again, because there is no effort
without error and shortcoming; but who does actually strive
to do the deeds; who knows great enthusiasms, the great
devotions; who spends himself in a worthy cause; who at
the best knows in the end the triumph of high achievement,
and who at the worst, if he fails, at least fails while daring
greatly, so that his place shall never be with those cold and
timid souls who neither know victory nor defeat."

— Teddy Roosevelt

I.

The overhead lights were bright and the odor of the locker
rooms filled the arena. The crowd was filing slowly in as various
cheers and hoots by teenaged students indicated a mood of
competitive spirit. The team members for the evening's event
were still in their locker rooms in last minute preparations for
their turns at glory or defeat. Each boy would have to face
his opponent alone on the green and white mat in front of
a boisterous crowd of spectators. High school wrestling is a
turning point. It is often the place where under intense lights
and in front of roaring crowds boys leave the last vestiges of
childhood behind and enter the first stages of manhood. Unlike

team sports, once on the mat, the competitor is completely alone to win or lose.

At age fourteen, we knew it was going to be a learning year for Chad as a new wrestler on the Conifer High School team. This was especially true because his high school had no one else to wrestle at his weight class. He would be the starting varsity wrestler for the 103 pound weight class. But Chad was a raw beginner with no previous competitive wrestling experience. Most of the boys he would face in his weight class would be at least one and more likely two or three years older. They would also be seasoned wrestlers. Regardless, our boy went into the season with a sense of adventure. He would approach this daunting challenge the same as he took on just about anything else difficult he ever faced. With a hopeful and positive attitude.

That first night of competition in November 1999 in front of the home crowd at Conifer was going to tell me quite a bit about the character of my stepson. I had encouraged him to try out for the wrestling team in his freshman year. Both his mother and I believed it would be good for him to become involved in a competitive sport. We could see that he was becoming too immersed in the popular computer games of the day as they had become his favorite pass time. He needed something to get him out into the real world. Into a world of learning how to work with and compete with others. Still, I was anxious about him in wrestling. He would be highly vulnerable in the sport because of his lack of experience and being so young. I knew there would be some pain and setbacks. I felt a great sense of responsibility as I saw the teams enter the arena a few minutes before Chad would wrestle his opponent. In front of the home crowd.

I studied the black haired boy in Chad's weight class on the opposing team. He was at least two years older than Chad. At that age, two years is quite a bit of difference in maturation and muscle development, not to mention the knowledge and experience the other boy would have. Our little man stretched and jogged around in front of his team warming up. The opposing wrestler did the same. The tight sinewy body and poker faced expression of Chad's opponent caught my attention. I figured he had to be sixteen and been wrestling competitively for no less than three years, maybe more. Then glancing back at our boy, I could see there were still traces of baby fat in his face and in his arms. His fuzzy reddish blond hair reminded me of a Teddy Bear. I wished I could somehow be inside his mind when that match started. I had wrestled in college and if he could have my knowledge, he'd stand a better chance.

All of a sudden the boys walked out on the match and shook hands. As the two faced one another the home crowd shouted encouragement to Chad. "Come on Chad!" his mother cheered just before the two wrestlers made contact. A lump arose in my throat. Then it began. The experienced boy had Chad down on the mat within ten seconds. A few deft twists from his foe had our boy on his back. Then almost before it began, it was over. The referee slammed his hand down signaling the pin. It was final and anticlimactic. My heart broke as I watched our little guy slowly rise to his feet. The referee held both of their hands and then raised the foes hand in victory.

I realized that at that moment would come the deeper and more meaningful test for Chad. How would he handle what could have been a humiliating defeat in front of the home crowd? In the next few minutes I was moved by what I was hoping I might see. Chad walked with dignity to the bench and took his seat. His head hung low for only a few minutes. Then he seemed to forget the loss and began to cheer ardently for his team mates as they went to wrestle one by one. I was lifted by his irrepressible spirit. This was the same spirit of fight and courage that stayed him as a 2 pound six ounce preemie some fourteen years earlier when doctors told his mother that there was not a good chance he would survive. But he did. The tough little man held on as a newborn at great risk against the odds. This night, that same character was revealed to me. I was made proud. I was made confident he would be alright in wrestling as well as many other challenges life would present him.

II.

The December evening in 2002 was cold and forbidding. As Chad's mother and I moved up the icy walk to the Alameda high school, I hobbled along slowly. The year before I had suffered serious injuries in a horse riding incident. By this particular evening I had had only one of three major surgeries I must have to repair broken vertebrae, pelvis, and numerous tears to cartilage and muscles in the core of my body. I had just come off the first repair to the pelvis and had two more to go over the next two years. Though in pain and always uncomfortable on the hard stands of the bleachers, I would attend every match I could where Chad was wrestling.

This first match of Chad's senior year was with the conference powerhouse. Alameda High School was a 30 minute drive for us as visitors. Alameda had just come off winning the conference championship the year before and had many of their team members returning. Conifer High School was still in a building mode but had some good wrestlers. Chad was now one of them. The two years between his freshman year and senior year had been up and down for our boy. He'd won his share of matches and lost some close ones. Most importantly, he competed with a sense of good sportsmanship and always a sense of adventure. He had fun wrestling. This was a function of his attitude. Now in his senior year he was one of the co-captains. We were proud of Chad. Regardless of how far he would go in wrestling, I was glad I'd encouraged him to join the team three years earlier. It had been good for him.

As the order of weight classes were determined for the evening, Chad now in the 130 pound class would wrestle the last match of the evening. Because Alameda was so highly rated, many from Conifer kept quiet about the fact that they did not expect our school to win the overall event that evening. But we did hope that a number of our boys would win their individual matches. Being the first match of Chad's senior year, I had high in hopes he'd get off to a good start.

As the evening wore on the individual matches before Chad's built a drama that none of us had expected. Somehow going into the last match of the evening, Conifer was behind Alameda by only four points. In the scoring system, if Chad could win his match by outwrestling his opponent, but not pinning him, Conifer would only be awarded three points for the overall score. Conifer would still lose the overall match. But if Chad could pin his opponent, his team would be awarded five points and become the unexpected victors over the Alameda powerhouse. The stage was set for what would become one of the most dramatic match's of Conifer high school athletics short life span. And possibly the most dramatic athletic event I ever attended.

III.

A passionate spectator when my loved ones are in the arena, it's difficult for me to not become part of the action. I can make a scene cheering for my kids. Tonight would be no exception. At the suggestion of Chad's mother and with complete agreement by me, I decided to climb down out of the bleachers and stand in the hall next to them where I could observe without making a spectacle of myself. Actually standing would be more comfortable for me because of the discomfort I suffered from being crammed into the bleachers with my damaged spine.

Chad and his opponent were warming up for their match. My stepson stretched and paced by his bench. I also began to pace. At one point before the match, Chad and I made eye contact. In that brief visual connection my expression might have telegraphed the passion I had for his challenge. Years before, even when he was in the earliest days of elementary school I had wrestled playfully and often with the little guy. His natural relentless spirit and the will to fight back were revealed to me even then. This evening I could not have been closer in spirit to him. I was as ready in heart for that match as he was. Maybe more so. Though my body was literally broken, my heart and will were at an all time high. In my mind I would be completely with him on the mat that evening.

Each wrestler, now both young men seasoned in the heat of battle before crowds, was charged with the will to fight with every ounce of their strength for victory. One boy in front of his hometown crowd to win the match for his team mates. The reputation of proud Alameda at stake. The other boy ready to do his all to honor the valiant effort of his team mates keeping their underdog team in the match to the very end.

The referee brought the competitors out onto the mat. After a few words, the whistle signaled the beginning. In an instant like a cat with its prey the Alameda wrestler was on Chad. Chad's opponent was successful with a take down. But Chad was not to be taken easily. In fact Chad reversed his opponent immediately and gained a brief advantage. The two were locked in intense struggle from that first moment. I sensed there would be no second or third period in this match. Both young men were giving everything and going for a pin. In the few ensuing minutes the crowd roared as the two boys put on an exhibition of what seemed to be a life and death struggle.

The wrestlers fought back and forth with one on top and then the other. And I was totally in the match. Though my body was racked with pain, I found my self leaping and cheering. Calling above the crowd I hoped my young man could hear me. I was sure I could help him through my voice. A few bystanders in the hall took note of my participation. I didn't care that they quite possibly perceived me as a crazed parent. I was. All of the years of sacrifice I had given to stand by that boy despite unusual and difficult circumstances that threatened to tear our home apart were somehow embodied in that match. As a stepfather I had given much more to Chad than I had bargained for when I married his mother. What he was participating in down on that stark arena floor somehow represented sacrifices I had made to stand by and encourage in him over many difficult years.

They two wrestlers were nearing the end of the first period. There had been no moments of backing off. But now the Alameda boy had finally gained what appeared to be the decided advantage on top. He had Chad in a near pin situation. I looked at the clock and saw there were just a few seconds left before the buzzer ending the first period. I was now leaping continually using every bit of volume in my voice telling Chad to break out of the hold and get up. Suddenly in that instant, our man reversed out of the precarious position and had the Alameda foe on his back. Simultaneously, though my throat now felt ragged I was yelling above the crowd. Never had I felt such passion for a sporting event. Or any other event for that matter. Chad's body straining, I could see the taught muscles and iron willed spirit of the tenacious fighter within him. He held fast, pushing his opponent relentlessly toward a pin. Chad would not be denied victory. The referee slammed his fist down signaling the pin. Our man won!

Chad's team rushed the mat. They boosted Chad above them and carried him in triumph. I became so overwhelmed by emotion that I had to limp into the men's room. In the solitude of that room I had become totally overcome with the spirit of the event. Somehow that victory reconciled much of what I had sacrificed for in the years of standing beside him in the face of events that had threatened to drive us apart.

IV.

After gathering my composure I returned to the arena. There I could see the Conifer wrestlers still jubilant. They were having fun celebrating. The Alameda crowd was quietly shuffling out of the building. I looked for Chad. Through the chaos we saw one another. I silently mouthed "That a boy!" to him as I squinted and gave a quick jab of my fist. He responded with a brief smile and then looked down. In this moment of victory, he demonstrated humility. My mind then revisited the first wrestling match of his career three years earlier. In that moment of loss three years ago, he had demonstrated dignity in defeat. He was now demonstrating dignity again with humility in victory. A few words from Rudyard Kipling's poem 'If' were illustrated on both evenings; "If you can meet with triumph and disaster and treat both those imposters the same . . . you'll be a man my son". How proud my stepson had made me on both nights. In fact over the years he would go on to make me proud many times beyond that evening.

Night of the Bears

> "You spend years trying to get them off the ground. You run
> with them until you are both breathless... They crash... You
> patch, comfort and assure them that some day they will fly.
> Finally they are airborne. They need more string and you
> keep letting it out, but with each twist of the ball of twine,
> there is a sadness that goes with joy. The kite becomes more
> distant, and you know that it won't be long before that
> beautiful creation will snap the life line that binds you
> together and it will soar as it was meant to soar - free and
> alone. Only then will you know that you did your job."
>
> — Anonymous

I.

A cool breeze in the late September afternoon sent a brief chill
down my spine. The sky was blue and the sun bright. But I
was reminded that fall would soon be upon us and with it
the change in leaves and all the things that made autumn my
favorite season. While cleaning up the yard I was thinking
that the kids were doing well with the move from Michigan to
Colorado. Unexpectedly and from behind me I heard, "Dad,
can I play hockey?"

Turning around, I faced my eleven year old son Eric. I
hesitated knowing full well what a "Yes" answer would mean.
Hockey was not a casual sports activity that kids could play at
when they felt like having a little fun. It was a lot of hard work
and sacrifice for the athlete. It was very demanding and took
serious involvement. It demanded the same of parents.

"Tell me about it, Eric."

"Vic plays Dad, and we've been talking about it. I think I'd like to play but I need you and Mom to agree that it's OK."

Vic Berlin was a year older than Eric. Having just moved to Colorado in the fall of 1992 we had hoped Eric would meet some boys that could be a positive influence. Vic was an athletic kid. He seemed to be good for our boy. Vic had been playing hockey in the Littleton South Suburban recreation league for a few years and that had evoked interest in Eric becoming involved. I had some inkling a few weeks earlier about the potential request. Eric and Vic as well as some other kids had been playing roller hockey for much of the summer. It was the kind of activity that would logically lead to something more sophisticated.

Still, I was concerned. I was an overprotective father in numerous ways towards my son and daughter. This was especially true since Eric's mother Cindy and I had been divorced for almost seven years at that point. While Cindy and I continued a strong alliance founded upon working together to do what was best for our children, the children of divorced parents are often more vulnerable to challenging circumstances when no longer living in a unified home with their mom and dad together. This coupled with my natural tendency to be especially cautious when it came to my children raised a red flag when it came to hockey.

Cindy and I had been uniquely bonded since the divorce. She came to Colorado from Michigan and worked with my business until she found a full time job on her own the next year. And we discussed everything in respect to the kids. We both supported one another in a lot of ways. But I still proceeded to be guarded about anything Eric and Melissa would become involved in. Add to this the fact that hockey is often a brutal activity both physically and emotionally as well as very demanding of time and financial resources for the athletes and their parents.

So, though I responded in the affirmative to my son when he made the request, and I encouraged him, I was steeling myself for what I figured was probably going to be a life changing event that I hoped would be positive for Eric.

II.

The echo of shouting and hockey pucks crashing against the boards filled the ice arena. I sat in the hard cold seats of the stands next to my brother George visiting from California. The boys were in two lines taking turns practicing skating up to and shooting at the goal. While just a practice session with instruction from the coaches, there was still obvious competition going on. Each boy was being tested for skill level, aggressiveness, and learning ability. George and I watched Eric at the end of one of the lines. Because George was especially important as my oldest brother and for whom I have enormous respect, I hoped Eric would do well in front of him. He was letting other boys cut in front of him which kept him near the back. It appeared he was uncertain. We were both a little concerned because through childhood Eric did demonstrate some hesitancy when it came to trying new activities. Still, I believed he had some purposeful reason for letting them cut in other than being timid. Most likely he was studying what was happening and reasoning out how to better do it.

Littleton South Suburban hockey was a premier recreational hockey program by any standard. The kids could begin in stages early in grade school and progress to different levels all the way though high school. The facilities and coaching were excellent. At the same time, the financial cost associated with registration fees, travel and equipment was steep. Practices and games could be anywhere from very early in the morning to late at night. The travel to play games may be local or as far away as Aspen or further. This was a big investment for families of hockey players in many ways. We noticed that for many of the people involved, it had become the top focus of their family life activity.

At the same time, the boys in the program received outstanding opportunities for development. Learning about hard work and sacrifice, team work, confidence, tenacity, good sportsmanship and having fun playing the game were just some of the benefits. There were more including meeting and making friends with some pretty good kids. I was encouraged by Eric having chosen to participate.

I liked the fact that hockey required Eric to take risks on his own. Years earlier I often had to coax and encourage him to try the slide board at the park, or ride a roller coaster, or just about anything he was unfamiliar with. Once he mastered something he usually seemed to become more proficient than his peers. The challenge was just getting him comfortable with new activities. Now hockey was another such test. However, it was far greater than anything before. Since I knew nothing about hockey, I could only watch.

During the practice session sitting with George we discussed whether or not it was a good decision to permit Eric to enter hockey. Though very careful with my children I had always operated on the philosophy that it was better for a kid to try something and take some bruises than become risk adverse and never test them selves. So, while we were a little concerned on that afternoon observing Eric approaching the challenge with what seemed to be more than warranted prudence, I believed that if treated in a patient and encouraging manner by me, my son would eventually do well. So, I stood my ground and insisted to George that Eric would eventually be fine after he learned what to do.

And in time, Eric did become very skillful at hockey. His hand eye coordination and reflexes were excellent. Even better was that he was a smart athlete. Playing on defense he could diagnose what the other team was trying to do and head off their efforts while making it look easy. However, the greatest characteristic he displayed was iron willed tenacity. Eric did not seem to know how to give up. Not ever. Once he made a goal of something he would do whatever it took to succeed. This characteristic has carried through on multiple fronts in his life. I'm convinced that involvement in hockey largely reinforced that characteristic.

Still, on that early afternoon sitting in the cold arena watching Eric at one of his first practices, I was challenged to have confidence that things would work out. As it turned out, Eric would surpass what either George or I hoped for as we watched his practice session on that day.

III.

The snowy night in January was unusually cold. Even for Colorado. I had come to the Littleton arena to watch Eric's team play a cross town rival. Now in his sophomore year of high school, his fourth year of hockey, it had become Eric's passion. He was consumed with hockey. There was even a summer league to ensure year round involvement. While I never understood the game very well and in fact did not have interest in hockey other than Eric's activity, I had accepted the routine and made as many of his games as was practical. By this time I could see he was able to compete on a high level and knew how to handle the disappointment of losses. I really had only one concern. It was that Eric might become injured.

In fact my highly attentive concern about potential physical harm to my son had begun in his first year of life. His mother's pregnancy with him had been routine. As with his sister Melissa, Eric had been delivered with little difficulty. In fact it had been expected that he and his mother would come home from the hospital early. However a botched minor procedure for newborn boys the day he was to be released had caused a complication that delayed when they could leave. By coincidence I had come to the hospital a few minutes after the procedure. Walking down the hall toward where I would find him and his mother, I could here a baby crying in pain. The child's cry was unusually plaintive. I felt much empathy for the child. The sound of the cry disturbed me. Shortly and to my horror, I discovered the child was mine.

I sometimes wonder if events during and shortly after birth affect a person's view of the harsh new world they have entered. I don't know. But I do know that our little boy received an unusually traumatic event shortly after entering this world. Even if the event did not have much affect upon him, it did on his father.

And then only four months after we brought Eric home from the hospital, on a wintery night he developed an unexplained fever. When the fever spiked above 107 degrees Cindy and I knew he must be taken to the hospital. Rushing him there in my car in the icy snow storm, I came close to being in a collision with a truck which further heightened the trauma of the night. As I carried Eric into the hospital he was completely limp and he felt hot. His little arms and legs dangled down as if he were a rag doll. Upon examination, the doctor decided we had to leave him overnight for observation. I had to return home to Cindy and Melissa without Eric. At one point that night, Cindy and I stood side by side looking into Eric's vacant room. It was a sad moment looking at that empty crib. I never forgot it.

The next day Eric was fine and home again. The mysterious fever subsided and he was himself. However, something about the event combined with the delay in bringing him home soon after birth encouraged deeply seated protective feelings toward my son. Also as a little boy prior to kindergarten, he demonstrated an extra cautious nature on his own. All of this had the effect to cause me to worry more about him than was natural. Over the years my obvious concern did cause Eric to rebel against my protective nature. I can't blame him.

And of course there would be many instances in childhood

before hockey when Eric would suffer routine injuries that all kids experience. They took an unusual toll on me. One event in particular I'll never forget was helping Eric overcome his anxiety about climbing the ladder on a slide board at a park near when we lived in East Lansing, Michigan. On this particular summer evening I had encouraged him to climb to the top by himself but while preparing to go down, he slipped and fell backward. As his head hit the ground his neck bent at an ugly angle. I rushed to him and inspected his ability to move his head and neck without pain. We was OK. But I wasn't. I had difficulty sleeping that night thinking about how close he had come to a debilitating injury. And I had been right there and believed I should have prevented it.

So as I sat in the stands that night of Eric's sophomore year watching the two hockey teams battle it out, I was my usual nervous self. The game was very physical. Every time I watched Eric collide with others, fall or battle against the boards, my heart rate increased. Finally I left the stands to go down by the Plexiglas shield surrounding the rink. I could watch the action from a closer vantage point. The sound of the skates scraping the ice, the breathing and grunts of the players, even the collisions of the player's pads were much more vivid there. But I could be closer to my son while he was in the middle of combat. While I yelled and cheered encouragement to him, I knew he probably couldn't hear me through the Plexiglas, but I felt closer to him.

The violence of the collisions and contact, while not a stranger to me from my own participation in sports, still was unnerving because it involved my boy. Eric could take it as well as dish it out. He was a strong young man, but I was still uncomfortable. At one point Eric was moving smoothly across the ice handling the puck and preparing to pass it to a team mate. Then from out of no where an opposing player came at Eric full speed from my son's blind side. The collision caused Eric's skates to leave the ice as his body flew in an arc backward and down onto the ice. His head hit the ice first absorbing the full weight of his body. The loud crack of his helmet against the hard surface led me to believe it was shattered. Wanting to leap over the eight foot Plexiglas barrier was not possible. I froze in fear looking at the prostrate and limp body of my son. I could see his face. His eyes were opened but blank. I could do nothing but watch as the action was stopped and his coach and an assistant went out to him.

Shortly my tough young son was on his feet and skating slowly off the ice. He took a seat on the bench but I have to believe he really didn't know where he was. I paced back and forth memorizing the number of the opposing player that had blindsided him. It was a display of poor sportsmanship that had escaped the attention of the official. But it didn't escape my attention. Overcome with anger I was prepared to grab the perpetrator when he came off the ice at the end of the period. Soon the realization of the embarrassment that would cause my son if I did it got the better of me and I settled down. However, I carried animosity for the rest of the evening. This was a usual occurrence as I attended Eric's hockey games. I just wanted to protect him from anything and everything. But I couldn't. And he was capable of taking care of himself.

IV.

Within a couple more years, by the time Eric was a senior in high school, his outstanding skill at hockey was obvious. It had become fun to watch him play. I was proud of his ability, leadership and courage in the unforgiving arena. Furthermore, I liked the young men he had developed friendships with through hockey. When he was selected to join one of the more elite hockey teams for young men his age I couldn't contain my pride. I told all of my friends and family about this achievement.

As it came time for Eric to attend college, we talked about whether or not he'd want to continue to compete in hockey.

His decision to enter the University of Northern Colorado in Greely was welcomed by me and his mother. The school was relatively close, not expensive, and while it did not have an intercollegiate hockey program, it had a hockey club that would enable Eric to participate without the level of time and stress attended by most intercollegiate programs. So, off he went as a freshman with plans to join the Bears Hockey Club of the University of Northern Colorado.

His mother and I as well as other family members often attended the games at UNC. Eric played regularly and well. Having finally overcome much of the trepidation I had earlier experienced with him in hockey, I was pleased that he was still playing. The fact is that like most hockey players he had experienced some injuries over the years. His knee, back, and shoulder all had been injured at one time or another. The shoulder separation and the knee injuries were the ones that I was most concerned about. They were the kind of injuries that often turned into lifelong chronic issues. Still, he continued to play well in his first year at UNC and I enjoyed going to his games.

V.

The Metro University of Denver Hockey Club, the Roadrunners, had a reputation as an aggressive and highly combative group. In actuality the team demonstrated more poor sportsmanship than any other team we knew of. Their fouls and penalties were beyond the norm and somehow they seem to pride themselves for that kind of play. The night they came out to play the UNC Bears in Greeley was no different. It seemed they came more to injure their opponents than to win the game.

Sitting in the bright but unusually cold arena that night in February of 1999 I was looking forward to what everyone had expected to be an exciting game. It was exciting. But it was more than that. It shortly became a battle of 'good guys' versus 'bad guys'. The play of Metro was shameful. I had never seen as much high sticking, tripping or blatant fouls in any game, ever. If the referees had called all the fouls committed by Metro, the game would have had to been called because they'd not have enough players left on the ice to continue.

At the end of the first period the score was close. As the players returned to the ice in the second period, the game became more a contest about brute strength and hostility than hockey skill. The action was intense. Eric held his own in the fray. However, due to the overtly nasty nature of the Metro team, I was beginning to feel hostile myself. As a parent and spectator it was good that I was insulated from the action. However, I knew if I was on the ice as a player I probably would have been ejected before the end of the first period. All during that second quarter the two teams seemed to be giving every bit to the game. The shots on goal were almost all hard slap shots. The collisions and contact between the players were as hard as I'd ever seen.

Though the action appeared to be almost chaotic, Eric was keeping his head. It was obvious by his play he was thinking strategically. He had not given in to the 'blood sport' mentality that defined this particular contest. I was reassured watching him skillfully perform like a leader instead of one of the out of control combatants.

There was one special feature that evening that helped keep me and many fans distracted from taking the whole spectacle too seriously. It was one of the fans on our side. In fact it was Eric's roommate Chad Foss. Apparently young Mr. Foss had imbibed in a little more liquid refreshment prior to the event than he was used to. The result of this was that he had become quite demonstrative of his support for his roommate and home team. The epitaphs and adjectives he employed in his spirited and unusually audible cheering garnered almost as much of the fans attention around him than did the game. He was highly entertaining. He did indeed help me feel less inclined to want to rush out onto the ice and take on a couple of the more insufferable Metro players.

As the third period began, the action began to seesaw in respect to scoring. Metro pulled ahead by a goal and some of their supporters as well as players began to boast. Regardless, Eric and the Bears continued to press on with a confident style of play. And sure enough midway through the third period, the Bears tied the score. At that point the Roadrunners began to pull out all the stops with their brand of hockey displaying any and all of the techniques from the book of hockey's dirtiest tricks.

With a few minutes to go in the game, the Bears had moved the action down to the Roadrunners end of the ice. There the majority of the players on both teams were fighting it out in front of the Metro goal with sticks and hockey blades flashing in the bright lights. The contact and speed of action was so fast it was difficult for me to follow what was happening. However, in the middle of it all Eric had positioned himself close to the goal hoping to get a shot or an assist. I couldn't keep track of the puck as it flew about in the chaos. Then from out of nowhere the puck did appear near Eric. He spotted it. In an instant Eric was on the puck and drove it hard past the Metro goal tender into the net. As it flew in for the go ahead goal, the home stands erupted.

As loud as the home crowd cheered, it was not loud enough to drown out one wild fan in particular. Young Mr. Foss exploded in unbridled enthusiasm screaming over and over "That's my roomie. That's my roomie!" as he sprinted up and down the steps of the stands. He eventually wore himself out but not until he made sure all in the arena knew that he resided with the Bear who had just scored the go ahead goal.

Down on the ice the Bear players congratulated Eric. But then they settled in to continue to play a smart and strategic game to finish and win when the time ran out. The kind of leadership and intelligent play demonstrated by Eric and a number of the more senior members of his team solidified the victory. That moment brought back to memory the cool September afternoon from years earlier when Eric asked me if he could play hockey. The concerns of that afternoon were finally completely put to rest.

VI.

As we waited outside the arena for the players to get cleaned up and dressed to leave, Eric's mother her husband Craig and I discussed how proud we were of Eric. While so many things had not gone right in the relationship between Cindy and me, one thing did. It was that we had held together fast through it all united to ensure our children would have the cohesive and united support of their parents. The unique bond that I felt with her as Eric finally emerged from the locker room had been in large part enabled by the noble and industrious efforts of our son.

As Eric came out, his girl friend Raquel was there to greet him. The two walked close side by side over to the group of us waiting to congratulate him. This was one of my most gratifying moments as a father. There is something rare and rewarding in watching your child compete and do well in sports that very few other activities they may participate in can match.

Finally, I was thankful that I had trusted in his decision years earlier and allowed him to join with Vic and the others outside my protection. It had been especially difficult for me to let go of being so shielding. But it was good. And in the coming years I would see the tenacious characteristics he built in the arena prevail in even more trying and challenging circumstances than any athletic competition.

The Choice

I.

The gray cold February day in 2006 had been uneventful. Cleaning up the dishes after dinner I was preoccupied by a number of unexpected events from the past year. One was the fact that during Christmas Melissa had become engaged to a young man that her mother and I were especially happy about. The couple had only begun dating in the summer of 2005 but by December they had become engaged. Chris, her fiancé was a guy I related to. He was athletic, kind, intelligent, had a great sense of humor, and everything indicated he had integrity. Most important to me, he was also a man of faith.

Shortly before the engagement in December of 2005, Chris had invited me to dinner to ask if I approved of their desire to become married. I was impressed by this demonstration of old fashioned courtesy and consideration on his part.

"Jim, I think you know why I asked you out to dinner tonight." I nodded. "I'd like to ask for your blessing. I'd like to marry Melissa."

"From what I know of you so far Chris, I'm very encouraged about you becoming Melissa's husband. What can I do to be of help?"

"I guess just wish us the best and stay close to us."

Among other things at dinner that night Chris and I talked about the challenges and rewards of marriage. He and I had both shared some similar painful experiences in our earlier marriages and he knew about the trials and threats that can often upend marriages conceived even with the best of intentions.

As I listened to him talk about his love and commitment to Melissa, little did I or Chris know that that commitment would very soon be put to a great test. The test would not come in years. It would come in just a few months. Melissa and Chris planned on being married in June of 2006. But much sooner than that, a great trial would befall the two young lovers.

While Chris and I talked that evening, images and memories of Melissa as a child flashed through my mind. Many cherished moments bestowed upon me by my precious daughter would be cued by something he said and then bring back vivid memories. Those memories wandered in out of my consciousness as I looked carefully into the young man's face while probing for any signs that might indicate how he truly felt about or understood Melissa. Visions of her as a baby; a little girl playing Cinderella with her grandmother; completing kindergarten . . .

Melissa's kindergarten teacher was talking with the parents of her class on the end of the school year as many of us had come to pick up our children on the last day. It was 1984 and our little girl had just finished her first venture into the East Lansing public school system. We'd had good reports about her during the year. Things like how cooperative she was and interested in trying hard at everything she did. But I could see this teacher had something additional to discuss with me.

"Mister Anderson, your daughter is a pretty special little lady."

"I realized that a long time ago. But why do you say so today?"

"Well, I noticed this year that often Melissa seemed to go out of her way to be kind or friendly to children that seemed to be having a tough time or maybe just didn't fit in as well as some of the others."

193

As her teacher and I discussed this characteristic, I was proud of my daughter. Her grandmother, Eleanor who raised us three boys had been that way. Mom was known to be unusually kind and likely to go out of her way to help others not only in our family, but in the community. I hoped that maybe Melissa had some characteristics passed down from Mom and I was happy about it.

I realized that my mind was wandering off a little as Chris and I talked. But our conversation was much about Melissa and what we both loved in her. The memories being evoked were to be expected. As long as I could stay focused enough on what Chris and I were discussing, I was not concerned about making him think I wasn't listening.

As he and I digressed into our own histories, particularly sports, I determined that Chris had an unusually good relationship with his father. Apparently his dad attended just about every baseball and hockey game possible during Chris's youth and even adult years. Chris having been an outstanding athlete, I surmised that the encouragement and support his father Duane demonstrated played an important role in his success.

This line of discussion got me thinking about how we as parents want things to go so well for our kids, but can't ensure anything other than we want the best for them. I could see that Chris's dad Duane did two things that seemed to me very important. First, he truly loved his son. And second, he stayed involved with him through all that the young man experienced. Chris's challenges, victories, heart breaks, joys or whatever, were shared as much as possible with and by his father. As I came to realize this fact, I grew even more encouraged about him becoming Melissa's husband. Again my mind began to wander back in time.

"*Daddy, do you think my princess costume will be right for the party tomorrow?*"

"*Yes, sweetheart, it'll be perfect. And I'll find your tiara and wand we made for you by this evening. You'll be beautiful and I'll be proud to be with you.*"

It was October of 1985 and I had been invited to a Halloween party at some friend's home in Okemos, Michigan. I was single and decided to take my daughter as my "date". The pretty yellow taffeta skirt and top with her blond hair and blue eyes along with the rhinestone tiara and silver wand would make her look like a child from a fairytale come to life.

The relationship between a father and daughter can be a revelation in a man's life. He is half of the human team that participated in God's work of creating a new person and therefore can feel that the person is part him. However, because the child is the countervailing gender she is often an enigma. So even though he may see, as I did, similar personality characteristics, he feels both foreign and united with the little girl simultaneously. She holds his heart and may carry a sense of royalty about her simply because of bloodline. The costume she would wear for the party was well suited to her role with me. She was my princess.

Melissa and her younger brother Eric aged four at that time were the highlights of my life in that period. While their mother Cindy and I were now parted, we worked at keeping all close and with some semblance of a feeling of family. Melissa never understood in childhood why her mother and I divorced. It would be years until she learned all of the facts, but still Cindy and I kept up a united front of communication and joint decision making between us in respect to our kids.

So, Melissa spent half her time at my place, as did her brother and I paid as much attention as possible to both of them. I relished the opportunity to do anything and every kind of activity I could with each. Taking Melissa to the party the next evening would be good for me. I believed it would be good for her too as it helped her see how proud I was to be with her.

It was during these early years after the divorce that both her mother and I tried to demonstrate to Melissa and Eric that there was nothing more important than our love and commitment to them. Of course that is not an easy case to make when two parents part. After all, if the family, which is completed in the act of having children, is the top priority, why would a man and woman divorce?

As ironic as it may seem, from the time of the breakup of the marriage all the way through our lives, Cindy and I had a unique kind of closeness. The closeness was as the children's parents. It did not go beyond that. But that was at least enough to provide some minimal stability that must have somehow helped Melissa keep sight of the fact that her parents valued nothing more than her and her brother. I often wonder if that fact influenced the kind of mother she would eventually become.

There were qualities in Melissa that began to surface very early. Even before the breakup of her parent's marriage. We saw them in how instinctively protective she was of other children. We could see that she had a strong sense of fair play and wanting to do what was right. Melissa always had principles that she lived by. A firm sense of self-reliance and taking responsibility for her actions also began to show itself early.

Chris and I talked more that evening in the restaurant about his childhood. He spoke with almost reverence about his parents. He told me of many instances how his father was close to him. I was touched by the obvious loyalty and connection between father and son. I had to believe that this same powerful value for a strong family bond must be part of what Chris was all about.

We laughed that evening as we discussed stories concerning how Melissa and Chris first met as well as the initial meeting between Chris and me. I learned that though Chris had a likeable and warm personality he was basically a shy man. That is why the first evening I met him at a party at my home in the foothills in the late summer of 2005 Melissa brought him to, I had to ask her where he was. Melissa had been inside at the party for a good twenty minutes, obviously alone.

"Melissa, I thought you were going to bring Chris out tonight so he and I could meet."

"Oh I did dad. He's still outside in the car."

"What's he doing out there?" I enquired.

"Well Dad, he's a little nervous about meeting you and he's working up the courage to come in."

Chris and I talked about this event over the dinner and it somehow made both of us feel a little closer. I liked him a lot that evening and hoped that he liked me. We laughed about stories related to family and I came to believe more and more that night that this man would be good for Melissa. And I hoped she would be good for him. Not that I feared she wouldn't. It was just that one never really knows what kind of match will occur until a man and a woman face challenges together.

"Dad, I have a favor to ask of you. My sorority is sponsoring a guest lecture on campus in February. This year we want a speaker who can talk about careers beyond college. Would you consider being our speaker?"

It was January of 2000 and Melissa was now a senior at the University of Northern Colorado. I was flattered that she had enough confidence in me to have me speak before her sorority. I would not only have to do a good job of speaking and making an excellent impression upon the guests, about 75 college women, but I was her father. That would place Melissa in a precarious position with her peers and close friends.

"Tell me more about what you need the speaker to do Melissa."

"Well Dad, we put together a program like this at least once

a year. We invite speakers that will be of interest to our sorority members. At a meeting a few months back, the subject of careers beyond college came up and quite a few girls wanted someone who was knowledgeable to come and talk about them."

"I'll do it. But aren't you a little nervous having your father speak in front of a large group of your friends?"

"No dad. I know you'll be good. I have faith in you."

That simple statement from my daughter had as much impact upon me as any compliment or show of faith in me that I had ever received. It was typical of how Melissa had the power to make me feel worthwhile. As long as she has been alive, my daughter has made me feel worthwhile.

II.

The stillness of the cold dark night in February of 2006 was broken by the ringing of the phone. I walked into the kitchen wondering who might be calling at this time of evening.

"Hello dad. Can you talk right now?"

I sensed tension in Melissa's voice. I knew instantly that something major was going on. I composed my response and did my best to become smooth and supportive.

"Yes Honey. What is it?"

"Dad, you and I need to get together soon. I have something very important to talk with you about."

The quaver in her voice cued my mind to suspect one of two scenarios. Either they had decided to call off the June wedding, or Melissa was pregnant. I more strongly suspected the latter. I knew better than to inquire on the phone. Whatever it was, there was enough gravity to it that it would be best discussed face to face.

"When do you want to get together?" I said in the calmest voice I could muster under the circumstances.

We agreed on a get together the next evening. She was to come over to my place. After I hung up the phone, the primary focus on my mind was how I could be supportive to my daughter. But at the same time I began thinking of all the possible options for what might be troubling her. Mulling things over, I concluded that she was pregnant.

Even though we were now facing a potential crisis, a very clear point came to mind. Because of what a great blessing she was in my and her mother's lives combined with the fact that she also was conceived at an unexpected time, I had a broad perspective upon the whole matter. I decided that if indeed she was pregnant, I must encourage her to look at the bright side. She had always wanted to be a mother. And the father of the child would most likely be a good father based upon the influence of his own parents upon his values.

Still, I was uncomfortable with the timing of everything. However, I was aware that how I felt was not consequential. What was of consequence was how Melissa felt and what I might do to help. I steeled my mind to the fact that whatever we faced; whatever she faced, that it must be taken on with a positive perspective. I began to pray for wisdom and strength to be helpful to Melissa. I also prayed for the ability to be helpful for Chris.

The following evening when the doorbell rang indicating that Melissa was at the front porch, I again prayed silently as I walked toward the door.

"Lord, please guide my words and actions as you would have me speak and behave."

When I opened the front door, I could see serious concern in my daughter's face. I gave her a hug and took her coat inviting her into the living room.

As we sat down close facing one another, she began.

"Dad, I don't know how to begin. I'm not sure how to tell you what I have to tell you. I'm afraid you might be very disappointed."

"Melissa, have I ever told you I was disappointed in you? Whatever it is, I'm on your side. It'll be alright."

Now I knew for certain what she was about to tell me. I

felt it ironic that she would be in such a predicament. During high school and college she was occasionally referred to as being prudish with men by her girl friends. There were in fact a few years here and there when she dated no one.

"Dad, I'm going to have a baby."

Because I had prepared for that distinct possibility, I first let her talk a little about how she felt and what was going through her mind. I was proud of the fact that her choice was to have the child. Even in difficult circumstances. After a short emotional monologue on the matter from her, I moved over and put my arms around her.

"Melissa, this may sound trite to you, but you have a choice beyond just keeping the baby. You can choose to see this as a great imposition on you and Chris. Or you can choose to see this as something positive. Sure, it's going to be very challenging and certainly not the way you planned for things to go. Regardless, let's determine what is best to make this go well for all concerned. What does Chris have to say?"

I was not surprised, but I was very happy to hear that Chris was responding in a positive manner. He had told Melissa that he was happy to be the father of a child with her and he would do his best to be a good husband and father.

After we talked a little more, I told Melissa that we would all work hard to do well with the unexpected turn of events. Then I told her she and I needed to actually go out to dinner that evening and celebrate. At first she was not keen on this idea. But soon she came around. I believe she was so relieved to see that I was not disappointed or upset, that maybe we could go out and talk about it all in a positive manner.

Later at J Alexander's restaurant we began to discuss what needed to be addressed and handled shortly. As we talked I could see she was coughing slightly. I asked her how she felt and she responded.

"Oh it's not much. I've had a sore throat for a few days

and I've got a cough. I'm just fighting off a cold. I'll be OK in a day or two."

I didn't like it. In my usual overly cautious manner when it came to my children, I decided that I needed to get her to see my family physician the next day. There was a debate about that. I knew she had no insurance coverage and that was part of the reason she was avoiding seeing a doctor. Thankfully I won. She agreed to go see Dr. Aiken the next day. I explained cost would not be an issue. Then of course it dawned upon me that there were about to be costs incurred during her pregnancy. I held off on mentioning that.

After she agreed to see the doctor, we turned the discussion back to what to look forward to in being a parent. I encouraged her as much as possible under the circumstances to think about the rewards of motherhood.

That evening we also discussed the fact that she and Chris must be married as soon as possible. There would be a waiting period for medical costs through the insurance program offered by his employer, so the sooner they were wed, the better. However, Melissa still wanted to have a formal marriage ceremony in May or June. The differences in opinion on the logistics of all of these matters would not be resolved for a few weeks. But with the help of Cindy, Chris's parents, and a little from me, it was all decided upon in due time.

The following day after the evening at J Alexander's, Melissa went to Doctor Aiken. I could not ever be more thankful for that fact when we learned she had strep throat. The threat of that disease and the antibiotics to treat it was definitely a hazard to the tiny child developing within Melissa. If she had waited and not gone to the doctor, the potential problems would have increased exponentially over the coming days and weeks.

III.

The civil marriage ceremony came and went in March of 2006. The formal ceremony came and went in June. All during that time the miracle of a human life was forming inside Melissa. Soon there was an ultrasound photograph of the tiny child. That picture further galvanized our commitment to the baby. We could see the tiny head and developing arms of the new person. And soon we learned the baby would be a girl. That was a delightful realization to me because I recalled the joy of my daughter as a baby and knew that Melissa would love to mother a daughter. Of course she would have loved to mother a son, and nothing was more joyful to me than the birth of my son, but I was happy her firstborn would be a girl.

There come a few moments in life when powerful realizations occur and define reality for each of us. In the good cases those moments are timeless and can be both meaningful and joyful. In respect to my experience as a father, the first was at the birth of Melissa in July of 1978. A minute or two after she was born the tiny child was handed to me as she heartily voiced her discomfort being thrust into the cold bright surroundings. However, when I announced softly to her who I was as well as my intentions about being her father, she ceased crying and became calm. In that singular and timeless moment, she changed the value and meaning of my life.

Then twenty eight years later in September of 2006 a related and powerful moment drove home an important realization to me again. I, Melissa's mother, her stepfather Craig, Cami, Duane and Carol Gentner and a few sat in the waiting room at Sky Ridge Hospital in Littleton, Colorado awaiting the delivery of Melissa's first born, a daughter.

The moment came shortly after the birth of Melissa's daughter Kyrah as she entered the same bright and harsh kind of world her mother had years earlier. Again, I was there. A little while after the delivery we entered the delivery room. The new tiny baby was lying on a table alone momentarily.

She had nothing on her to keep her warm, though the room was a comfortable temperature. She was squirming on her back as I walked over to her. As I introduced myself to her quietly, I lightly moved one finger in circles on her stomach. She immediately quit twisting and relaxed. That moment, similar to her mother relaxing when I first spoke to her when she was born had enormous impact upon my role as a grandfather. I believed she would become comfortable and involved with me as she grew up.

Both daughters demonstrated the same power to imbue me with appreciation, wonder and meaning. The 28 years between these two events seemed only an instant. In essence the two events were one and the same though two different individual souls were involved.

As the years rolled on since the birth of my granddaughter Kyrah, I was fortunate enough that her and her mother were geographically near enough that I could be a part of their lives. I know of nothing that could ever surpass this blessing. I continued to pray always that I could be good for both of them. The have been more good for me than words can describe. And Chris far exceeded my hopes as the husband of my daughter and father of my grand daughter.

Blackie

I.

The first time I saw him was in the late summer. Early that morning the woods were moist from a rain the night before. Wild flowers and mosses covered the hillside among the ponderosa pines and blue spruce. The earth smelled damp as I hiked up the hill through the forest. I had to stop occasionally to catch my breath. At eight thousand feet of elevation and on steep terrain, this was an excellent though taxing early morning exercise regime I had developed since acquiring the property.

A regular resting place was the granite ridge that jutted out above the hillside looking over the valley of Turkey Creek Canyon. I took a seat on a vantage point that afforded me a good view as the early morning sun began to light the valley with yellow and white hues. Sitting silently I listened. After remaining still for a few minutes the birds and squirrels resumed declaring their territories. It was as I remained still that I caught sight of him. The large jet black cat was perhaps twenty to thirty yards below my perch. Stealth fully climbing among the rocks he was stalking something I couldn't see. Feral cats were common in this part of Colorado, but not this high on the ridges. They typically inhabited the pastures and lower lands of Turkey Creek Canyon as well as the entire southwest region of Jefferson County. It was unusual to see one at this elevation in the woods.

Sitting motionless I watched him slow down to move in slow motion as he zeroed in on his prey. He was obviously close to whatever he was stalking. His ears and eyes were focused like a laser upon his target as he moved ever closer. Possibly a small mammal. But then unexpectedly he froze. His focus slowly shifted directly toward me. Though I had not moved or made a sound the entire time I had been observing him, he had become aware I was there. Large yellow eyes locked directly onto mine. We sat staring at one another.

There was something in that gaze that was mesmerizing. Clearly this was a wild animal. No collar or little bell on this predator. His eyes communicated a keen sense of alarm though he indicated no sense of panic. The creature completely forgot about his prey and fixed his total attention upon me. As we looked into one another's eyes, I sensed something primal and natural in his being. The distinct vertical scar on the left side of his face was a clue that his was a tough and unforgiving existence. I deduced that here was a creature that was completely a loner and independent spirit. It had no warm home with a loving family to feed or pamper it. There was likely no security other than what it afforded itself by tough resourcefulness. I was curious about what caused the large battle scar on his face. This was a tough animal. He obviously survived solely upon whatever he could catch. Possibly the only comfort he had was an old barn or dilapidated shack where he found refuge from the elements year round.

As the large eyes stayed locked upon mine I wondered what was going on in the consciousness behind them. Was he wondering about my intentions? I was reminded of the poem 'The Tiger' by William Blake.

> *In what distant deeps or skies*
> *Burnt the fire of thine eyes?*

How had he realized I was there? Was it through sense of smell or some mysterious sixth sense that enabled him to detect me? I knew that if I attempted to make any motion of friendship toward the animal it would be perceived as a threat. I guessed this was not a creature that would easily trust anything. I believed that to him, most things must either be a potential threat or something that demanded action. Though lean, he obviously wasn't starving. The smooth muscles and definition of the wild creature had been honed by the challenge of raw survival.

> *And what shoulder and what art*
> *Could twist the sinews of thy heart?*

I smiled as we continued our silent connection. Perhaps it was me breaking into the smile that caused him to dart away. Whatever caused him to bolt, I wasn't surprised. A creature like that would not be won by a smile. In fact, I suspected that it would not be won by anything. As he disappeared across the hill behind a ridge I remembered the prey that had almost met its demise had I not been sitting there. Whatever it was, it had unknowingly been spared by my presence. The black cat was gone and therefore the reason for me to continue to sit silently. I rose and resumed my trek up the steep slope.

Though I observed other animals that morning including a few white tail deer, an elk, a coyote, and a red tailed hawk, I couldn't forget the cat. There was something about that gaze that stayed with me. I wondered if he had any social interaction of any kind. I determined that if he was this high in the canyon, away from the pastures and houses lower in the valley, he must be a solitary creature with no companion of any kind.

II.

As the summer gave way to fall I began to enjoy my favorite time of year in Colorado. My home was surrounded by aspen and conifers. Though my lot was only 14 acres it bordered public lands that were as undeveloped and unspoiled as any primeval forest. In all the years I owned my home and property there and traveled in those woods, I had never seen another human being. In the fall, I increased my hikes up the hill through my woods to as often as two to three times every week. But now the hikes were in the sunny warm afternoons instead of the mornings. Many evenings when I didn't hike, I would sit out on the stone entryway of my home and watch as evening turned to night.

It was one evening in late September that I had decided to bring out my night vision scope. I had learned to employ the scope often after the sun would go down to observe wildlife. This night I planned to simply sit out front and see if anything would show up. I knew there was a red fox that came often but he usually did so boldly while it was still light. In fact he was so comfortable with me that I could speak to him without him leaving.

Soon after dark I turned on the scope and scanned the open space between my front porch and the stand of trees beyond the clearing. Because my home was completely surrounded by woods I had no lights or distractions of any kind. I detected what I thought was a vole scampering around. But there was nothing else. Soon I grew bored with the scope and was about to turn it off to gaze at the stars. Because there was no light pollution in that area, hundreds of stars were easily visible with the naked eye on cloudless evenings.

As I was about to turn off the scope a shape appeared on the edge of the viewing field. I watched as it glided across in front of me. I didn't recognize what it was for a moment. But then the familiar outline of a large cat became apparent. This one was black and would have been impossible to see without the infrared technology of the scope. Then he stopped and looked directly toward me. Huge eyes focused upon me. On the left side of the face I thought I could detect a vertical line of some kind. It was then that I recalled the feral cat I had encountered maybe a month earlier hiking in the morning. I wondered if this could be him.

Again this creature knew I was there. But this time in the dark he seemed to be emboldened by the night and rather than freezing or running off, he strolled around in the field in front of me. But as he did so, another shape appeared in the scope moving in behind him. I recognized that it was a fox. Probably the one that I had become familiar with. *This should be interesting.* I sat quietly to see what would happen. *OK, Blackie. We're going to see how tough you really are.*

On the one hand I wanted to warn the cat as the fox crept up behind him. On the other I was intrigued by the real life drama I expected to occur and I felt it would be wrong to interfere. So, I watched. The cat seemed to saunter nonchalantly toward me as the fox, now low to the ground followed closer and closer. *This is gonna be good! C'mom Blackie, get ready to show me what you got!* It was just then that the cat whirled unexpectedly and sprung high above the other animal and landed on him! He had known all along the fox was there. The larger animal turned and ran in a small circle with Blackie on his tail. Just as suddenly they both halted and the fox give chase to Blackie. It then became apparent; these two were playing! Like a couple of puppies. They frolicked some in my scope and then finally stopped to rest.

To say the least I was surprised by what I had just observed. Two wild animals of completely different species that obviously knew one another and enjoyed playing together. *How could this be? What would cause these two to become friends?* I then recalled seeing a wild life video on television a few years earlier about a domesticated husky and a wild polar bear that in essence did the same as these two. If I had been mystified by the black cat the day I first saw him, this far exceeded that mystery. Then the mystique was even further driven home as the cat and the fox both trotted off together out of sight! They were companions.

Did He smile His work to see?
Did He who made the lamb make thee?

III.

When I had left suburbia years earlier and built the home in the woods of the foothills I and an architect friend designed, I naturally expected that I would enjoy the peace and beauty of being in the wilds. I anticipated that I should enjoy watching the wildlife first hand. But I had no idea of the lessons I would learn from being so close to the various wild animals. There was a bear, many elk, deer, coyotes and others that I came close enough to touch or talk with routinely. All imparted lessons that no book or nature program could describe. So Blackie was not the only animal that I was surprised in observation of him. But he was one of the most memorable because of the opposing behavior I saw him demonstrate. On one hand being uniquely a loner and independent spirit. But on the other, demonstrating camaraderie and even playfulness with a completely different and competing predator.

He did appear once again the following spring. But then only fleetingly. I was sitting out on one of the redwood decks of my home. This one facing the pond. I saw him above the pond for a moment moving through some brush. He had stopped and looked back at me. Again, this animal somehow knew I was watching him. He convinced me that he had senses beyond what we humans can experience. Be it a sixth sense, or just incredibly honed sense of smell and hearing, Blackie was a beautiful and uniquely gifted spirit of the forest. Watching the little beast resume his stalking, I recalled the beginning of Blake's poem.

Tiger, tiger, burning bright
In the forests of the night,
What immortal hand or eye
Dare frame thy fearful symmetry?

'Bugsy'

I.

The open field on both sides of the drive was covered with dew as I pulled slowly up to the farm house. A light breeze swayed the old white oak next to the stable. It was early Saturday morning September 29, 2001. Though only eighteen days before America had been shocked and changed forever, this fall morning seemed untouched by that event and held the promise of a peaceful beautiful day. The sky was a stunning clear blue. A red tailed hawk circled slowly overhead. It seemed a good day for my first ride on a horse. I'd been on a pony as a child but this was to be my introduction to riding horses.

Having been invited on a trip in October that would include horse back activities at Jackson Hole, Wyoming, I wanted to be well prepared. A childhood friend by the name of Mark Grievas who now happened to reside in Colorado agreed to let me have a lesson on one of his family's horses stabled at his friend Reggie Shanholtzer's place.

I slid out of my gold Pathfinder and strolled up to the door of the house with high spirits. Ringing the doorbell chime brought a slim sandy haired lady to the front door. "Hi. I'm Jim Anderson. I'm here to see Reggie."

"Good morning, Jim. I'm Marsha Shanholtzer. I'm happy to meet you. Come in."

Stepping through the hallway and into the kitchen, I could hear and smell coffee bubbling in a percolator. Marsha asked if I'd like some before meeting Reggie. Not being a coffee drinker I declined and spoke with her for a moment before she invited me to walk out back toward the barn where I'd find Reggie.

Walking toward the barn the smell of hay and fertilizer filled my senses. The kinds of smells one would expect at a place where horses are stabled. It was a bit intoxicating, in a pleasant way. I looked forward to my experience and expected it to go well. Mark had told me I'd be in good hands. He had spoken with Reggie and told him to saddle up 'Boo', a small mare that Mark described as gentle and ideal for a first lesson.

"Good morning. Are you Reggie?" I called to the "cow hand" looking gentleman with the Stetson hat I found carrying a saddle.

"Yep! Are you Jim?"

"I am. I'm glad to meet you Reggie."

I liked Reggie immediately. He looked genuine and friendly. About 5' 10" his warm smile and twinkling eyes made me feel at home right away. Perhaps seventy he was still very fit and looked as tough as an old weathered saddle. His warmth was accented by a distinctive sense of humor. He smiled a lot and was gracious. In time those same characteristics would be demonstrated by him over the next four years through times that would try the patience and emotions of anyone else in his position.

Reggie and I chatted a little about his place, the horses he stabled for other people, and some basics on riding. While he spoke he walked me over to Boo and introduced me. Boo was a friendly little animal and swished her tail as Reggie and I both patted her. She had large brown eyes and unusually long lashes. I felt good about her and she seemed to take to me. Her ears were far forward as she nuzzled me. While Reggie and I talked and he began to saddle her, I noticed a large beautiful dark brown stallion in a stall close to where we stood. The powerful horse stood staring out the back of the stall toward the field between the barn and the house. He was focused upon a small athletic young lady striding toward the barn.

As the young women entered the barn, Reggie introduced me.

"Jim, this is Mark's daughter Channing."

"Hello Channing. I've heard a lot about you from your Dad. I'm happy to meet you."

The trim young lady responded in a detached manner, "Hi. Dad told me you'd be coming over this morning for a lesson."

Turning toward Reggie she said, "Reggie. I'm thinking it might be good to have Jim ride 'Bugsy. What do you think?"

"Well, Mark told me that I should saddle up Boo for Jim's lesson."

Channing responded, "Yeah, I know. But I think Bugsy will be better. Let's use him."

Reggie hesitated a moment. I could see he was pondering the situation. Possibly because he was being paid by the Grivas family to stable and take care of the animals, he felt some obligation to go along with her. "Well, OK. If that's what you want."

Reggie took the saddle off Boo. He then began to prepare the sleek stallion for me. Knowing nothing about riding, I didn't know that a temperamental thoroughbred like 'Bugsy' should have been warmed up before putting an unfamiliar rider on him. Channing busied herself with raking in the stall while Reggie threw a pad and then the shiny new saddle Channing had brought with her over the horse's back. The stiff saddle was also something 'Bugsy' had not become accustomed to yet. All the while Reggie talked about what to do when I got on the horse. As Reggie spoke, Bugsy seemed calm enough and I figured they knew best about conducting the lesson. I cast a glance over at Boo and kind of wished it was her I'd be riding. After placing a bit in Bugsy's mouth, Reggie led the large powerful animal directly out into the open space behind the barn. Channing and I followed.

"OK, Jim. Now you'll put your left foot in the stirrup,

grab the saddle horn with your left hand and swing your right leg over and fall into the saddle. Then I'll hand you the reins and tell you what to do from that point" said Reggie.

As I stepped up to the left side of the big animal, I noticed that his ears were angled back sharply and his eyes were darting around. Other than that, he stood still and steady and I assumed this was all business as usual for him. I reached up grabbing the saddle horn, put my foot into the stirrup and swung up into the saddle. The leather of the new saddle creaked slightly as I sat down. Reggie handed me the reins up to me. I settled down into the saddle and relaxed.

Suddenly for no apparent reason Bugsy reared up vertically on his hind legs. Startled by the move I leaned forward and hung onto the saddle horn to not fall off backward. The big animal then came down on his front legs and began bucking wildly. It all happened so quickly I didn't have time to think about anything but holding on. As the horse's massive body jolted up and down my mind became a blur. All seemed to be moving in slow motion and as if it was a dream. I heard yelling somewhere off in the distance but couldn't discern the words. As the horse exploded repeatedly up and down my body was out of sync with him and became like a rag doll bouncing in the opposite direction of his motion. In a last great thrust through his powerful back he propelled me far above him into the air.

Like an aquatic diver with arms outstretched above head before striking the water I fell to earth. The force of the impact caused my arms to buckle and my face struck the hard ground. My neck was snapped to the side and my right shoulder was jammed back toward my ribs. I collapsed into a heap. For a just a moment I lost consciousness. But quickly I came to my senses and rolled up into a sitting position. Stars and ringing in my ears were accompanied by a feeling of spinning.

"Jim! Jim! Can you hear me?" Reggie called as he ran over to me. I swayed side to side as I struggled to become fully consciousness. I looked up into Reggie's face. I saw a look of alarm. He wanted to help me but didn't know what to do at that point. Then I looked to the side and saw Channing. She simply stood there with a look of alarm on her face saying nothing. Having much experience earlier in life with contact sports, I was familiar with violent collisions with the ground. I automatically struggled to my feet. For a few seconds I felt dizzy. Reaching up I put my hand to my face wiping a mixture of blood and dirt from my nose and eyes. From out of no where, Marcia appeared. As I stumbled beside her back toward the house I could tell something was very wrong with me but I didn't know what.

"Your nose is broken", Marcia announced as we got near the back porch. Meanwhile Reggie took Bugsy back into the barn. Channing simply disappeared. I headed immediately into the bathroom on the first floor near their living room. Now nauseous and faint I leaned heavily on the sink and looked into the mirror. The pale white face staring back was that of a man who was going into shock. Blood trickled from the nose down across the chin and began to collect in the sink. I leaned over, turned on the cold water to begin splashing it onto my face in an attempt to revive myself and keep from fainting. Now the spinning resumed so much I sat on the closed toilet seat to keep from falling on the floor.

Get it together. Don't faint. Stand up and get cleaned up then walk out under your own power.

Soon I did stand. I cleaned up my face and hands. Finally I opened the door and stepped out into the hall. Reggie was there waiting for me. He put his arm around my shoulder and guided me into the living room and a large reclining rocker. I fell into the chair and leaned back.

"Jim. What can I get for you?" asked Reggie. His eyes flashed deep concern as he leaned down to look carefully at me. Marcia also asked if there was anything I'd like. I requested a glass of orange juice knowing that my blood sugar might be off as a result of the trauma. I wanted to avoid going into shock and believed the OJ might help counter that.

"Would you like me to call an ambulance?" Reggie offered.

"No. I definitely don't want that" I responded emphatically.

"But Jim, you may have some broken bones or have a concussion. You don't look good at all", Marcia said.

"I just want to sit here for a little while and see what happens over the next few minutes. Then I'll decide what to do."

II.

"So, how are you doing?" Mark asked as he walked into Reggie's living room?" Reggie had telephoned the Grivas's and Mark and his wife Angela drove over immediately. Because I was still dazed I had no idea how much time had elapsed since the event and Mark showing up. Everyone except Channing was now in the living room around me. I learned later that Channing had taken 'Bugsy' out for riding as soon as I was back in the Shanholtzer home. I never did see her again that day.

"What time is it Mark?"

"It's getting near 10:00 Jim. We should get you to a hospital to be checked out."

"I'll drive myself to the Littleton hospital and let them look me over."

"Well, I can drive your car Jim and Angela will follow in our car."

"No. You can ride with me if you want though."

"Man, you're not too damn stubborn, but you're pretty damn stubborn. Look, you're hurt. You better let us help."

"Right. But as I said, you can ride with me if you want. That will be helping."

Soon Mark and I were headed toward the hospital with me behind the wheel. I felt a little groggy but by this time I believed I was alert enough to drive safely so I wasn't a hazard to Mark or anyone else on the road. I actually stopped at the bank, which was on the way to the hospital to make a withdrawal. The clerk looked oddly at my face and though the bleeding had stopped I'm sure she wondered if I'd been beaten up in a fight. And of course I had been beaten up; by Bugsy. But I had no idea at that point how badly.

Once we arrived at the hospital, Mark and I were advised to sit in the waiting room and a doctor would check with me when my turn came. I knew enough to tell the attendant that maybe I shouldn't be kept waiting too long as I believed there could be some broken bones. My body ached everywhere but no where in particular. I felt like a mass of ground hamburger.

"I'm sorry, sir. But you'll have to wait your turn. There are a number of people before you." Mark then chimed in, "OK. But I think this guy may be injured more than it appears. He could have a concussion."

Mark's appeal fell on deaf ears. It would be over 45 minutes until a physician checked on me. When he did, he quickly became quite concerned. He determined that there was indeed major injury and trauma. In fact he decided they were unable to handle the extent of the injuries there at Littleton. He had me strapped to a stretcher and placed in an ambulance to be taken to St. Anthony's Trauma Center in Denver.

This has to be a dream. I was just walking under my own power. Why do I have to be tied down to this damn board? I wonder how much all of this is going to cost?

I was whisked off in the ambulance and soon was being inserted into an MRI scanner at St. Anthony's. All of me from head to foot was scanned. After that I was removed and placed in a room where I was subjected to perhaps the most humiliating exam I have ever endured in front of four or five nursing students and a 'Nurse Ratchet' clone supervising the spectacle. Why she felt a need to insert a glass rod into that highly private and strategic place in front of onlookers I will never know. Lying with my legs spread uncovered in front of that group with the glass rod protruding from me, I tried to demonstrate some humor. "So, what are you hoping to find in there? What I drank last night?" My joke was completely ignored. Had I not been in such a precarious position I might have been tempted to test the impact resistance of her skull and then walk out.

Soon afterward a physician introduced himself. "I'm Doctor Elliot. I've looked at your results from the scanner. Mr. Anderson, you are going to have to stay here. And in fact, I want to ask you for permission to prep you for a surgical procedure today."

"Why? What's going on?"

Over the next few minutes the doctor explained that I was suffering from a broken pelvis, crushed disc in my spine, one broken vertebrae, extensive muscular and ligament tears in the abdomen as well as other issues related to my shoulder and hernia areas. His words were like a bad dream. How could all of that have happened so quickly? I wondered how I had been able to rise, walk and talk as though it had just been another collision on the gridiron or basketball court.

"Doctor with all of this, why am I able to walk. And I don't feel as bad as you just described."

"You don't feel it yet Mr. Anderson. But you're going to quite soon. In trauma cases like this the body often masks pain to enable the injured person to escape danger. I'm sorry, but you are injured badly and it's going to be difficult for you unless we take you into surgery soon."

Call it tenacity or just plain stupidity but I was resistant to entering surgery that afternoon. In the forefront of my mind was a trip I was scheduled to make to Atlanta Tuesday of the coming week. It was not just another business trip coaching or advising my clients on sales, leadership or management issues. This one was special. I was to facilitate a critical meeting between a division head and the president of the client company. The division head, a friend of mine by the name of Chip Groom was on the verge of being terminated. I was going to meet with him and Tom Sinkbell the president in an effort to save Chip's job. I was confident that meeting would spare Chip.

"Doctor, do I absolutely have to have surgery?"

"We can't force you without your permission. However, I strongly advise it in your case. I definitely can not release you from the hospital. You'll have to remain here at least tonight. If you like, tomorrow we can discuss your options if you still refuse surgery."

I agreed. If I could have a night to see what developed and make a decision the next day, I'd take that option and hope for the best.

III.

Dr. Elliot was right. I woke up the next morning after a drug induced sleep feeling the way he predicted. By that time, they had applied a large elastic brace around my hips. It was like a giant knee brace made of elastic and Velcro extending from my stomach to the tops of my thighs. Basically it held my pelvis together and added much support to the lower back for the damaged vertebrae and crushed disc. But it didn't do anything for what the nerves in those regions were communicating to my brain.

I found that I could slide out of bed to my feet and shuffle slowly to the rest room. That gave me some hope that perhaps I could get out of there that day. Chip Groom's predicament was on my mind. If there was any way I could get out of there, I would.

Possibly around 9:30 AM I recognized a voice in the hall. It was Dr. Elliot making his rounds. I knew he was headed my way. Turning slowly and letting my feet dangle toward the floor, I slowly slipped out of the bed. Standing at the foot, I braced myself while leaning against the frame just before he entered the room.

"You're out of bed!" he exclaimed when he came through the door.

"Good morning, Doctor Elliot."

"How are you feeling?"

OK, time to do some Oscar quality acting.

"Well I'm sore. But I don't feel too bad."

"Were you able to sleep?"

"Yes. I did pretty well with that. I ate breakfast and have gone to the bathroom a couple of times already."

"Jim, we need to make a decision this morning. I still recommend surgery. It will be best to get this done now rather than later."

"Well, is there any chance I can heal up some if I keep this brace on? It seems to really help. I admit, I don't want surgery and I want to leave the hospital today."

Dr. Elliot examined me and we talked about my options. If I left that day I'd have to return to see him or one of his partners in a couple of weeks. He said that there was an outside chance I might begin to heal the split in the pelvis, but it was not likely. Definitely the back would not heal. Regardless, once I could see there was even a small chance I could get out of there that day I lobbied hard to make it happen. I said nothing about wanting to fly to Atlanta that week. He finally agreed and said I could be released.

Thankfully, later that day I was driven home. Once I arrived, I went directly to my bed. I determined to stay down until having to go to the airport Tuesday. Maybe I'd start to feel better if I just took it easy and let the brace do its job. And maybe I'd win the lottery. I figured the chances of both were about the same. Over the next couple of days, trying to rest up for the mission to Atlanta I lived on Tylenol and a prescription for valium Dr. Elliot had written for me. All that time I tried to convince myself I could rise above this challenge and save my friend's job. I had to go; like it or not.

IV.

The trip to Atlanta was a success. At least for Chip Groom. We got a reprieve for him. He would keep his job for the time being. For me, it was just plain hell. In fact the next six months were much the same. But because I was self employed and had no way to earn income when laid up, I kept going. To Atlanta, Philadelphia, and other places where I had consulting work. In the meantime, nothing healed. So in April of 2002 I finally turned myself in and entered Swedish Hospital for the first of three surgeries over the next three years to repair some of the damage. That first surgery was having a steel bar bolted to my pelvis to hold it together. While the pelvis would be improved right away from the insert, I was told the torn ligaments and muscles would take at least a couple of years to heal. And then they would never be the same and there would be discomfort always. I didn't believe that. However, it turned out to be true.

Because measurements from X-rays after that first operation indicated that the broken vertebrae was 8 millimeters out of alignment with the rest of the spine, and one disc was almost completely crushed, the next surgery would be the back. However, it would be the following year after the pelvis and abdomen had some time to heal. Apparently the jack hammer pounding I took from Bugsy before being catapulted in the air did most of the damage. It was going to be a long ordeal. A life changing ordeal though I didn't realize it for a long time after the incident.

In the meantime, I continued to travel and work. Being self employed, there was no way I could take time to convalesce. If I didn't work, I didn't get paid. So, within three weeks of getting out of the hospital for repair of the pelvis, I was on a plane again hitting the road to visit client companies. And over the next two years which included back surgery to repair that injury and then a double hernia surgery as a result of the damage done in the abdominal area, I struggled to keep my business alive. But I lost much of it due to having to turn down the normal level as well as I was not able to perform at 100%

The continual physical pain took a toll on my overall health. I was not as sharp as before the accident. And to make matters even more interesting I began to use steroids to keep going. They masked some of the pain but affected my memory and general mental state. All in all, it was like an ongoing bad dream. But I survived. I was able to stay in business, though minimally and debt free. My income suffered significantly and medical bills not covered by my insurance plan were large. But, I took some consolation that I prevailed in the face of circumstances that could have ruined much more than just my general state of health. I didn't feel prideful; but I believed I had at least stepped up in the face of overwhelming circumstances.

If it had just been the challenge of the physical pain, financial set backs and losing the strength and vitality I had before it all began, that would have made for enough of an adventure that my life would have been dramatically different. However, there was to be a much different kind of challenge that took an emotional and mental toll that would also make this entire episode something that would change everything for the balance of my life. It came from an unusual and unexpected source.

V.

Almost a year after my ill fated encounter with Bugsy I received a telephone call from a close friend. Jeff Brinen was an attorney I had met years earlier. We had examined some career change options for him around 1994 and shortly after that we became fast friends. His call came on a morning in early September of 2002. He was asking me how I was feeling, as everyone had come to do in those years. During the conversation he uncovered the fact that I had lost a considerable amount of income because of the accident as well as incurring significant medical bills not covered by my insurance.

"Jim, doesn't Mark Grievas have insurance that should cover this accident?"

"I haven't talked to him about it Jeff. I don't want to cause him inconvenience. He had tried to do me a favor and is really feeling badly about the whole thing."

"But Jim, if he has insurance, this is what he's been paying for."

The conversation went on for awhile without me agreeing to call Mark to open the subject. But ironically, later the same week I received a call from another attorney friend. This was Tom Derederian in Michigan. Tom asked the same questions Jeff did. A debate between me and Tom ensued. However, Tom with unknowing support from Jeff won. I agreed that I would telephone Mark to discuss the matter. I did so the following week. I reached Mark at work one afternoon.

After our 'Hello's' I opened the subject with him.

"Mark, I'm going to ask you something and if you don't want to deal with it, that'll be fine. I'm going to leave it up to you."

"What is it?"

"Well, a couple of friends suggested to me that I ask if you have insurance that may cover some of my medical expenses or lost income from the incident with 'Bugsy'."

"We have a policy. I'll telephone my insurance agent and ask him about it."

"Mark, I'm leaving it up to you. If you want to drop this, we won't go any further with it."

"No. I think I should talk with him and I'll call you back."

It was the next day that Mark called back. He told me his policy through Farmers Insurance did cover this kind of loss and that I should submit a claim. He explained I'd hear from a Farmers claim representative who would take the information and work with me on it. I was greatly relieved. Already the financial losses were mounting and I knew I still had more surgery to undergo.

When I heard from the Farmers claims representative he took information by phone and told me he'd send a form for me to complete describing the incident, what I estimated my expenses to be beyond my medical coverage and any other costs. When I did get the form I only listed the out of pocket medical expenses to that point. I didn't want to get into lost income because I was self employed, and those would be estimates that were not absolute. After submitting the form I spoke with both Jeff and Tom and told them that I had indeed pursued the matter and that Farmers told me I'd hear back from them in a couple of weeks. My hopes were up. Anything Farmers would do would help a lot. I told Mark how much I appreciated him looking into the matter.

Then a couple of weeks later I did receive a letter from Farmers Insurance responding to my claim. The letter bewildered me. It explained that my request was denied. I learned shortly thereafter the principle reason was that Channing Grievas and her mother's description of the entire event conflicted directly with mine. In essence the two ladies claimed that I had been an experienced rider and told them I was experienced. Channing also stated I had not been bucked off the horse but had fallen off just after I got in the saddle. Furthermore she stated her opinion that I was making a much bigger matter out of the entire affair and was simply attempting to "cash in" on the incident. There were other reasons Farmers denied the claim, but they were incidental. However, it was clear by the wording in their letter that Farmers treated my case as bogus and they were rejecting it.

VI.

A few days later the phone in my home office rang. I limped over to pick it up. "Hello?"

"Hi Jim. It's Jeff. I'm calling to ask if you heard back from Farmers yet about your claim."

"I did Jeff. They denied it."

Jeff was incredulous. "What? For what reason?"

"Well, it seems that they think I'm faking."

"So, you faked a broken pelvis and broken back?"

"According to them I just fell off the horse and am trying to just cash in on it."

Over the next few minutes as Jeff asked more questions, he became increasingly bothered by what he was hearing. Though a mild mannered and gentle man, I could hear anger stirring in his voice. It was reassuring to know that someone believed me instead of Channing Grievas and her mother Angela.

"So what did Mark say when you told him about this Jim?"

"He said he was sorry. He had no explanation. It appears he's got to side with his wife and daughter."

"But does he understand that it will cost him nothing if Farmers pays your claim and that's what he's been paying premiums for all along?"

"He understands that. But it seems the ladies in his household have decided for some reason unknown to me that I should not receive anything from Farmers. And Farmers seems more than happy to believe them and deny the claim. I guess that settles it."

Jeff and I talked awhile longer and then we hung up with me resolving that would be the end of everything. When I spoke with Tom Derederian in Michigan he became much more agitated than Jeff.

"Jim, I think you have just cause for getting a lawyer to represent you now."

"Tom, you know me. That's something that is so foreign

to me; I can't even begin to consider it. Especially since the guy at the center is a childhood friend who was trying to do me a favor by letting me have a lesson on one of his family's horses."

"Look, I understand you don't want to put Mark on the spot. But the truth is that his daughter and wife are putting him on the spot by lying. If he was a real friend. . . . "

A debate ensued and went on for some time. I got nowhere with Tom and he got no where with me. At least until he made one point I couldn't dispute.

"Jim, you suffered serious life changing financial and physical set backs. I want you to ask yourself if that will have an effect upon your family in the long run."

As I thought that point through it was pretty clear this was eventually going to affect not only my net worth which would flow to my children but in the near term I was hindered to do certain things for my family. Additionally, they already were suffering as they saw the change in their father's quality of life and even my personality. Again, Tom was making points with me that Jeff had that I didn't want to reveal to him. More importantly, both Tom and Jeff were good friends. Both men of great character whom I had much respect for. I knew they were rational and well informed. I knew in my heart they were right. But taking such action was foreign to my nature. I had to think about it more.

VII.

The phone rang one morning in mid October. It was Jeff again.

"Hi Jim. How are you feeling?"

I had already adopted the habit of dodging that never ending question from everyone who knew me.

"Hi Jeff. What's going on?"

"Well, I know an attorney who thinks you have a strong

case against Farmers denial of your claim. I think you ought to meet with him and at least hear what he has to say."

"Jeff, I really am not comfortable with initiating any kind of legal action."

Though I knew neither Tom nor Jeff knew one another, it seemed as though they had been talking. Jeff wasted no time making the same solid points Tom had a few days earlier. It didn't take Jeff too long to wear me down. I conceded. I agreed to meet his attorney friend who specialized in representing clients with valid injury claims. Jeff told me the name of the gentleman. It was a name that would eventually become seared into my consciousness. Not so much because of the role he would play in this matter. But more so because of his nature. His name was Bruce Fierst. A meeting was arranged between me, Jeff and Bruce.

The day of the meeting Jeff had me come to his office in Denver. There Bruce would meet me and learn more about the incident and the facts surrounding the denial of the claim. Jeff and I talked for a few minutes and then he went to find Bruce and bring him into the large brightly lit conference room.

Soon, Jeff came back with a middle aged man a little less than medium height. The solidly built man had short light blond hair and piercing blue eyes. While he was very professional, there was an aura of intensity about him that you could just feel by being in the same room with him. Even when he was not speaking. Instantly the atmosphere between Bruce and me became charged. Almost as though we were two opposing poles on a generator emanating sparks between them. Two highly charged and competitive characters that seemed to be competing even though there was nothing overt to compete upon. Yet.

In the discussion, I was impressed by Bruce. He asked direct and obviously important questions. I saw that he was very intelligent and more than competent. During the discussion, Bruce wasted no time in making a few facts crystal clear to me. One was that Farmers was denying a just claim that they should by all rights pay. Another point was that my real financial costs as well as lost income cost were just beginning. There would be more surgery as well as time away from work. Additionally, physical rehabilitation and related incidental costs yet unrealized were likely to be substantial. Beyond that, and most importantly, Bruce made a strong case that the Grievas women were unjustly behind an effort that would ultimately undermine any settlement.

I left that meeting with a lot to think about. What occupied my thoughts the most though was that all of this was definitely having a detrimental affect upon my loved ones. And it promised to get worse. That was the most significant consideration.

The next day I telephoned Jeff to review everything to that point. I told him that I could not take any action without first calling Mark Grievas and telling him what I was considering. I felt that Mark needed an opportunity to correct the actions of his daughter and wife before anything else could happen. Jeff agreed. I telephoned Mark and reached him on my first attempt. As he and I spoke, I asked him if he had seen a copy of the letter from Farmers denying my claim. He told me he had.

"Mark, what do you think about the parts stating that I had not been bucked and simply fell off the horse or that I had told you and Channing I was an experienced horseman?"

"Well, I can't speak to any of that. I guess it's all a matter of interpretation and whose perspective you look at things from."

"Mark, you know it's not a matter of "perspective" but a matter of facts versus untruths."

We talked a little while longer and finally I offered him the chance to right things.

"Mark, because of the position Farmers has taken and I have a family to think about, I have no option other than to get legal representation. You do understand that if I do, whatever happens, you will not have to pay for anything."

"I understand, Jim. I guess you have to do what you have to do."

"Mark, all that has to happen here to solve this, is for the truth to be told. If it is, Farmers will do the right thing and it'll be over soon."

"Well what do you want me to do?"

"Just tell the truth and have your daughter tell the truth."

"But what do you want me to say."

"Just the truth." I was not going to attempt to coach him in this matter. I knew if the facts were offered, things would work out. If not, there was going to be a long ugly battle and I would be in the middle of it. And a lot of people were going to be affected.

Though I suspected that Mark and his daughter and wife were not going to clear the matter up I was a little comforted that I had been upfront with him before I engaged an attorney to represent me. Mostly I was comforted by the fact that Mark still had an opportunity to bring everything to an end even before it began. All he had to do was ensure that the truth was told. It was in his hands. I told him I would not do anything until the following week and he had time to work things out at his end. We hung up amiably.

VIII.

Unfortunately, the Grievas women and Farmers stood their ground. As a result, I was left with no choice. Bruce, Jeff and I agreed to meet again to discuss our options.

In our meeting it soon became apparent that what were about to embark upon was something that would likely take years. It would be a very demanding challenge to all concerned. Me, my family, the Grievas family, Reggie and Marcia Shanholtzer, and others. Many innocent people were about to be put through very trying and uncomfortable circumstances. Simply because two women, for a reason that seemed to defy common sense, would not be truthful. And Channing's father had no authority.

When it became obvious that we had no recourse other than to seek litigation, Bruce talked to me by phone about what we could expect over at least 24 months and very possibly much longer. He described depositions, routine and expected delay of formal court proceedings, likely negative and false information presented about me and the expenses. He told me that I would probably be characterized as the architect of a frivolous law suit; and worse. And during all of this, I knew I would be having more surgeries. One to repair the broken back and the other a double hernia. It is a euphemism to say that this would be a daunting task. It would be an ugly battle.

In early November 2002 Bruce, Jeff and I sat in the conference room at Jeff's law firm again, discussing the sequence of events and what must be done to prepare for the battle. Jeff had already done his job. It was getting me to understand that a law suit was necessary and bringing Bruce and me together. He would have to do little else other than encourage me at critical points where I might be weary during the conflict.

It was going to be Bruce and me taking on Farmers' legal representatives, the Grievas family, the Grievas family lawyer and even the lawyer that would have to represent the Shanholtzers. Even though Reggie Shanholtzer was completely innocent, we knew that if he was not named as a co-defendant with the Grievas family, it was possible that Channing Grievas would claim that Reggie had made the decision to place me on Bugsy instead of Boo and that would undermine the whole case. So, Reggie, an innocent and good man was going to be dragged into the sordid matter simply because he was present. The whole thing smelled rotten. I learned that's the nature of litigation.

The formal law suit was written up and registered in November of 2002. I telephoned Mark and Reggie both to tell them that they would be served. Because I cared about both men, I wanted to do everything I could to minimize the trauma of what they were about to experience. Especially Reggie.

Again Mark asked me what I wanted him to do. I repeated, "Mark, just tell the truth and get your daughter to do the same." But it was apparent he was going to do nothing but hang on through whatever would happen. His wife obviously had an oppressive hold upon him. I told him I regretted what was about to happen. But I knew that no apology was really necessary from me as the cause was squarely on his side of the equation.

IX.

Between November of 2002 and August of 2005 there were numerous depositions and other information gathering efforts performed. I was deposed and questioned by Marks attorney Teresa Seymour and Reggie's attorney Jan Spies. Teresa was a heavy set unpleasant woman. She was not very formidable. Jan was a lovely but keen defense attorney in her mid thirties. She was tough. I had to be especially sharp when being deposed by her. Surgeons and experts were also deposed. The cost of the time for those depositions was steep. Bruce and I had to pay for them. However, Bruce carried most of that load. I was very grateful to him. Also, his time and expenses were substantial over those years. But he passed none of it along to me as he was confident we would eventually prevail and then I would be able to pay him. I expressed my gratitude to him often.

Over three years beginning in 2002 there were the depositions, rescheduled trials and various administrative complications. I entered the hospital again in 2003 and had back surgery to correct the spinal injury. I participated in physical therapy. My insurance covered only part of the medical costs so my out of pocket expenses mounted. And I continued to lose business income as I was unable to sustain the same level of effort that I had previous to the injuries and surgeries. I was losing my edge mentally, which is the core requisite of my business, due to the constant physical pain, sleeplessness, dependency on steroids and continual emotional strain of the process.

I would need more surgery for the hernia but that would be held off until after the outcome of the case. The physical discomfort during all that time was unrelenting. Because I was unable to tolerate narcotic based pain relievers then, I relied heavily upon Tylenol, ice packs and the steroids to keep me going. They were not terribly effective, but they were better than nothing. I'm confident the steroids undermined short term memory as well as day to day mental focus. I was told often by more than one member of my family I just was not myself. Often I appeared to be in a daze. And I was.

However, the most trying and difficult challenge I faced was not financial, physical pain, or even the erosion of my quality of life. The most difficult gauntlet I faced had to do with the emotional and mental stress attending the entire process. And the greatest cause of that stress came from an unusual source. It came from Bruce Fierst.

Bruce had some issues in respect to how he perceives and related to others. One of the central themes of his nature was intolerance for people who did not agree with his political views. His intolerance was overt. He demonstrated animosity in an aggressive manner which alienated others as a direct result of his sometimes hostile and contentious manner. It would be bad enough if he had restricted this behavior to personal relationships. But to do this with a client while attempting to serve as my advocate multiplied the difficulties. In a case like mine, the client is almost totally at the mercy and whim of the attorney. Everything rests upon the attorney's ability to win the case and protect the client. So Bruce had enormous power in respect to me.

To my dismay, when Bruce became aware that I did not ascribe to his political views and causes, he began to attempt to promote them to me. I explained that it was his right to have whatever views he held but it was inappropriate that he would try to get me to agree with him. This was especially true in his role serving as my attorney in one of the most traumatic and painful times of my life. However, Bruce was unrelenting.

Often he would take up the crusade after seeing something in the news that criticized President Bush or some other highly visible person in a different political camp than himself. One memorable call in particular between Bruce and me occurred early in 2003. I was at home when Bruce telephoned to discuss a minor detail having to do with depositions. After we addressed it, he chose to challenge yet again the fact that I had voted for George Bush in the preceding election.

"Did you see what Bush said on the news last night?" Bruce asked.

"Bruce, as I've said before, I don't hang on every news byte that is spewed out daily about President Bush. More importantly, I thought I'd made clear that I don't want to talk about politics or President Bush, ever."

Bruce sputtered, "But I can't believe you voted for him! Why did you vote for him anyway? Do you support this illegal war we're waging in the Middle East?"

"Please Bruce, we're not going to get anywhere with this. Let's just agree that we disagree on a lot of issues outside our case against Farmers and simply not go there."

"Well Jim, you seem to be an intelligent and highly educated person. I just don't understand why you don't want to hear the truth about Bush. Look, let me . . ."

I was becoming frustrated and I interrupted Bruce.

"Bruce! That's enough. Would you please let this go?"

But he pressed on. Without missing a beat he began to

recount a series of what he described as mistakes President Bush had made since coming to office. I twisted in my chair holding the phone away from my ear just far enough that I could hear him speaking but not make out the content of what he was saying. This particular day my back was hurting more than normal and I had a headache. My frustration was slowly turning to anger. Yet he was my attorney and I was dependent upon him. I struggled to keep my composure and remain patient and able to tolerate his tirade. Regardless, his voice was raising and when I heard the question, "What is wrong with you?" I exploded.

"Bruce! I've heard enough of your indictments. We're done here! I'm hanging up now. Good bye!"

Right after I hung up, I knew I shouldn't have. I thought of calling him back and apologizing. Then I realized he was pushing my buttons purposefully and he is the one who should be apologizing. I tossed and turned all night revisiting the call and thinking about how I should have handled it differently. That dialogue was not the only one of its' kind. They seemed to increase in frequency as the months and then the next two years dragged on. All the time Bruce was driving a wedge deeper and deeper between us.

In hindsight it's obvious that Bruce knew all along that me being in the throes of a law suit which dragged on for years and being so dependent upon him he was in a powerful position. My future relied heavily upon him and I was at his mercy. But he showed no mercy. He continued the political crusade during our entire four year long relationship. While he handled the legal case in a competent manner, he handled me in a demeaning manner. I had to fight hard to keep my sense of dignity. It would be a continuous battle all the way through to the conclusion of the case.

When we were granted a trial date in the middle of 2004 I was encouraged that Farmers and the Grivas family would finally have to appear in court in front of a jury. As we got close to the trial date I was hopeful that one way or the other, the horrendous series of events would finally be over. If we didn't win our case, I would at least be released from the torment of dealing with Bruce, the constant conscious awareness of the court room battle to come, and the never ending anxiety that attended all facets of the lawsuit.

However, when we came close to the date of the trial in 2004, it was delayed. Another trial took precedent over our trial and we were assigned a date the following year in 2005. And again, that trial was called off at the last minute and the trial was delayed yet again. We were assigned a date later that year in October. The let down before each of the delays took a significant toll upon me. Each time getting close to the date the tension and excitement would build as a function of expectations and the potential of just having everything finally come to end. Regardless of the result it would be better than living with the specter of it hanging over my head. Then at the last minute each time when the trial was cancelled, the frustration was maddening. But I could not let my family and certainly not the opposition know what a toll it was taking upon me.

X.

Ironically a few weeks before our rescheduled trial date in October, I was called in as a possible jurist in a criminal trial in Arapahoe County. It would be at the Arapahoe County Justice Center. The same place our trial would be held; if it ever did make it to trial. The criminal trial was an ugly affair having to do with the accusation of a young black man raping a child. I was not inclined to want to serve on the jury. It came at a very inconvenient time with my own trial supposedly to occur a couple of weeks later.

After the first screening of candidates for the jury through written questionnaires we completed, about fifty of us remained in the jury pool. We were then led into a court room where the attorneys for the defense and the District Attorney would speak with us.

Eventually, one of the questions the attorney for the defense asked the potential pool of jurors was, "Is there anywhere in the United States where a person is ever guilty before being proven innocent?" I could see he was trying to make the point we should consider the defendant innocent to begin before the evidence was analyzed. Pondering the question, I had to raise my hand and be recognized. When identified, the defense attorney said, "Mr. Anderson, do you think there's a place in our country where a person must prove their innocence and is treated as guilty before being proven innocent?"

I responded, "Absolutely."

"Well, what is it Mr. Anderson?"

It's with the IRS."

The courtroom broke up with laughter. Including both the defense attorney as well as the District Attorney.

Good. They'll think I'm a clown and I should be out of here soon.

A little later the defense then stated, "As you can see, my client is an African American. As I look at this pool of jurors I don't see one face of color. I have to ask if there is anyone here who ever had a bad experience with an African American."

Mine was the only hand that rose.

"Mr. Anderson. Have you had a bad experience with an African American?"

I responded, "Well, to me all citizens of the United States are simply Americans versus hyphenated Americans, but that's a whole other issue. However my answer is yes."

"Was the experience a function of being of different race?" the attorney queried.

I came back, "No. It had nothing to do with the fact that we belonged to different races. And frankly I'm surprised no one else in this group raised their hand."

Many in the room hung their heads. A few looked away.

Now they have to think I'm too outspoken. That should definitely get me out of here.

Ultimately after the screening process I was surprised that my name was the first one called to be a member of the jury. I was perplexed. On the written questionnaire I had made it clear I was not sympathetic to anyone accused of rape as someone close to me had been raped and that greatly affected my feelings on the matter. Also, the questionnaire asked questions about our values and even opinions on various issues. My obvious strong conservative values, the same thing that Bruce Fierst railed against, might have made me seem less supportive of the liberal defense team organized to represent the defendant. And my outspoken comments in the court room made me, if nothing else, stand out as unique.

During that entire week, we jurors were exposed to various revolting accusations and details as well as a number of witnesses that were about as unsavory a crew as I've ever seen assembled. For some reason the family members of the defendant as well as a number of people on both sides of the courtroom battle watched me more than any of the other jurors carefully looking for clues in my face. Did they think I was a bellwether for all the jurors? Maybe they could see something I didn't as ultimately I was selected by the rest of the jurors to be the Foreman of the jury. In that role, when it came time to render a decision, I would facilitate the jury through the process.

When it was time for the decision to be announced, the defendant, and his family had their eyes glued upon me. Based on the evidence, or lack thereof, our verdict acquitted the defendant. When the defendant's team heard the decision, they exploded into tears of joy attended by much hugging. Even their defense attorney, a tall distinguished looking black man was moved. Then the defendant looked across the room at me and smiled. I'll never know why they focused upon me. Interestingly after we were excused from the courtroom I happened to encounter the defense attorney in the hall. As we walked up to one another and stopped I said, "Walter. I'd like to ask you a question."

"What is it?"

"After reading all I had written on the questionnaire as well as my comments in the courtroom during the screening, how did I ever make it on that jury?"

He responded, "Mr. Anderson, you were the first person we selected."

Dumbfounded I asked "Why?"

"It was simple. We believed that your responses on the questionnaire and comments during selection indicated you were honest. My experience is that honest jurors are objective jurors. That's the best we hope for."

We shook hands and moved on. I don't consider myself especially honest. I try to be but know that often I avoid details or sometimes misstate things like anyone else does. However, Walter must have known what he was doing as he won that case. I learned later he was considered one of the most successful defense attorneys in the country.

XI.

As it turned out, my unexpected participation in the criminal trial actually prepared me in some important ways for my upcoming trial a couple of weeks later. I had witnessed first hand the kind of lies as well as underhanded tactics that attend court room histrionics. I had also experienced first hand how a jury behaves behind closed doors and the kinds of non-verbal clues they look for outside the evidence. I believed knowing that would help me conduct myself judiciously for our trial. It appeared that providence had thrust me into a timely preparatory experience. Against all my efforts to escape jury duty.

We did indeed go to trial a couple of weeks later that October of 2005. I was greatly relieved and actually looking forward to getting on with it. The nightmare would finally end. However, I had no idea of how demanding that week would become. While I had anticipated there would be lying and character assassination directed toward me, I was completely unprepared for the worst source of distress that would befall me. It began Sunday night before the first day of trial when my cell phone rang as I was getting off a plane returning from a business trip.

"Hello?" I said surprised to be receiving a call that late on a Sunday evening.

"Jim. This is Bruce."

"Hi Bruce. Are we still on for tomorrow?"

"We are. I want to meet you in the parking lot in front of the Justice Center at 7:30. I want to go over some last minute details with you then."

I was optimistic about our chances and said, "OK. I'm really glad we're finally going to get our day in court."

Ignoring that remark, Bruce unexpectedly turned the course of the conversation.

"You know Jim, before we begin tomorrow, I just have to tell you that it has been very frustrating working with you. I don't know how this will all come out, but I'll be happy when it's over and I won't have to work with you anymore."

His statement was like a fist in the stomach. I recoiled, not sure I had heard him correctly. I tried to compose myself and respond diplomatically.

"Bruce, I'm sorry for anything that has been an issue for you. But tomorrow you and are going into this fight as partners. I'm hoping we can be mutually supportive."

Again ignoring my response he stated simply, "I'll see you tomorrow morning at 7:30", and he hung up.

I stood in the airport silently without moving. I was shocked. All of the optimism and energy I had about facing the upcoming week had just been knocked out of me. I found a chair on the concourse and sat down. I tried to collect my thoughts and figure out why Bruce had done what he did. I thought carefully trying to determine what strategy he was using with me and how it would serve our cause. I found no answer. I stood up and slowly trudged through the airport suddenly feeling tired and discouraged.

The following morning I waited for Bruce in the parking lot outside the Justice Center. I was determined to behave as though the strange conversation with him the evening before hadn't occurred. I decided to smile and be upbeat when he arrived. Soon he did. I walked over to him in the lot and greeted him in a friendly manner.

My "Good morning Bruce" was met with an impersonal, "Jim, I have a couple of things to go over with you before we walk in there."

Bruce succeeded in making me feel like a non-person. Almost an inanimate object that he would use as necessary through the process. He proceeded to instruct me on how to conduct myself that week. He told me to avoid eye contact with our adversaries, the jurors, and the judge. He told me not to speak to him unless he asked me a question. In essence, I was to follow carefully any dictate he had for me and do nothing of my own volition. After we proceeded into the building and passed through the metal detectors at the security station I suppressed the urge to drag him off where no one would see me and express my growing outrage toward his behavior. I became resolute to keep a stoic posture through the entire week. Two weeks earlier I had seen first hand what a cauldron a court room could be. I would have to remain focused and as aloof as possible in order to endure Bruce as well as the indictments that would surely be launched by our opposition. I would be battling two separate adversaries.

XII.

The courtroom was a spacious and well appointed venue. Rich oak veneer panels accented the walls and the jury box. The witness stand was stately and elevated. I felt comfortable in the room. Despite Bruce I was regaining confidence in our case. The first day in court much of the basics of the events surrounding the incident four years earlier and evidence would be delivered. There would be some testimony with attorneys for both sides examining those persons who were called to the witness stand.

It all began with a touch of humor, or disgust depending upon how you looked at it. As all filed into the courtroom, Angela Grievas was actually carted into the room in a wheel chair. It was not because of her obesity. Her attorney explained that she had a rare debilitating condition that is aggravated by stress. I knew this was bogus, and I would learn later that apparently so did some others in that courtroom. I discretely watched the jurors' non-verbal responses to the spectacle of her in the wheel chair. All that was missing was a violin accompaniment to dramatize her sad expression. Because I was being watched simultaneously by some of the jurors I stifled my urge to laugh and would not even allow the slightest twinge of a smile to touch my lips. That took some effort.

For the most part, Bruce and I didn't speak much that day. Occasionally he told me to sit up straight, or don't look so tense, or don't look too relaxed. Or he would direct me to go and get him some water. Regardless of what I did, it was never right. I complied with his dictates only because it promoted the image that I was subservient to him. I wasn't but I wanted him to think he had authority over me. I'd reconcile that misconception on his part later; after the entire debacle was complete. In the meantime I'd try to avoid any confrontations with him. He had a critical job to do for me and I would allow him much license for the time being.

At the end of the first day, I was relieved to get out of that courtroom and the Justice Center. Mostly I was just relieved to get away from Bruce. His contentious and demeaning manner with me was trying my patience to its limit. He clearly had an agenda in addition to winning this case. Unfortunately I was the target of that secondary agenda. As I drove out of the parking lot that Monday I realized I was exhausted. Though I had not been called to the witness stand and merely sat next to Bruce or ran his errands, the tension in my body the entire day drained all of my strength. It was going to be a long week.

The next morning, in part because I was unable to sleep the night before and in part because I was becoming unable to respond to Bruce with a positive demeanor, I greeted him coolly.

"Hi Bruce, what's on the agenda today?"

Not even saying 'Hello' he just responded, "Today we're going to begin to get into the meat of the testimony. Based upon what came out yesterday and my read on the jury, I think we're off to a good start."

I just nodded and followed him into the building. I knew that regardless of what I'd say, he'd either take offense at it or tell me why I was wrong. I decided to not speak at all that day unless he asked me a specific question. I wanted to be neutral toward him and as helpful as I could be. However, my attitude was becoming almost hostile. Because I don't hide my feelings well, I knew I'd better be careful to not do or say anything that might agitate my nemesis any more than he would naturally agitate himself.

Over the next three days leading up to Friday, all of the tricks I suspected and more were unveiled by our adversaries. If even one half of what they other side said about me had been true, I should have been locked up in prison. I listened with amusement Tuesday as I heard Channing Grievas give her version of what happened with Bugsy.

"Ms. Grivas, would you tell the court specifically what happened right after Mr. Anderson mounted the horse?" her attorney asked.

"Yes. Well, as I stated earlier, Jim had told us that he was an experienced rider and would not need any instruction. But we wanted to be helpful and suggested he take it easy at first once he was in the saddle. However, as soon as he got in the saddle he gave Bugsy a nudge with his heels."

The attorney went on. "So, what happened then Ms. Grivas?"

"Bugsy began to move forward slowly and Jim just fell off."

"What caused him to fall, Ms. Grivas?"

"I don't know. I guess he just lost his balance and slipped over and fell."

"What happened after Jim landed?"

"Well, he got up right away and dusted himself off."

"How did he look?"

"He looked embarrassed at first. Then he became angry. He said that had never happened to him before. I believe he wanted us to think he was an accomplished rider and was upset when we could see he wasn't."

I could not help but look directly at Channing as she wove that tale. When she finished she looked directly back into my eyes and smiled. Her smile was as phony as her words. I felt a little nauseous but at the same time was encouraged that she must look transparent to the jury. At least I hoped that was the case.

Her attorney went on with more questions, and she went on with more fabrications. When it came time for Bruce to cross examine her he made a few notes then hesitated before rising to address her. Under his breath he whispered, "This is gonna be fun." And indeed Bruce expertly dissected her. His questions soon had Channing contradicting herself and illustrating the implausibility of her stories. Though Bruce was no friend of mine, it warmed my heart to watch him handle her. Again I stifled the urge to chuckle. Later in the week he would accomplish the same with Angela Grivas. And then after that it was Marks turn. I felt sorry for my old childhood friend. Though he betrayed me, and was not doing the right thing, I still recalled happy visions of him in our old hometown of

Coraopolis. As I watched him squirm on the witness stand, I felt sorry that the road of his life led him to this place.

XIII.

But the most challenging thing that week in trial was the unrelenting badgering of me by Bruce. He found a way to take issue with everything I did. It was infuriating. On Wednesday, when we came out of the cafeteria after the lunch break, I couldn't help but respond to it. We were standing alone in a hall near the men's room. He was berating the way I was dressed as he said it might send the message to the jurors that I was too affluent. Suddenly I stepped to within an inch of his face and spoke in a low determined voice through clenched teeth with my eyes drilling directly through his.

"I am more than tired of your continual criticism of me. We're on the same side here!"

I was breathing low and hard with my chest heaving and both fists clenched so tightly I felt the skin stretch over my knuckles. Bruce quickly recovered and responded, "Jim I'm only trying to help you win this case. My advice and suggestions are based upon years of experience dealing with juries."

"No! The fact is that you're attempting to torment me."

Bruce was no more intimidated by my outburst than if I had been a house cat hissing at him. In fact, I believe he took some perverse delight in seeing me vent. He had been trying to rattle me all week and try as I might to hold it in he seemed satisfied once I expressed the anger. I hoped that would finally cause him to let go and lighten up on me the rest of that day and the next. It didn't.

On Thursday it was my turn to take the witness stand. I had testified many times over the years since my early twenties not only as an expert witness for various client companies, but in battles with union representatives attempting to unionize my workforce at Michigan State. I was comfortable with being on the witness stand. The only preparation I needed was to brush up on the events surrounding 'Bugsy' and simply state them factually when asked. It was much easier for me than the Grivas family. While they had to concoct fiction and then attempt to make it all sound plausible and fit together all I had to do was tell the truth.

My testimony began in the morning before lunch. Bruce had told me the night before what he would be asking me so I was ready. My testimony proceeded for perhaps 50 or 60 minutes up to lunch and then was to resume after lunch. I felt fine about it and thought it was going well as Bruce and I left the courtroom around noon. Again, I was unprepared for what I least expected to hear from Bruce, though should have known better. Once we were safely out of hearing range of anyone he began.

"Jim you're doing badly. The jury doesn't like you. You're too uptight and stiff."

Yet again Bruce had caught me completely by surprise and demoralized me. I took a deep breath and composed myself before responding.

"How do you know they don't like me?"

"I can read a jury like an open book. They're not responding well to your carefully paced direct responses. You look so stiff and uptight there's no way you can evoke their sympathy. As it stands right now, I think we're on pretty shaky ground the way you're handling yourself."

"Well, I wasn't trying to evoke sympathy. I simply wanted to relate the facts in an objective manner. I'm sorry, Bruce. I thought it was going OK. Maybe we can regroup over lunch."

"Look, I'm not going to have lunch with you. I've got some more preparation to do for the afternoon. I'd recommend you go somewhere outside the building and get something to eat. You've got to loosen up before we go back in there this afternoon."

I was crushed. Bruce had not only undermined my confidence, he had pretty much convinced me we were losing and it was because of me. I walked to my car and got in. At first I sat there not sure of what to do. I had no appetite but I knew I wanted to drive somewhere if for nothing else than a change of scenery. I started the engine and drove slowly out of the parking lot and eventually east on Arapahoe Road with no particular goal in mind. I wound up at '3 Margarita's' at Clinton and Arapahoe. Still not hungry I sat in the parking lot wondering what I could do differently in the afternoon.

Too uptight and stiff. They don't like me.

The words kept repeating in my mind. Staring at the colorful '3 Margarita's' sign I got an idea. Maybe if I had a margarita or two with my lunch I would loosen up. If not, at least I wouldn't feel near as lousy as I did. Finally with an audible sigh I succumbed to the fact that I needed to put something in my stomach. I had to eat to replenish my recently sapped energy before returning to the witness stand.

Looking the menu over, not much of anything appealed to me. By the time the waitress arrived at my table I had made a decision. It had more to do with what I'd drink than what I'd eat.

"I'll take two chicken tacos and a margarita. Make it a double."

"Yes sir. That'll be coming right up."

Soon I was munching on a taco and some black beans. The margarita was excellent. Somehow the tequila in it seemed to be just the thing to salve the emotional bruises that Bruce had inflicted a few minutes earlier. I enjoyed the margarita so much and I had not come close to finishing lunch so I ordered another forgetting that she'd make it a double again. I've always been able to hold alcohol pretty well. A trait passed on from my father. I expected it to serve me in this instance.

You're not doing well. Too uptight. Too stiff. They don't like you.

I couldn't forget Bruce's words. I needed to loosen up considerably. Maybe the margaritas would do it. After finishing my food and the second drink, I ordered one more. Just for "the road". As I sat enjoying the final drink, I did feel that I was relaxing. In essence I unknowingly packed the equivalent of 6 Margarita's into my meager 170 pound frame. Leaving more than enough cash on the table for the tab and a substantial tip I got up and strolled out of the restaurant to find my car.

Now where the hell did I park that thing?

Finally realizing that I had walked out a different door than I had entered and was in the wrong parking lot, I eventually made my way to the gold Pathfinder. Luckily I did get back to the Justice Center just before it was time to reenter the court room. Bruce met me outside the door. Somehow he and the rest of the trial just didn't seem all that important to me at that moment. When Bruce asked, "Jim, are you ready?" I simply stared at him for a long moment and then chuckled. That prompted him to respond, "Are you OK?" I came back with "Yep. I'm good. Let's get on with it." Bruce stared at me queerly for a moment and then turned to enter the room.

Soon I was being reminded that I was still under oath and I took the stand. As I sat down I leaned forward slightly and braced myself against the side of the stand. I then realized I was more than "relaxed". I was actually dizzy. I knew I'd better not weave around as all eyes were on me. That might give the jurors and judge the idea that I was not in full possession of my faculties. I believed I was. At least that's what I told myself.

OK man. Now get it together. Don't look so uptight.

Frankly I was in a condition where the last thing in the world I could have managed was to look uptight. As Bruce began his questioning, I felt good and quite capable. However, I was informed later that half of my responses to him were "I can't recall." And that was true, I really couldn't recall much about anything as he queried me. Soon he was looking perplexed as he was not getting what he wanted and needed from my testimony. However, I wasn't concerned. I was feeling great and actually enjoying the attention I was getting. As I surveyed the crowd I was heartened to spot my friend Jeff Brinen in the audience. I was tempted to raise my fist and call out "Hey Jeff!" but I still had enough presence of mind to know better than to act on that desire.

And then it came time for the highlight of my testimony. It was the point where Bruce asked me to step down from the witness stand and describe to the jury some of the details of how the injuries had affected my professional work and ultimately my business. We had planned this earlier. Because a significant part of my work has to do with professional presentations and I've coached many executives on how to speak publically, Bruce thought it would be a good idea to have me give a short presentation in front of the jury. He was in for a memorable surprise. Poetic justice one might call it.

Leaning against a table to steady myself to keep from keeling over I began rambling to the jury something about the nature of my work. I tried to make it clear that my clients were national which required I travel to many locations. I explained that because of the debilitating affect of the injuries not to mention the continuous stream of drugs I had fed myself while traveling, I simply had been unable to sustain my regular pace. Not to mention the dulling effect the pain and drugs had upon my mental capabilities. I tried to relate that the overall affect of it had been to cause my business to dwindle to a fraction of what it had been before the injuries. All the while I rambled on I had to stifle an overwhelming desire to start giggling.

Perhaps the seminal statement of my bizarre testimony came when I was referring to the discomfort of the titanium rods and bolts in my lower spine. I turned around with my backside aimed toward the jury pointing out where the hardware was while admonishing them not to let their eyes proceed below my belt. I cast a glance toward Bruce as I delivered that brilliant point just in time to catch the look of horror on his face. Again I had to stifle an enormous desire to begin laughing. Somehow I did manage to not laugh and get back to the witness stand without stumbling though it took a deliberate effort.

At that point Bruce could see it was time to get me the hell off that stand. He had no more questions. But I still had to be cross examined by opposing council. However, that seemed to go alright. I simply responded with either the truth or "I can't recall" to everything I was asked. However, I somehow rallied enough of my faculties in that portion of my testimony to completely exonerate Reggie Shanholtzer of any responsibility for the dire interaction with 'Bugsy'. I knew that it was too late for the Grivas trio to implicate him and I wanted to be sure he was not in any way held responsible for what happened. I was quite successful with that strategy as would be revealed later. During that portion of my testimony the few times I looked toward Bruce, his head was down with his hand covering it as though he was trying to hide. I just figured since he had skipped lunch he must have been low on energy.

Finally, and thankfully, after what seemed like minutes to me but must have seemed an eternity to Bruce, I was excused from the stand. Feeling proud that I probably did well because I had so much fun on the witness stand after lunch I walked carefully back to take my seat next to Bruce. For a reason unbeknownst to me at the time Bruce would neither look at me nor acknowledged my presence in any way. That was fine with me as I received no further admonitions from him until we finally left the building at the end of the day. However, by that point I was feeling no pain and probably nothing Bruce could have said would have bothered me. I do remember seeing him talking at me in the parking lot waving his arms with a look of exasperation on his face but I simply couldn't comprehend what he was trying to communicate. I just stood there grinning at him and nodding like I knew what he was talking about. Finally he just shook his head, turned and stomped off muttering something else I couldn't make out.

XIV.

Friday morning dawned cloudy and cold. As I drove to the Justice center I was heartened by the knowledge that the entire farce should come to an end that day. No more Bruce. No more lies or character assassination by the Grivas clan. No more courtroom and on and on. Even if we lost, everything would finally be over. As I pulled into the parking lot I looked for Bruce. He had not shown up at his usual time. I hoped he was OK. But then I reminded myself that people like Bruce Fierst usually don't have many bad things happen to them. He'd show up alright. And eventually, though at the last minute, he did.

During the morning there was some final testimony and evidence submitted. And the attorneys for both sides had to get in a last word before the jury was excused to go off and begin working on a verdict. When the jury did depart it was about lunch time and Bruce told me he would remain in the building. I decided to leave for awhile and made sure my cell phone was on so Bruce could call me when the jury was to return with their decision.

Again I headed east on Arapahoe Road but not to '3 Margaritas'. I'd had quite enough of that establishment to last me a long time and went instead to the Target store to pick up some things. I had packed a sandwich in my car so I consumed it before going into Target. As I left Target I was surprised by my phone ringing. It had not been a full hour since the jury had been excused. It was Bruce.

"Jim. I'm afraid I have bad news for you."

"What is it Bruce?"

"The jury is returning in a few minutes with their verdict. When they take such a short time to reach a verdict in cases like this, it is usually in favor of the defendant. You'd better come back right away as we'll need to get into the courtroom shortly."

At that point some strange sense of compassion gripped me in respect to my tormenter and I offered, "Bruce, listen to what I have to say. You've done an outstanding job regardless of the differences between you and me. Whatever happens, I want you to know I appreciate all of your efforts."

He only responded with, "See you in a few minutes."

As everyone filed back into the courtroom, Channing Grivas walked close to our table. Our eyes met. She flashed the same arrogant smile I had seen more than once before in the courtroom. Her head was held high and she appeared more than a little confident.

As she passed, Bruce muttered an unsavory descriptive term of her under his breath. I just kept my gaze fixed upon Channing until she took her seat next to her mother, perched in her wheel chair. And then it was time for the big moment.

The judge asked the representative of the jury if they had reached a decision. They had and it was recorded in an envelope that was passed to the judge. He opened the envelope carefully and took what seemed an inordinate amount of time to examine the contents. Bruce sat next to me nervously tapping his foot. Channing and her mother sat smiling toward the jury members. I sat back in my chair with one hand folded over the other calming waiting for whatever would happen.

The verdict was not simple because it involved Reggie and Marcia Shanholtzer as well as the Grivas family. But as soon as the judge began to read, the basic outcome was obvious though there would be specifics that attended the decision. We won! Almost instantly Bruce's head jerked toward me and his mouth dropped open. Not only did the verdict go in our favor but it completely exonerated Reggie Shanholtzer and indicted the Grivas's. As the judge read it, the award to me was more than we had hoped for. It would cover the medical expenses I sustained, the lost income, and the fees for Bruce as well as all other expert witness costs and expenses we had paid. In summary it made me whole financially and paid Bruce well for his hard work. While it could never make up for the pain and suffering or the physical limitations I'd face the balance of my life from the injuries, it at least made our efforts over the years seem worthwhile.

As Angela Grivas sat in her wheel chair sobbing, Channing walked quickly out of the court room wiping her eyes and avoided looking at anyone. Mark began talking with his legal council. Reggie looked at me with a beaming smile on his face and then hugged his attractive attorney Jan Spies. Bruce actually let his guard down for a brief moment and shook my extended hand. Mostly I was feeling relief. Relief that Bruce would be paid well, I'd never have to deal with him again and the entire drama was hopefully at an end.

A few minutes later out in the hall Bruce advised me that Farmers would likely file an appeal to the verdict. I knew that, but I still was relieved this chapter was over and we had won. As Bruce and I talked about subsequent steps, the foreman of the jury and a couple of other jury members happened down the hall in our direction. I smiled at them and they smiled back. As they neared I said, "Thank you!" That comment halted them and we began to chat. I couldn't resist the urge to ask the foreman how they had reached a verdict so quickly.

He responded, "It wasn't difficult. We all concurred almost right away that it was obvious the defendants were not telling the truth and you were. So most of our work had to do with figuring out what the award would be."

"What was most indicative of the fact that they weren't being truthful?"

"You know, when we saw the mother being wheeled in a wheel chair, we were immediately suspicious of her. Then as we listened to both her and her daughter's testimony, we could see they were a matched pair. Both phonies."

We talked a little more and I thanked them again. Shortly

after they departed I asked Bruce if he'd be willing to take a few minutes to go have a beer or at least a coke or coffee to celebrate. He coolly declined my invitation. That was OK with me as I was feeling tired and ready to drive home and relax for the first time in weeks. I stopped in the cafeteria to get a soft drink and by coincidence encountered Mark Grivas by himself looking for a snack. I said 'Hi" to him. I felt good knowing that Farmers would be obligated to pay the entire sum of the judgment and Mark would pay nothing.

I felt no animosity toward Mark. I still felt sympathy for him. What a pitiful life he must be leading being married to Angela and having Channing, now age twenty four and obviously quite maladjusted still living at home. We spoke briefly and I told him I was glad it was all over, at least for now. He made mention of the possibility of an appeal. I responded in a cavalier manner, "That's OK if it happens. I'll just look forward to seeing you in court again in a year or two." I wanted him to understand that I would be unrelenting and also that I was prepared to take whatever happened in stride. I learned later that he relayed that comment to his attorney and it was one reason, though not the only one, that caused them to abandon an appeal.

XV.

One morning early in January of 2006, about three months after the trial, I picked Reggie up at his home and took him to breakfast. He talked away in his usual upbeat manner about nothing in particular. I enjoyed being with him and wanted to tell him again that I was sorry I had to name him as a codefendant in the lawsuit. In a classic Reggie response he stated,

"Jim my attorney said you were right. If you hadn't named me in the lawsuit and then exonerated me with your testimony, Channing likely would have implicated me. No problem. It's over now. We'll move on."

I couldn't resist asking a question.

"So Reggie, whose idea was it for Angela to pull the wheel chair act for the trial?"

He began to laugh then responded, "Oh man that was something wasn't it? It was her idea. Mark was embarrassed because he knew the rest of us thought it was ridiculous though Angela tried to convince us she really needed it."

"Reggie, I spoke with the foreman after the trial was over and they caught on to that right away."

After Reggie and I finished breakfast I took him home and we agreed to stay in touch. And then the following year I gained even more insight on the case when I encountered Jan Spies, Reggie's council at Elway's Restaurant one night in the Cherry Creek district of Denver. We were both surprised to see one another. She walked directly over to me smiling. We hugged immediately before we began talking. It was ironic. Here was a lady that had been an adversary for years in the interest of protecting her client as I had named him as a co-defendant. Yet here we were hugging and laughing like old buddies.

"You know, you were pretty tough during those depositions and then during cross examination in court", I said. "But I knew you were just trying to protect your client and respected you for the good job you were doing."

"Well, I didn't enjoy having to do that. It would have made it easier if I'd known all along you'd let Reggie off at the end."

"Yeah. Like I could have called you behind the scenes and told you that."

We laughed and went on recounting with humor the events in the courtroom. I then asked her what she remembered about my ill fated testimony after lunch.

"You know, you were not the guy I had deposed earlier. It just didn't seem to be Jim Anderson. I couldn't say for sure but something was different. What was going on?"

"Jan, let's just say that at that point after everything, I was ready for it all to be over."

"Have you seen Bruce since the trial?" she asked.

I paused for a few moments looking directly at her with a slight smile. I said, "We'll leave it that Bruce is an excellent attorney but it's unlikely he and I'll see one another again."

She gave me a knowing smile nodded and then tipped her glass against mine.

The Actress

I.

We were close to the front row of the theater. As I sat in the
dark staring at the screen with my neck craned back, I wasn't
especially entertained by the plot. Three teenage boys on a
summer vacation experiencing the trials of puberty. I watched
only with mild interest. But about a half hour into the story,
something engrossed me. A beautiful vision of a young woman
captured my attention. She was on a beach watching waves
breaking on the shore. Bewitching large almond shaped eyes
set above classic high cheekbones framed by the lovely curve
of her face. The young woman's long walnut hair tossed by the
ocean breeze.

The plot of the story was the classic fantasy of a fifteen year
old teenage boy. Admiring a goddess from afar and dreaming
that somehow he may make love to her. And in fact in this
award winning production of 'Summer of 42' the boy did
have an encounter with the woman due to an odd sequence of
circumstances that set the stage for the realization of his dream
after the death of her lover at sea in the Second World War.

255

In the darkened theater during 1972 I began wondering about the lady on the screen. There was a quality in her that transcended the story. I pondered what she was like in real life outside of Hollywood. On screen she was absolutely captivating. But what was she like off screen? Was she a self-focused attention seeking prima donna like so many in Hollywood? Or was she a genuine person who just happened to be a star? I considered how fascinating it would be to actually meet her. But what would I say if I encountered her? It occurred to me that I would probably be so enraptured I would inevitably find that I had nothing to say; or even offer that might interest her. I quickly decided it may be best that our paths never cross.

At that time of life and aged twenty five I was about as likely to meet her, Jennifer O'Neill the star of the movie, or a celebrity like her as winning the lottery. I was functioning as a placement officer at Oakland University in Rochester, Michigan. Not the most exciting career path for a restless young man from Pittsburgh. Far removed from ever meeting any celebrity let alone a movie star. As I sat in the theater I considered that it would be more than a little interesting to have an opportunity to talk with her about her career. Or anything else.

As the story on screen progressed the absorbing lady seemed to get more under my skin minute by minute. Something about that face. The deep soulful eyes and the vulnerability. By the end of the film while leaving the theater I was a little bothered to think that I had become intrigued by the simple presence of a Hollywood actress in a movie. The old Frank Sinatra version of 'I've Got You Under My Skin' played in my mind thinking about her. But I remembered she was only a fictional character who in real life was functioning in a world of glitter that was completely foreign to my reality. I resolved to put that face out of mind immediately. It only took a month or two.

II.

Driving north on Monaco Avenue in Denver in the spring of 2003 the annoying sound of my cell phone was ringing somewhere in the car. I fumbled and found it buried in the pocket of my jacket. Pulling it out I hurried to answer before it moved to voicemail.

"Hello?" I hurriedly offered after hitting the talk button.

"Hello. Is this Jim?" the husky and intriguing feminine voice responded.

"Yes. This is Jim."

"Hi Jim. This is Jennifer O'Neill."

In an attempt to sound cool and composed I eased the car off the road into a convenient parking lot as I responded, "Hi Jennifer. Thanks for the call. I'm assuming you heard that we're interested in bringing you to Colorado for our 'Light on Life' fundraiser."

"Yes. I'm excited about the possibility. What can you tell me about what you'd like me to do?"

By now I was stopped in the parking lot. As I explained what our Pro Life fund raiser was all about I was envisioning the memory of the young woman staring at the waves from the beach in the movie thirty one years earlier. But I indicated nothing of my excitement in talking with her. Though cordial, I was all business. My goal was to help Colorado Right to Life build more presence and credibility and at the same time raise money by bringing a big name celebrity in for the fund raiser in the fall of that year. And Jennifer O'Neill was one of the biggest if not the biggest name on the Pro Life scene at that time.

I explained what the program would include with her being the keynote speaker. I also talked with her briefly about her ministry. 'Jennifer O'Neill Ministries' primary focus was to promote healing for women who had suffered the trauma of abortion. Our paths were crossing due to a common cause. We were both strong Pro Lifers and by a set of coincidences, we were to become more than a little involved as partners working to save unborn children as well as their mothers from the nightmare of abortion.

Near the end of the discussion, she asked, "Who will coordinate my visit to Colorado?"

"I'll pick you up at the airport and take you to your hotel which is where the event will be held. It's the Denver Sheraton West and you won't leave there until I return you to the airport the following day. Does that sound alright?" I asked.

"Yes. That would be great. I won't have to get a shuttle or rental car?"

"No. I'll be with you through the entire event if you like."

"That sounds good. I'm looking forward to meeting you. Let's talk the week before I come out to discuss any last minute details."

"I'll call you. What number do you want me to use?" I asked.

After she provided me her cell phone number we said 'Goodbye' and hung up. I made a note in my planner with her number on the date to call. I was elated we'd get her to come out for our fundraiser. And I was definitely looking forward to meeting the real life character I had wondered about so many years earlier.

III.

The years between seeing Jennifer on screen in 'Summer of 42' in 1972 and talking with her on my cell phone in 2003 were chaotic years. For both of us. In her case the kaleidoscope of her life as chronicled in her autobiography 'Surviving Myself' as well as an episode about her on the television series 'Biography' was beyond what most fiction authors could imagine.

The twists and turns of her life were so numerous and complex that they almost seem to be a condensed record of unrelated soap operas. During her life in addition to numerous marriages and divorces, a stunning modeling career, becoming a highly respected actress though eventually shunned by Hollywood because of her Christian activities, she gave birth to a son, Reis and a second son Cooper. More than once she amassed money and lost it either because of irresponsible husbands or poor investments. By the time she and I met, she was again without significant financial resources but had created 'Jennifer O'Neil Ministries' in the midst of everything.

Despite all her great successes and dramatic set backs, I learned she was a kind and giving woman. None of the trials washed away a spirit of compassion for friends or even strangers. After her children grew up and left home, in addition to still being cast in many made for television movies and guest starring roles in various weekly series she gave unselfishly to numerous charitable causes. She served as a chairperson for the American Cancer Society, and worked for other organizations such as the March of Dimes, the Retinitis Pigmetosa Foundation and the Arthritis Foundation. Ultimately she became a born again Christian and decided to form her ministry in the mid 1990's. Her national presence and passion for the cause of those injured and lost to abortion is ultimately what brought her to my attention in my efforts to help Colorado Right to Life.

IV.

Friday September 26, 2003 my cell phone rang shortly after lunch. It was the day I was to go to Denver International Airport to meet Jennifer in person for the first time and bring her to the fundraiser.

"Hello?"

"Jim. This is Jen."

"Hi Jennifer. So where are you?"

"I'm in San Diego right now waiting to meet my agent. I'm supposed to catch my flight to Denver in about three hours."

"OK. Anything else we need to discuss before I come to pick you up?"

"Well, I'm having a rough time. I believe I'm suffering from food poisoning. I think I'll need to see a doctor before the event tomorrow night."

Because I normally hope for the best and prepare for the worst, I did have a back up speaker for the event. So, I played the chivalrous role and said, "Jennifer. If you can't make it, we'll understand. I have someone to fill in if necessary."

"Jim, I plan to be there. But I'm really feeling poorly. When you meet me at the airport I'm not going to be looking very good."

Her comment inspired me to inject some humor into the tenuous situation to see if I could lighten things up a little. I responded, "Well let me make something clear, Honey. If you aren't lookin' good when you show up here, I'm afraid you'll be lookin' for a standby ticket to get back home the same day."

My attempt succeeded. She probably was not used to a stranger speaking with her in such a cavalier manner. She laughed. Then she said, "OK. But I warned you."

I asked, "How long have you felt bad and what kind of symptoms are going on?" Again, a direct appeal ignoring the fact that even though she was a celebrity I was going to treat her like a regular person.

"Well, I haven't eaten anything today and I feel pretty weak. But I have a bad stomach ache."

"Have you put anything into your stomach at all today?"

"Just the handful of vitamins I usually take before lunch. I did that around noon but since my agent hasn't shown up yet, I've had nothing to eat."

"Are you sure you're going to be able to make it?"

"Jim, come whatever, I'll be there. Just understand I may not be doing very well."

"OK Jennifer. I'll look for you. I'll be the guy with the black knit shirt, grey crew cut and well trimmed Vandyke. I'll look for you where the passengers come up off the escalator from the subway. Got that?"

"I'll be there" she said as we hung up.

I thought a little on what she had told me about her condition. Though I have no medical training other than dealing with my own health challenges and a lot of reading on health matters and first aid, I had raised three children and that prepares one a little for things such as stomach issues and the like. I made a deduction about her feeling badly and came up with a strategy that I hoped would help her when she arrived.

Because she hadn't eaten anything but a handful of vitamins on an empty stomach, I guessed that she simply was suffering from acute indigestion. The fact that she also told me she was feeling tired seemed to fit. Maybe some good food and a chance to relax would perk her back up. Regardless, I stopped by the drug store and picked up some elixirs including a few concoctions for gastro-intestinal problems. And due to the fact that I had just had major back surgery three weeks earlier I was well supplied with valium. So just to make sure she'd get good nights sleep, I grabbed a few 10 mg valiums from my supply to employ if necessary.

V.

Jennifer's plane was due in after dinner. I came to the airport early to find a convenient parking space inside and close to where we would come down the escalator. Instead of carrying the electronic remote lock, I took the key off and put it in my pocket. I don't like a lot of bulk in my pockets anytime but especially when I wanted to look a little better than normal to meet a movie star. I went up the escalator and found the baggage claim carrousel for her flight which was due in about another 30 minutes.

Because of the back surgery just three weeks earlier, I was very sore and still weak so I decided to sit down and relax on a bench seat in the waiting area. However, trying to get comfortable on a hard bench seat with an eight inch incision in my spine and enough titanium hardware under the wound to build a small bridge was taking its toll on me. I decided to go back down to the car and get some Tylenol. I knew I had plenty of time and figured this would reduce the impatience I was feeling about the wait.

As I reached the silver Cherokee, I found it odd that I had put the windows all the way up. I usually like to leave them cracked a bit to keep fresh air in the vehicle. I decided that once I got the Tylenol, I'd open a few windows. As I inserted the key in the lock and turned it I was shocked to see that nothing happened! Could it be that there was some high tech security system glitch that was locking me out because the electronic remote was in the car? I tried again but to no avail. Not one to panic I just stood there fuming while considering my options.

Option one was to call airport security and see if they could help me get into my car. With that would go looking like an incompetent dope in front of the celebrity. And time was short. Option two was to tell her I'd locked myself out of my own car and we'd have to get a taxi to take her to her hotel and then me home. That seemed even worse. The third option was to break the rear window, clean it up quickly. My overly aggressive manner combined with ego had me ranking this option as the most likely strategy. But wait! Maybe the sunroof on the top of the car was still open. I distinctly remembered opening it on the way to the airport.

Placing my foot on the step by the door and painfully elevating my body with bad back and all, I peered across the top of the Cherokee. As soon as I detected that there was no sun roof on the car I froze. *Am I losing my mind?* I held on staring with disbelief. Then, coming to my senses I looked across at the next row of cars. Incredibly in the next row there sat a silver Cherokee. This one had the windows cracked open. I carefully climbed down and walked around to what I knew was my car. The door opened when I inserted the key. I considered what had almost happened. Visions of smashing out a stranger's window, of airport security, my attempts to explain, what Jennifer would think and worse all flooded my mind in a nanosecond. I stepped back, looked heavenward laughed and said, "Thank you, God" as a couple of teenagers passed by staring at me as though I was strange. Then I laughed. *Man that would have been an awesome screw up!*

Grabbing the Tylenol and locking up, but bringing the electronic remote entry just to be extra safe, I walked away shaking my head. *Well, this whole affair is off to a great start. My speaker may not be well enough to speak; I almost broke into a stranger's car; my back is broken and hurting like Hell. What's next?* Proceeding up the escalator I was determined to get things in hand from this point on.

After chewing up and swallowing three Tylenol without water as I didn't have it in me to walk another 50 yards to a fountain I took my seat back on the bench. There I collected myself and thought carefully about what to do to make the lady comfortable as soon as she arrived. I recollected that I read something in her autobiography, 'Surviving Myself' that might come in handy. She had written that whenever she is feeling stressed or anxious a hug was one of the best remedies for her. I also recalled that my treating her with humor and quite naturally on the telephone worked. *OK. Let's see what we're dealing with when she comes up off the escalator and then just do what comes naturally.*

The older couple sitting next to me was friendly and I figured if I paid attention to them in the meantime that would help fill the few minutes left before the lady arrived. As we chatted I actually lost track of the time and when I finally looked at the clock, I realized she might have come up already. I decided to check her baggage kiosk and then stand near the escalator to make sure I couldn't miss her. After seeing there was no one from her flight at the baggage claim I headed for the escalator.

Walking back from the carousel I felt the strange sensation of being watched though I didn't know by whom. I began to scan everyone in the crowd flowing toward and by me. I discovered there was indeed someone walking forward with their eyes upon me. And as soon as I got a clear view I recognized the face. It was the same one I had gazed up at in the darkened theater thirty two years earlier. And it looked amazingly the same! There were slight crow's feet near the eyes and a few grey strands of hair, but her face left no doubt about how this lady had held on to her role with Cover Girl for so long. She was in a word, lovely.

I realized that Jennifer had recognized me and knew immediately who I was before I saw her. As we walked toward one another she was smiling in an almost childlike shy manner. Her head was cocked slightly to one side and the corners of her mouth indicated that it was a genuine and comfortable smile. Though she had told me she wasn't feeling well, you would never guess that as she moved gracefully forward with her palms facing toward me. *Do what comes naturally.* Without speaking I slowed and smiled as I walked up to her. I simply spread my arms and gave her a long hug. Still not speaking I kissed her on her right temple. We stood there for a moment as though we had been too old friends that required no formalities. I spoke up first with, "How are you feeling? Do I have to carry you now?"

She laughed and responded, "Well, maybe. But what do you think these folks will suspect were up to if you do that?"

I ignored her comment and offered, "I'm really glad you're here. And I'm not the only one. The others are very happy you're doing this for us. C'mon, let's get your bag."

As we walked slowly toward the carrousel, I kept my arm around her waist and could feel that she really was tired as she placed some of her weight against me. I asked about the flight and then asked if she had eaten anything on the plane. While we spoke I resolved that I would handle her bag and there was no way she would learn about the condition of my back. When we got to the baggage claim, I kept my arm around her as we waited. I was amazed that this lady, who I had only just met, seemed so comfortable with me. While I have often been characterized as more than a little intense and occasionally with a tough demeanor, for some reason most canine and human strangers seem to take to me pretty quickly. And thankfully it was working with Jennifer.

VI.

When she pointed out her bag sliding down the chute, I almost bobbed my head in disbelief. It was the largest suitcase I had ever seen. *Man, you better 'suck it up' here and make like it is no effort to carry at all. I hope Doc Lankenau put those rods and bolts in my back firmly!* I stepped over and hoisted the damn monstrosity as though it was a mere overnight bag. We strolled off toward the parking lot. By that time, though still subdued by her stomach, she was chatting away about the fact that this was her first visit to Colorado and how the view of the mountains from the plane had made a strong impression upon her.

I was feeling pretty comfortable with Jennifer but doing most of the listening. After pretending it was no problem hauling her oversized trunk into the back of the car, I helped her in on the passenger side. As she got into her seat, I spontaneously leaned in and hugged her again. She went silent. When I got into the car she looked directly at me and made one of the more unforgettable statements I have ever received from a member of the fairer sex. She said, "You know Jim, this will sound odd. But honestly I feel like I have known you my whole life. I've never felt so comfortable with a person so quickly." I had no come back to that remark. But I smiled and took hold and squeezed her hand briefly before I fired up the Cherokee.

As we drove out of the parking lot she reclined in her seat a little and became quiet. I then put a CD of movie theme music from the forties and fifties into the sound system and turned it on low for her. Soon she was humming along. After a few minutes of quiet time, I suggested a bland snack might be good for her. I offered her some crackers and a kiwi Snapple. She only nibbled at the crackers put she drank all of the Snapple. Then she began to speak a little about her last couple of days. Obviously they had been hectic. I deduced she must have been pretty stressed by it all.

"Jennifer, we should be at the hotel in about a half hour. I'm assuming you'd like to go directly there and get unpacked and settled."

"I would. But I have one request, Jim."

"Yes?"

"I like my friends and family to call me Jen."

"Sure Jen. And I like my friends and family to call me Sir."

Again she laughed. Then she responded, "Well, I may not use that name, but I could easily think of a few others depending upon my mood."

"I guess I won't even enquire about that."

We bantered back and forth a little in a playful manner. I was guessing that the soft music, reclined seat and the little bit of food in her were beginning to help. I was careful not to place my guest under any more stress than she had endured that day. So I didn't ask her many questions and let her talk or remain quiet. She was actually comfortable enough that she closed her eyes a few times when not talking.

Soon we pulled into the Denver Sheraton West parking ramp. I believe she had dozed off for a few minutes which I took as a good sign. It meant she was comfortable and able to relax with me. I wanted very much for her to get a good night's sleep and be rejuvenated for the next day. Her role in the banquet was critical to the level of support we would gain from the first time fundraiser.

After checking her in at the front desk, the three of us, her, me and that oversized trunk she called a suitcase ascended in the elevator to the top floor suites. Earlier that week I had carefully chosen her the best accommodations the hotel had to offer. It was a beautifully appointed Oriental two room suite with a hot tub that overlooked the Denver skyline in the distance. I helped her get settled in and then we sat for a few minutes while she had some Celestial Seasons tea to settle her before I left. We talked about our children and she asked if I'd bring pictures of mine the following day. I agreed. But as we talked I could see I'd better not stay much longer as she was obviously low on energy. I offered her valium to help her sleep and she opened her hand. As soon as I placed a couple of the little orange pills in her hand, she washed them down with tea.

She was so gracious, I believe I could have stayed longer and talked until sleep overtook her. However, I told her I'd better get moving and let her get off to bed or whatever she wanted. Then we agreed to meet for brunch the following morning around 10:00 AM. I told her not to get up as I left, but she did. We walked to the door and she reached out and gave me a long hug with no words. I planted a kiss on her cheek and said 'Goodnight'. As I walked down the hallway toward the elevator I was confident that she never had food poisoning to begin with. This was just a lady who burned the candle at both ends too often and the last couple of days leading up to our event was typical. At that point I had no idea how chaotic her life was not just for the past week, but always. I would learn about that in time.

VII.

The little silver and black Nokia cell phone rang around 9:00 AM the following morning. I had it in my pocket as I was expecting a call.

"Hello?"

"Hello, Sir Jim. Good morning."

"Hi there. Did you get any sleep last night?"

"Yep, right after you left I went in to lie on the bed for a moment before I got undressed. I didn't get undressed. I fell deeply asleep and didn't wake until a few minutes ago. Do you still want to come over?"

"I do. Would you like me to bring anything?"

"No. I'll sit in the hot tub for a while and then be ready for you around 10:30 if that will work. I'm feeling hungry. But I don't think I want to go out. Maybe we can order something in the room. Is that OK?"

"Lady, whatever you want will be fine. I'll see you in awhile", I said as we hung up.

The fact that she had an appetite was an encouraging sign. Before my cell phone rang I had talked to the event coordinator for the evening's program. I had not told any of the Colorado Right to Life people our keynote speaker was not feeling well. All they knew was that she was here and everything was proceeding as planned. I arranged some materials for the evening and brushed up on my opening remarks for the program. Then I left to see my new friend.

Upon arriving at the hotel I called up to her room and told her I was on my way up. She said she was starving now and was glad I was there.

When I knocked upon her door it took a few minutes for her to open it. I was surprised to see the glamorous Jennifer O'Neill with no make up and in a cotton robe and fuzzy slippers that looked like bunnies! Her hair was brushed but hung loosely around her face. With no eye make up, lipstick or anything but what God gave her she still looked damn good. However, I was struck, and in fact impressed by the fact that she was so unpretentious and would let me see her looking so natural.

"Good morning Lady. So, I assume you're not planning to go out for awhile. Or are you?"

"I think I want to stay in all day until this evening. I like this suite and see no reason to go out. Are you hungry?"

She's hungry. Thank you, Lord!

We looked over the in room menu and made our choices. She called down the order and we went into the living room. Apparently she had prepared for me. There on the coffee table was a small pile of pictures of her children and grand children.

"C'mon over here. I want to show you something", she announced.

Sitting on the couch next to me with her fuzzy bunny slippers now up on the table she immediately began to take me through the photos one by one explaining who I was looking at and a little bit of color or a story on each.

So, the movie star is an ordinary proud mama below the exterior after all. And she's comfortable without makeup.

Then it was my turn. Since she had requested the night before that I bring pictures, I had them. She seemed to take quite a bit of interest in each and asked questions. I was again impressed by the natural and even domestic side to this woman. We sat comfortably next to each other and eventually she turned and pulled her feet up under her to face me. Soon the discussion turned to the evening program and I prepped her on what would happen and when. I gave her a printed agenda just as a knock came on the door.

"Oh boy! Food!" she said as she got up and made a beeline for the door. I was delighted to see her show enthusiasm for eating and walked behind her to see if I could lend a hand. Shortly we were set up at a small dining table at the far end of the living room. She did not eat quickly. But she ate everything. As she did so, her cheeks grew rosy. Obviously this lady just needed some decent food to get back to normal. It was touching to see her eating her chicken soup and roll like a little girl home from school for lunch break.

"So, Sir Jim. Tell me about your work."

I was surprised that she would take an interest in what I did for a living. I was delighted. But I knew better than to get too carried away about me and gave her just enough to allow me time to turn the tables comfortably.

"Jen, how did you ever get started as an actress?" I queried. Though I had read her autobiography I still wanted to hear her in person version. Suddenly I recalled that 31 years earlier leaving the theater after seeing her the first time I had hoped for an opportunity to interview her about her career. And here it was actually happening.

Hmmm. Wonder what would have ultimately happened if I had wished for some other type of interaction with her? Good thing I didn't. Not sure I ever could have kept pace with this one.

She was quite open with her account. And she was genuinely humorous. Her ability to make fun of herself and the adventures she had experienced was more than a little entertaining. I couldn't resist asking how she was cast in her most famous roles and what John Wayne was like as well as many of the other better known highlights. She seemed happy to oblige. I decided it was best that she do most of the talking. Then unexpectedly she stopped and stared at me and finally asked, "Jim, why did you choose me to come to Colorado?"

"You know Jen; you're just about the biggest name in Pro Life these days. I know you are a primary spokesperson for National Right to Life and I wanted someone with your reputation and drawing power to give this event the level of credibility it needs. But there was another reason I invited you. I've read your story and I know about the work of your ministry. Your real life experience with this issue is just what I wanted to connect with the people who I expect will be there."

"So, how and why did you become involved in Pro life?"

"Like you, I had direct experience with it. In fact a child of mine was lost to abortion. My attempts to change the mind of the mother when I realized what a mistake it would be failed. It's the darkest moment of my life. Most simply I believe that if I can do some things that save lives of unborn, my child will not have died in vain."

We both sat quietly looking at one another for a few moments. I looked deeply into those eyes. They stared directly back at me. There were no words. Finally she reached over and took my hand and said, "Let's say a prayer."

She said a prayer of thanks and then sat quietly for a few minutes looking at the pictures of our kids. Soon we began to talk again. We covered Pro Life issues, politics, and stories from our childhoods and a few other related subjects. The time flew by and when I finally looked at the clock it was after 1:30 PM.

"Jen, I believe I need to go now to help the others get ready for tonight. Is there anything else you need in the meantime?"

"No. I have a pretty good idea of what will happen and what I need to do. I just want to spend a few hours relaxing. What time will you come to get me?"

"Well, we need to go to the early reception for you at 5:45. That's what time I'll be back. Sound OK?"

"I'll look for you then. And Jim thanks again for inviting me out to Colorado and being so nice to me. I'm already glad I came."

Again she walked me to the door and gave me a good hug.

VIII.

Shortly before 6:00 I got off the elevator on the top floor and strolled toward her room. On the way a young couple, arm in arm and looking like they were honeymooners waltzed passed me laughing as they looked at me. I felt a little self-conscious and wondered if maybe something about my dress was not "complete". I checked everything on me. Nope, all was in place. I was ready to pick up my friend for the evening.

When she opened the door she was glowing. *Man, this is one good looking woman!* Even at the time when the vast majority of women her age have given into accepting a matronly presence, this lady was down right eye catching attractive. However, she never acted that way. An aura of humility and pleasant grace exuded from her. I told her I would stay close to her until the dinner began. We walked down to the reception. On the way she stated that she wanted to do a good job with her presentation. She hoped to promote a strong response to my appeal for donations from the audience which would follow directly after she was done speaking. Regardless of all of the high profile Hollywood events, movies, television appearances and other activities this celebrity had participated in, she appeared to be as keyed up for this event as anything.

After we met and spoke with a handful of board members, supporters and some politicians at her reception, we entered the hall for the welcoming address and dinner. Walking into the large brightly lit room it was immediately obvious that the turnout at the event was great for a first attempt. Colorado Right to life had managed to fill the banquet room at the Sheraton with over 400 people.

The program officially began with the lights going down and a spotlight on center stage. I walked out into the light and began.

"Ladies and gentleman, I'm Jim Anderson and on behalf of the Board of Colorado Right to Life, welcome to our first annual 'Light on Life' program. Tonight we are here for one purpose. It is to serve to protect those who have no voice and would be forgotten if it were not for those like you who support and honor the gift of human life."

The audience erupted in a loud and long round of applause. After the applause died down I provided a brief overview of the evening and made reference to the program agendas on their tables. We had a local celebrity by the name of Dan Caplis as the MC for the program and I introduced him and turned it over. Dan had outstanding stage presence. I was more than happy I had invited him to MC the program.

After about 30 minutes for dinner, Dan got back up to introduce Jennifer. Even before she spoke as she walked up to the podium she got a thunderous round of applause. Jennifer began by talking about how she came to be involved in the Pro Life cause due to the experience with the abortion she had as a young woman. She recounted the circumstances, confusion, deception and betrayal of the event. Though the circumstances made a case for the procedure in the first eight weeks of her pregnancy, she made it clear she believed there was no good excuse for allowing it. Jennifer's address was powerful and passionate.

At one point, with emotion causing quavering in her voice she stated, "You have to be numbed to go through with this unthinkable act. And there are so many things that force that numbness upon you. Lies such as the life in you is a mass of tissue with no personhood or awareness of anything; that you will not think about the "procedure" after it is over; that the "tissue" within you is only a growth of your own body that will not become anyone until birth; and that you will face lifelong humiliation and regret if you don't end this "mistake" now".

She went on to explain that human life is human life at any stage and even at the earliest, the full set of genes and make up of the person is in place. She referred to the fact that the tiny heart is beating at six weeks. The feet formed at eight. And the tiny person is moving on their own within the amniotic fluid by ten weeks. But most powerfully she talked about God's plan for protecting the little living being within the safest place He designed for it; the mothers womb. She emphasized that what is good for the child is ultimately what is good for the mother as she was designed to forge life within her; nurture it to birth and beyond.

She talked about the regret and guilt that plague most women for the rest of their lives after making the heinous decision of turning a cold heart toward the beautiful creation within them. While many do not get in touch with these feelings right away, she referred to the conclusive research that confirms eventual anguish; though it is not reported by the media or disclosed by Planned Parenthood. Building upon the case against abortion as an alternative, no matter how much of a crisis the woman faces, she made a compelling argument for the forgiveness and healing available through Christ. Finally she offered an emotional and moving call to action describing what the guests can do to participate in overcoming the consequences of abortion in America. She was magnificent. When she finished, the audience stood and applauded for what seemed at least five minutes.

She had set the stage well for my appeal. As I stepped up to the microphone in the spotlight I could see there was a significant portion of the audience still overwhelmed with emotion from her memorable address.

"Guests, members of Colorado Right to Life, and all that have just heard the message of truth and hope that Jennifer has provided, I'll now ask something of you. We may not win this battle to protect the unborn in the courts or the legislative halls. We face an unfriendly media that is not sympathetic to the cause of the unborn. But we can win it by spreading the light of truth in every corner of our culture. We'll do that though education and directing the truth about the horror of abortion to women in crises who are considering making this mistake."

I based my case upon the importance of action for the unborn as well as the mothers who would face a similar nightmare as Jennifer with guilt and regret that would haunt them. I built upon the emotional context of the issue and told them how their support would lend itself directly to positive results. I did not talk long. However, as we would learn later, the contributions from the appeal both at the dinner and then following soon after the banquet far exceeded what we hoped for.

After I finished with my appeal, I turned the podium back

over to Dan Caplis. I walked down off the stage and left the banquet room briefly to go out into the hall for a breath of fresh air and some water. While outside the banquet room I unexpectedly encountered Jennifer in a small hallway by the drinking fountain. As I walked over to her, she demonstrated the same shy childlike demeanor as when I first met her in the airport the day before.

"Did I do OK?" she asked.

Taking both of her shoulders gently in my hands I looked her directly in the eyes and responded, "You couldn't have done better. You were perfect!"

We stood looking into each others eyes. There are few moments in my life in which I felt such a deep and powerful connection with another human being. There was no need for words at that point. We were in that moment two people who were tied deeply by something that was as meaningful and important as anything could be. It was the cause of honoring, protecting and fighting for the precious gift of life bestowed upon us and others by our creator. We were a man and a woman who had a connection beyond most experiences between men and women. What I felt in that moment was as meaningful and fulfilling as anything I ever knew.

We hugged for a long moment gently swaying side to side almost as if dancing but without our feet moving. Then she said. "Thank you for bringing me here."

It was obvious that this was a woman who was deeply compassionate. She also needed affirmation. Though she had achieved great fame during a period earlier in her life as well as still carrying the status of a celebrity, she craved validation. I thought about how challenging life must be for someone who requires so much continuous affirmation of self worth. While her intellect was unusually high and her physical presence and personality far surpassed most, because of her kind heart and need for approval, it was not difficult to see how she could be taken advantage of. My awareness of this fact at that moment made it clear to me why she had been used at various periods in her life. I felt a strong protective caring urge for her in that moment. Not caring about how she felt toward me. But caring about her. I felt a desire to validate and encourage her. I resolved I would always do my best to be kind and a good friend toward her. I did not then anticipate how difficult that would eventually become.

We returned to the hall holding hands and I escorted her back to her table and then returned to the back of the hall where I could watch the rest of the evenings' program. After the program ended Jennifer was seated outside at a table where we had arranged for a signing of her latest book 'From Fallen to Forgiven' as well as the earlier autobiography 'Surviving Myself'. A number of the guests stayed to meet her and have her sign books we had available for them. Her gracious and patient manner with everyone was heart warming. Later, a number of people who met and spoke with her related to me how impressed they were by her gracious and kind manner.

By around 10:00 most of the guests had left and Jennifer was obviously quite tired. She and I went back up to her suite and talked for a little bit about the evening and then what she had coming up in the next few weeks. We agreed on what time I'd be back to drive her to the airport the following morning. After reaffirming what a good job she did that evening, I gave her a good long hug and then left.

IX.

The following morning she was already downstairs with the crate masquerading as a suitcase as I entered the lobby. Once more I hoisted the monster and put it in the car wondering, *Why does this thing have to be so huge? What does she have in here?*

On the way to the airport she was bubbling with enthusiasm. I'm not sure if it was because the venue was outstanding as well as the people she met, or whether she just felt so much better after another good meal and another night of sleep. Regardless, she talked about she and I doing other things together in the future. I told her I would look for opportunities and was pleased she wanted to do something else if it came up.

When we got to the airport I dropped her off at curbside and went to park the car. I met her back at the ticket counter and then we went to have some OJ and a roll which we shared. She seemed to like me. Of course, having been a Hollywood actress she was quite skilled at making people feel just about anything she pleased. However, her energy and interest appeared genuine. It was a strong warm friendship type of feeling.

I savored the last few moments with Jennifer O'Neill. She was funny and serious at the same time. As I sat listening to her talk over food and drink we passed back and forth, I remembered a particular scene of her in 'Rio Lobo' with John Wayne in which she played the female lead. In the scene she was sitting at a table like the one we were using but it was in an old western saloon. Across from her was a villainous character who was threatening her. Suddenly from under the table she pulled a concealed pistol and employed it in a dramatic and memorable fashion on a strategic target on the poor guy.

"Jen, you don't happen to have any concealed weapons under the table do you?" I asked.

"What?" she responded as she tuned her head and looked at me like a man from Mars.

"Oh, just remembering a scene from 'Rio Lobo'", I responded.

"Oh yeah. I think I know the one you mean. No, you're safe. At least for now."

And then without missing a beat due to the interruption she resumed where she had left off with her previous line of conversation. We talked and laughed some until it was time for her to take the escalator down to security. Finally, we walked over near the escalator to say our final goodbye.

Sending her off was almost as memorable as the first time I

met her. We hugged and she held onto my hand for a moment. Then in true Hollywood fashion, she looked up at me and said, "Jim this was really was the best trip I've made in a long time. And much of that had to do with you. I believe we're going to be good friends."

"I hope so", I said.

Again with a flourish of drama straight out of an old Bogart - Bergman movie she announced, "I love you", gave me a kiss and turned to take the escalator. It was a good friend's kind of "I love you" but made me feel that maybe she really enjoyed my company. While a little skeptical, I still told myself that she was sincere. In time she would prove that she was.

X.

Sure enough, about two weeks after Jennifer's departure, my cell phone rang as I was heading into a business meeting I was conducting at a Denver based client company. I had about five minutes until the meeting would begin so I answered.

"Hello?"

"Sir Jim. This is Jen. What are you doing? Did I get you at an inconvenient time?"

"Hi! Good to hear from you. I am about to go into a meeting but I have a couple of minutes. What's going on?" I said.

"Well, I wanted to see how the contributions came out from our event a couple of weeks ago."

"We exceeded our target by over 50%. No small thanks to you."

"That's great! I'm so happy to hear it went well. As we discussed, it's not easy raising money for this cause. My ministry continues to struggle from year to year."

We talked briefly about what she was trying to accomplish with 'Jennifer O'Neill Ministries'. I could see she might be looking for advice on contacts that could possibly help so I offered to call her back later and brainstorm ideas with her. She welcomed that offer and I told her I could later that afternoon.

When I did call her back that day we talked some about potential contacts and fund raising strategies for about ten minutes. Then the conversation turned toward her children and some of the challenges of parenting. Before I knew it, about a half hour had elapsed. She thanked me for talking and we agreed to stay in touch.

After another couple of weeks Jennifer called again. This time it seemed she just wanted to talk. The conversation covered a number of unrelated subjects including her activities with National Right to Life, the horse property she had for sale, some of the trips she had coming up and she asked how things were going with my family. It was a pleasant conversation with no specific agenda. It seemed she just wanted to talk. I welcomed it as I liked her and found her to be a great person to talk with about family and faith. She demonstrated wisdom on matters of faith that were highly enlightening. The telephone conversations with her became regular over the next few months with her initiating calls every two to three weeks. Occasionally I would call her.

As we moved into 2004 we had become good telephone friends. In fact she had a trip to Colorado coming up in the spring of that year to speak at an event in Highlands Ranch and I agreed to take her to a restaurant near the location. When she did visit, we had a great time. Over a few glasses of wine and sharing a salmon dish we discussed the Right to Life movement, our families and miscellaneous other subjects from health and fitness to travel. It was a thoroughly pleasant time. We shared with each other about our similar individual idiosyncrasies as we both lived with intensity and drama. Among other similarities we discovered that many of the trials we faced in our lives were in large part because we both led with our hearts too often on matters that demanded more caution than we chose to use.

Of course we also discussed developments in respect to the Pro Life cause. We were both largely in agreement on the abortion issue in promoting spiritual healing of women who had abortions as well as the need for more education aimed at women before they committed the atrocious act. We discussed the fact that if women who were considering abortions knew about the likely long term emotional and psychological effects as well as had options to either keep their child or place them in adoption, abortion would decrease significantly. Where we differed had to do with the role of Pro Life organizations attempting to promote changes in law as well as sponsoring politicians. She believed that strategy was worthwhile. I disagreed. Eventually that difference would divide us.

After the meal I drove Jennifer back to her hotel and we talked for a little while before I left. We spoke about continuing to stay close and agreed I'd visit with her in Nashville later that year. In part because we both had other relationship commitments in our lives at that time, there was never a thought about pursuing anything along a romantic angle. I was good with that as I ascertained she was not a person that ever would have made a good long term partner for me. Or I for her. We were both simply too independent and strong willed. We did discuss the possibility and agreed that had we met much earlier in our lives there would have been a high likelihood we could have become involved. Secretly I was glad that had not happened as I was sure it would have never have worked for long.

XI.

As Jennifer and I stayed in regular communication having to do with our Pro Life activities through 2004, Steve Curtis, a board member on Colorado Right to Life and I had begun to discuss the ineffectiveness of the Pro Life movement. Abortion on demand had been legalized in Colorado in 1967 making Colorado the first state to formally approve the dreadful act. Then the infamous 'Roe vs. Wade' case in the Supreme Court made it national law in 1973. And during all of that the strategy of most of the Pro Life organizations, as modeled by National Right to Life, the umbrella organization over all the state affiliates, had failed miserably.

In essence, National Right to Life and their state affiliates had tried to sponsor and promote changes in laws regarding abortion. They collected hundreds of millions of dollars between 1973 and 2004 from well meaning supporters nationally. They used the money to conduct lobbying campaigns, sponsor various bills, support politicians who claimed to be Pro Life, and attempted to gain fair coverage in the media as well as other unsuccessful activities. However, over all that time the incidence of abortion had simply expanded exponentially in Colorado and nationwide. National Right to Life and their affiliates had mostly become successful only at building large bureaucratic self maintaining organizations and little else.

Steve was a former Chairman of the Colorado Republican Party who had prior to his Pro Life activities hoped to rally the party to better represent the principles of conservatism including reinstating the death penalty for murder and revoking abortion on demand in Colorado. In fact Steve had two friends murdered by Denver gang members who had been repeat offenders. Those same two murderers had also gunned Steve down but he miraculously survived two bullets to the head. The trial over the incident actually became the biggest court case in Colorado history. His story was so significant a good friend and talented author by the name of Lee Martin authored a book on the murders and trial titled 'Ten Minutes till Midnight'.

But after a short stint as the Republican Chairman, Steve could see that the values of true conservatism were absent in the Colorado Republican Party so he left the Chairmanship. It was then that he became involved with Colorado Right to Life hoping that he could channel his effort and talents into saving lives of unborn children. Though Steve was unusually intelligent and knowledgeable about politics as well as crafting proposed bills in Colorado, his efforts along with the rest of Colorado Right to Life came to practically nothing.

However, on his own Steve did write and produce a powerful television commercial titled 'Roe, Roe, Roe' in 2004. The commercial was targeted toward making woman in crises pregnancy as well as the public at large aware of the effects of abortion on demand upon mothers as well as the culture. In fact the video won "Best New Commercial of the Year" in it's category from the National Religious Broadcasters.

Because I was convinced that chasing politicians and attempting to get balanced coverage on the issue in the media was a waste of time and money I began to try to convince Steve there were better uses of his talents. As he and I built our friendship I suggested to him that going directly to the public with the truth rather than attempting to gain support from politicians may be a much better strategy for reducing the incidence of abortion. My thought was that putting the truth in powerful messages aimed at women in crises pregnancies may cause them to think more carefully about their alternatives. I suggested that since his commercial was so successful in raising awareness it might be a better investment of our time to produce another commercial and pay to have it aired.

In fact, later that year, Steve came to me with a proposal to launch our own pro life foundation that would produce and air television commercials aimed at education of women and the public upon the consequences of abortion. At first I resisted joining him in this endeavor. I was concerned about the amount of time, effort, and cost it would undoubtedly require. However, Steve was undaunted and persisted in persuading me to join with him in the venture. He finally wore me down and I consented. We formed The Foundation for Life in Media in July of 2004. Steve resigned from Colorado Right to Life at the same time. I left CRTL shortly after. While we were ambitious about the potential success of the foundation, we had no idea the enormous success that would soon be yielded from our efforts.

Shortly after forming the foundation Steve learned how close my friendship with Jennifer had become. He got an idea to use her in a commercial. This one would be targeted specifically at woman who either were considering abortion or were suffering the after effects of abortion. He asked me to see if she would have interest in working with us on the project. If we could get a big name like her to do something with us, it would not only add a lot of credibility to our foundation, we believed it would open important doors in a number of respects. When I called her to promote the project and discuss the costs for her time and efforts, I was pleasantly surprised. She agreed immediately. She would do it for nothing but we insisted on paying her. Once again I was impressed by the gracious and magnanimous nature of the lady.

'Jennifer's Story' was produced by Steve through our foundation early in 2005. In the one minute production, Jennifer spoke in front of a black background about her experience and the regret she carried from her abortion. Her soulful and powerful message to women considering abortion or suffering the aftermath encouraged life saving options as well as healing. The outstanding commercial was recognized that year as the best in its class by the National Religious Broadcasters. This made Steve a two year in a row winner for his efforts. Jennifer was elated. She then agreed to be the keynote speaker for our first annual banquet for the foundation in September of 2005. In essence, with her commercial, coming to be our keynote speaker and subsequent efforts she breathed life into our new foundation.

XII.

When I went to the airport to pick up my Pro Life lady friend in September of 2005 for her engagement at our foundation's first annual dinner she was wearing the classic garb of a celebrity not wanting to be noticed. Wrap around sun glasses and clothes that would not draw attention. Truth was she probably drew more attention in that get up as she looked great and like a movie star who was attempting to go incognito. But it didn't matter. At that stage of the game most of the persons that would take note of her were simply too young to recognize who she was and what she was famous for.

As I walked over to her I opened with, "Hey. I never would have recognized you behind those wrap around glasses if I wasn't looking for you. Great disguise."

She ignored my snide remark and planted a big kiss on my cheek and gave me a long hug.

She finally spoke by stating, "You know what?"

"What?"

"Are you hungry?" she asked.

I figured that was her nonchalant way of making it clear we'd be heading somewhere quickly to get something into her.

"Oh man, I'm hungry! Can we go somewhere soon and get something to eat?" I retorted.

"OK. You talked me into it", was her response.

After collecting the same enormous hulk of a suitcase she had brought the first time she visited Colorado we headed out to the car. *What the hell does she have in this thing?* Driving on our way to Littleton I put on some Frank Sinatra which she obviously liked as she began to warm up her pipes. I had not known she had recorded some albums along the way of her career but should have suspected it out of the multi-talented entertainer.

"Would you like to hear my all time favorite?" I asked.

"Sure. Will you sing along with it?" she challenged.

"Listen Darlin. I do feel like I know you pretty well and we're buddies and all, but I'm not sure I'm ready to go that far with you."

But when Frank came on and belted out 'Night and Day'

she and I got into it. We seemed to do fine as a duet. In fact that was so much fun, I put on 'Old Blue Eyes' again with 'I've Got You Under My Skin'. It suddenly occurred to me that many years earlier I had felt for a few days that the lady actually did get under my skin and here we were singing the words together many years later. *Ironic how life seems to connect in such unexpected ways if we just keep going.* The ride to the restaurant in Littleton went quickly.

We shared an excellent cut of prime rib and a carafe of cabernet. I counted her having two glasses against my one. I wouldn't describe her as inebriated from the wine but she definitely became more animated. She was more humorous and entertaining than I had ever seen. To complete the scene she even kept those ridiculous glasses on in the restaurant.

"So. Did you have laser surgery recently?" I asked

"You're referring to my glasses. You got a problem with them?"

"No. I don't have a problem with anything. You got a problem?" I responded.

"Nothing I can't handle. And that includes you, Sir Jim. So, maybe you better watch yourself" she said feigning reaching under the table as she had done in 'Rio Lobo'.

"Yeah? Well' I'd rather watch you. You're interesting and not too bad too look at either."

"Flattery will get you everywhere. Keep it up sir."

We bantered on some more in a harmless manner. I knew I could get away with it as nothing out of place was going to occur between me and my keynote speaker for the next night's program. Besides, Steve had primed me to offer her to be a board member for our foundation and I just wanted her to have a good time with a guy she would always see as a buddy.

During the meal we did make time to discuss the banquet the following evening and what we were hoping she would address. As we talked I could see that she was very much behind

National Right to Life. She played a major role in their strategy for visibility and promotion. While I knew they were actually counter productive to progress in the cause, because they were channeling millions into do nothing efforts, I kept quiet at that point. She did have an excellent ministry for women who were suffering from the long term emotional affects of abortion and that was very constructive. If she wanted to waste time and effort supporting NRTL, that was her business. Besides she was helping us and I was not about to raise any issues with her. I was very aware by this point that the 'Jennifer's Story' commercial was a decided turning point to build the presence and credibility of our foundation.

The following evening, as expected she did an outstanding job for us. As it turned out, even though it was our first annual banquet, we had over 200 guests so it was a good crowd. We surpassed the hoped for level of contributions. After the event I took her back to her place as we'd be heading to the airport early the following morning. We talked a little about her ministry before I left. I tried to encourage her about her ministry which by that time was in serious financial difficulty.

The next morning on the way to the airport I was happy when she accepted my offer to become a board member of our foundation. Her name would add to our credibility. We talked about doing more things together. Also, I agreed to drive over to Nashville to her home the next time I would be in Atlanta. We shared some breakfast at the airport waiting for her time to depart and just enjoyed talking about whatever came to mind.

XIII.

Between 2005 and 2007 we stayed close. I visited her in Nashville as well as spent more time with her when she came back to Colorado in 2006 for an engagement with Cherry Hills Community Church in Littleton. Again we shared a meal and much laughter. However, I could see that things were getting very difficult for Jennifer O'Neill Ministries due to lack of funding. In fact during 2006 and 2007 things took dramatic turns with both of our ministries.

Things got tougher for her. But due to Steve's enormous talent for producing videos as well as his astute grasp of how to leverage the Internet, the influence of our foundation grew by leaps and bounds. And the "Jennifer's Story' commercial was helping promote great response to our foundation. Also, one of the smartest things Steve did was link us with CareNet, a national network of counseling clinics for women in crises pregnancies. CareNet provided women life saving options to allow their unborn to escape abortion. They were very impressed by our online offering of 'Jennifer's Story' and that was significant in cementing our tie with them. Jennifer's involvement was definitely pivotal in our success.

During 2006 and 2007 thousands of women who had been considering abortion reconsidered and decided to allow their child to live as a direct result of seeing our 'Jennifer's Story' commercial and then being linked by our website to CareNet. Some months we had as many as 60,000 hits per month which translated to as many as 300 "saves" per month. Our click through rate to CareNet documented that. The knowledge of this fact made my involvement in forming and sustaining the foundation with Steve unquestionably the most worthy thing I ever did outside parenthood. If I had had nothing else of value in life, this would have made it worth living.

Additionally thanks to a large contribution from an anonymous donor with roots in Pittsburgh we did a special billboard campaign in the greater Pittsburgh area. Our campaign there was aimed at women considering abortion to go online to see the 'Jennifer's Story' commercial. The click through rate to our website from Pittsburgh was huge during that campaign and we know hundreds of babies and mothers in Western Pennsylvania were saved from the specter of abortion as a result.

Another milestone occurred early in 2007 when I was invited by CBN to visit their headquarters in Virginia Beach on January 22 of 2007 for an interview. That date was the 34th anniversary of the passage of Roe vs. Wade. CBN gave me a four minute spot on their 6:00 PM evening report as well as did a special 15 minute feature on the work of our foundation with me. We know that millions around the globe saw the interviews and the traffic to our website increased even more. Those appearances were one of the high points of my involvement in the entire effort. I traced them and other successes directly to bringing Jennifer to Colorado years before and working with her to boost the credibility and presence of our foundation. I'm convinced that without her involvement, we never would have achieved so much. Because of her, literally thousands were saved. Both children and mothers.

But the fortunes of Jennifer O'Neill Ministries headed in the opposite direction during 2006 and 2007. The lack of funding and support undermined her attempts to offer much support and service to her constituents. Additionally, she took a major risk that did not pay off. She wrote and directed ten talk show episodes similar to a Dr. Phil or Oprah format. But the major networks displayed little to no interest in picking it up. And the Christian broadcast stations didn't have the level of audience required to make a go of it with her. In fact I was one of the guests during one of those episodes.

Jennifer was back into a financial crises; yet again. It occurred because of her well meaning efforts to do something good for others combined with almost blind faith that there would be good results if she produced a quality program. Again she followed her heart above all else. I saw some of the episodes she produced. They were outstanding. But because they were Christian faith focused the major networks wouldn't touch them. So, unfortunately the risks she took on the program and the costs she incurred hindered her ministry.

By 2008 Jennifer had refocused much of her efforts and attention toward National Right to Life. And at the same time, Steve Curtis along with Pastor Bob Enyart, one of our board members and a national activist figure in the Pro Life movement created a new organization called American Right to Life which would compete with National Right to Life. ARTL had nothing to do with our foundation which continued on placing our messages on the Internet.

One of the first activities of ARTL was to demonstrate how the failed strategy of NRTL as well as similar organizations that attempted to gain favor of politicians as well as attention through the major media were actually hurting the cause of the unborn. As NRTL siphoned off hundreds of millions of dollars from well meaning constituents, they channeled much of those funds to politicians that did next to nothing to curb abortion. The major "achievement" of NRTL over a 15 year period was the passage of a ban on a certain partial birth abortion technique that did not save one life. Abortionists simply used other techniques in the place of that procedure.

Steve and our board member Bob Enyart went national with reporting the facts about the failed strategy of National Right to Life. Because our foundation supported the indictment of NRTL, and Jennifer worked with NRTL she perceived us as adversaries. As a direct result she ultimately perceived me as "on the other side". She did not say that in as many words. But when it became clear to her that I was not in concert with her efforts to support NRTL it undermined our relationship. We began to talk less. Additionally, there was nothing I could do to help resurrect her ministry and when she began to call me less, I was simply too stubborn to be the one to attempt to keep things going between us.

Eventually by early 2008 we ceased communicating completely. It was ironic that it was not because of anything specific that happened within our relationship. But similar to the civil war between the North and the South, we just happened to be on opposite sides of a battle line. Our relationship was over. But I continued to feel great appreciation for her role in building our foundation which ultimately led to saving a great many lives and mothers from a lifetime of regret.

Epilogue

In the middle of a sleepless night in late summer of 2008 I was flipping through cable channels for something to do while battling insomnia. Various infomercials and reruns were about all I could find. Then by coincidence I happened to hit on *Lifetime*, a woman's channel that runs movies almost continuously. I recognized a familiar face in the made for television movie. It was a lady playing a role about a mother whose child had been abducted. Receiving no help from the authorities the undaunted heroine had taken matters into her own hands and was hunting down the person who had taken her child.

As I lay in the dark staring at the screen, the same bewitching face I had seen in 'Summer of 42' many years earlier mesmerized me yet again. I reclined and enjoyed watching the actress with whom I shared some of the best moments I've known. Moments from a real life drama more meaningful than anything I ever would have been able to script without her.

The Aviator

I.

As the young man marched his cadet platoon through drills, though not yet sixteen years, he had the bearing of an adult. Iron rod posture, confident stride and assured voice were indications of natural leadership abilities beyond his years. And the auburn hair and sharp angles of his face gave him a distinctive look that set him apart from the teenagers he led.

I and my other squad members stood observing the smooth coordinated maneuvers of his platoon as they drilled in the early afternoon sun. Our squad leader had just put us through drill. We were there at attention while the squad leader took a moment to speak with our platoon leader.

Only two weeks away from home and uncertain about how I'd fare at Greenbrier Military School, I was just beginning to become acclimated to the rigorous military training. As a new cadet, and not accustomed yet to life in a military school, almost everything was foreign to me. The young officer drilling his platoon before us seemed so well suited for his role as a cadet leader. Would I ever be like that? I decided that I wouldn't. But I somehow believed I would prevail even if it meant only not being sent home.

"Anderson! What are you looking at?" yelled Joyner, our squad leader.

Apparently I had become so mesmerized watching the smoothly oiled platoon and its leader drilling that I forgot I was supposed to be standing at attention with eyes forward.

"Anderson, step forward!"

I did so wondering what fate I was about to meet.

Joyner walked over in front of me. I wondered if he was about to make an example of me. I felt embarrassed. But I wouldn't show it as I was by nature a defiant kid who wouldn't be intimidated. Over Joyner's shoulder I watched as the marching platoon moved off into the distance. For a moment I wished I had the rank of its leader so I could make this guy drop and give me twenty push ups.

"What were you looking at, Anderson?"

"I was watching the A company platoon drill, sir."

"Anderson, when you're at attention you will keep your eyes directly forward at all times! Is that clear?"

What's even more clear to me Joyner is that I could mop up the ground with you if we weren't at this stupid military school.

"Yes sir!" I retorted at the skinny teenager yelling at me.

We returned to our drills for another half hour before being released for free time before dinner. Though for me there would be no free time as I was on the junior varsity football team and practice would fill the void between afternoon drill and dinner.

Later that afternoon I trudged to the upper practice field where the junior varsity practiced. I noticed something when I passed varsity players preparing for practice on the lower field. The young red headed lieutenant was on the varsity. That didn't make sense as the varsity was composed almost exclusively of cadets who were post high school. These students had graduated from high school and were receiving academic preparation for college. A large proportion of them were star athletes from high school that were being seasoned another year before entering college. So, why was the lieutenant on that team? Later I would learn that he was a superior athlete that had been "drafted" from the junior varsity, the high school team.

So, I didn't know who he was, but I was impressed. Later I learned that his name was Waldo Beaman Cummings. He went by Beaman. He was a junior class member at GMS but had been there since the seventh grade at age twelve. His record in athletics, the military and academics was superior on all counts. Though I was not the type to defer to anyone, he did earn my attention by his achievements. I made a mental note to stay on the good side of him if I ever encountered him as he was a cadet officer and someone I respected because of how he conducted himself.

II.

The following year as a junior at GMS I unexpectedly had been pulled from the high school team myself along with three others and placed on the varsity football team. Because of a number of injuries to varsity players they needed a few more of us to fill the roster. So I was brought up. Beaman Cummings was now a senior and co-captain of the varsity. Though he was not large, he was a fearless, tenacious and smart athlete. And an outstanding leader for our football team. Unfortunately because injuries had decimated our team, we had a poor season. But it was a great year for me. I actually got to play some and was mentored by our outstanding coach who built my confidence as well as skills on the field.

In addition to coming to know Beaman on the football team, I had been transferred into A Company, which he now commanded. That turned out to be more fortuitous than I could have imagined. Beaman placed me in the role of a squad leader. Watching him and fulfilling my role as the head of a squad taught me much about leadership.

Though not very vocal, he had an aura of presence that filled any room he entered. He was cool and self assured yet in a humble way. When he spoke, which wasn't often, he was worth listening to. He was selfless. And he was patient. Characteristics that set him apart. But I liked him not because of his achievements or even his presence. I did so because of his attitude of service. He always seemed ready to do his best to advance others. As it turned out, in the entire core of cadets in the three years I attended GMS, he was the cadet I had the greatest respect for.

The following year I was a senior and had been chosen as a cadet officer myself. I believe to this day it was because before he graduated and left GMS, Beaman recommended me to the military department heads. The leadership lessons I learned from that role at the age of seventeen would ultimately serve me far beyond GMS. In fact what I learned then became a cornerstone of my professional life many years out.

III.

I lost track of Beaman after he left Greenbrier. I learned later that he had gone on to graduate from Amherst College in Massachusetts in 1967. That is where his father and grandfather had graduated.

The small Ivy League like environment of Amherst was the antithesis of GMS. Liberal, dominated by intellectuals, and a laid back campus life, it was markedly unlike Greenbrier. But Beaman adjusted, and again distinguished himself in the classroom as well as on their football team where he became a standout. In large part he had selected Amherst because of his loyalty to his father combined with the fact that upon leaving Greenbrier he wanted an experience outside the military for awhile. Otherwise it would have been far more likely he would have attended West Point or the Naval Academy.

But while at Amherst Beaman was drawn back to the military. He applied to and was accepted into the Marine Corps Officer Candidate program. This program for college students required attendance in summer basic training at Quantico, Virginia. Satisfactory completion of the program plus a college degree would qualify the graduate for a commission in the Marine Corps. Ironically it was the same OCS program I participated in when I was in college. However I was honorably discharged before being commissioned an officer at graduation because of a physical defect in my lower back.

The majority of the commissioned college graduates from Marine OCS either went back to Quantico or to San Diego to be trained as platoon leaders. However, a small group applied to be accepted as flight officers. Very few were selected to become Marine aviators. Beaman first missed the written test score requirements by one point and became a navigator for the Marine Corps for his initial tour of duty. But he persisted and later met the qualifications to become a pilot.

At the time he was commissioned in the USMC the United States was firmly mired in the quagmire of Viet Nam. After completing his training at Pensacola he was assigned to service in Viet Nam. There he served his country first as a navigator and then as a flight officer over the jungles and villages of Viet Nam. He completed two tours of duty defying death in that ill conceived struggle America eventually lost. Finally Marine aviator Cummings returned to the States and continued on to serve as a flight officer in the Marine Corps until his eventual retirement in 1998. After finishing his active service in the Marine Corps Beaman would join Southwest Airlines as an airline Captain.

In the early years of his USMC duty the aviator had become married. He became the father of a little boy named Waldo Beaman Cummings III. In 1989 participated in Desert Storm. As he did in Viet Nam, the aviator served with honor and distinction. While he never did seek attention or even recognition, he was recognized as an uncommon example of outstanding leadership as a Wing Commander in the Middle East war.

After returning home from duty serving in the Iraqi war, a heart warming story about Beaman appeared in the Daily Gazette of Schenectady, New York. Published on My 23, 1991 the story told about Beaman's visit to a group of school children that wrote to him while he served in Desert Storm.

*Marine Pilot Personally Thanks Albany Students
for Their Letters*

*By Jeff Wilkin – Gazette reporter of the Daily
Gazette, Schenectady, NY Thursday May 23, 1991*

For weeks Joe Schaller and Nadia Samuel wrote to
a friend far away. And they worried. Lt. Col. W.
Beaman Cummings was flying over the Persian
Gulf, on night bombing missions against the Iraqi
army. He read the letters from the two ten year
olds and some of their friends.

And he remembered.

On Tuesday Cummings rumbled into town
with his A-6 Intruder bomber landing at Stratton
National Guard Air Base. Yesterday the Marine
pilot from Havelock, NC visited the Albany
School of Humanities and personally thanked 17
fourth graders for keeping him in their thoughts
during the war.

A school assembly followed and then
Cummings led the 375 students to Stratton to
show off his sleek gray aircraft. The kids asked
about all the electronic controls, the ejector seats,
and the feelings a pilot gets flying between 550
and 600 miles per hour.

Sandra Preston who teaches the fourth graders
who developed a friendship with Cummings
said the children first wrote letters to "Any
Serviceman". Cummings, nicknamed "Stinger"
wrote back several times and became their hero.

When the 45 years old pilot came home he
made plans to fly the 1 ½ hours from Cherry point
Marine Corps Air Station in North Carolina to

Stratton. Taking the plane, in which he logged 34 combat missions, was not a big problem. Every pilot has to log training hours.

Preston said neither she nor the students ever thought they would meet Cummings. "It is something that will live in our hearts at the Albany School of Humanities forever" she said. "This is the most heartwarming experience I have ever participated in. I will always treasure the memory. Not only for myself but for the children."

Cummings, who also flew in Viet Nam, will also treasure his visit. He said he never expected the large reception from his young fans. "My eyes were watering", he said.

Then years later in the book titled '*The Gulf War Chronicles: A Military History of the First War in Iraq*', author Richard Lowery highlighted the service of Beaman. A passage referenced one of the exploits of the aviator.

> *Lieutenant Colonel W. Beaman Cummings, Jr. led a flight of four A-6 intruders in one of the attacks against the Scud maintenance buildings at Qurnah. "As we penetrated Iraqi airspace I looked down and saw the biggest light show I had ever seen. Continuous lines of red and orange tracers covered the black void below us. It seemed like every Iraqi who could put his finger on a trigger had it pressed down and wouldn't let it go." Colonel Cummings' strike dropped twelve two thousand pound bombs on the Scud facility and left it engulfed in flames.*

IV.

Many years rolled by from the time the war hero came home in 1991 until he became reacquainted with the roots of his education at Greenbrier. In the meantime from 1998 until 2006 he served as a Captain for Southwest Airlines until mandatory retirement at aged 60.

Ultimately Beaman was asked to serve as the President of the Greenbrier Military School Alumni Association. Though the school had closed in 1972 after over 150 years its alumni association remained vital and active due to the uncommonly high proportion of distinguished and loyal alumni. His two year term began for him in 2007.

Then in 2007, forty four years after I had last seen the aviator when he graduated from GMS in 1963, he and I encountered one another. It was Homecoming for the GMS alumni in 2007. By coincidence he and I saw one another on our former gridiron then an empty field behind the West Virginia School of Osteopathic Medicine. WVSOM had purchased the campus of the defunct GMS and refurbished it to make it a state of the art and well respected school of osteopathic medicine.

I was standing and reminiscing on the edge of the former football field in front of the GMS Alumni Center that WVSOM agreed to let our alumni build and maintain on their campus. Coming toward me I noticed an iron straight form, with graying hair but sharp features and a confident stride I instantly recognized from long ago.

As he walked toward me, I said. "Hi Beaman. Do you remember me?"

The retired Colonel stopped and looked at me for a moment. "I'm not sure", he stated tactfully.

I smiled and walked over and took his hand. "We were in 'A' Company together Beaman. When you were the Company Commander. And back then we both played for the 'Fighting Cadets' under Coach Ritchie."

When he recognized me he beamed and the bright smile and dimples I recalled from long ago quickly lit his face. We began to reconnect immediately. There was some common characteristic between us two that I can't define. It enabled us to pick up where we had left off years earlier. I liked and respected him. I would learn a few years later that he felt similarly when I called upon him to shoulder yet another leadership responsibility.

It was a few months after the Homecoming that fall I next spoke with Beaman. It was a Sunday evening in December of 2007. My cell phone rang.

"Hello, this is Jim".

"Jim. This is Beaman. How have things been going since Homecoming?"

"Pretty well Beaman. It's great to hear from you. Where are you calling from?"

"I'm in Tucson right now. In between hops for the company I fly for. Are you in Colorado?"

"Yep. I'm at a friend's home and we just finished dinner so the timing of your call is good."

"Well, I'm glad. I'm calling to see if you'd be willing to serve on the Board of the GMS Alumni Association."

"Damn it Beaman. Did they have to get you to call? I think they knew you're the only one who I could not refuse."

That was true. I had so much going on at that time that I couldn't see how I would be able to commit to any more responsibility. Even one as light as I thought the demands might be for a position on their board. I had no idea the amount of time and effort that my becoming involved in that organization would ultimately require. And I had no idea of the enormous rewards that it would eventually bring.

V.

Over the next couple of years I became actively involved in the GMS Board and alumni association. And by coincidence I was asked to head a leadership development program for the Greenbrier County Schools with the GMSAA. Quickly that involvement resulted by 2008 in a formal partnership between the Greenbrier Military School Alumni Association and the Greenbrier County Schools of West Virginia. Our alumni were enthusiastic because it gave the association a real purpose for the first time since the closing of the school beyond just social and minimal community service efforts.

By the fall of 2009 I got the idea of forming an institute from the partnership as I knew it would lend much more credence to the leadership programs I was putting together through the alumni association. And thanks to Beaman and a few other influential alumni I was fortunate enough to gain the concurrence and commitment of the total alumni association in endorsing and funding the Institute. That's when I was afforded the opportunity to turn the tables on Beaman.

It occurred in the fall of 2009 one year into the formal partnership between our alumni association and the Greenbrier County Public Schools. It was the afternoon of October 16 after Beaman and I conducted a leadership training program. I had got him to agree in leading one of the programs I designed for the schools. Beaman began the conversation. He was just about to step out of his two year term as President of the alumni association. The timing was perfect for what I had in mind.

"Jim. The alumni association has asked me to ask you if you would take over the Director role of the leadership group as Ted (Admiral Ted Parker USN retired) has completed his commitment."

"Beaman, I'm flattered. But I don't think it's the best thing for the long term effort. Because I've designed and run the programs for the past couple of years and will continue to do so, if I also become the Director I see a problem."

"I don't understand Jim. What do you mean?"

"Well, we're going to need to raise a fair amount of money as well as build a bigger team of guys to join in the effort. If it appears I'm at the center of everything, it becomes too much of a one man show. Any guy that steps into a multi-faceted role like that in an alumni association is going to have to cover a lot of bases and he's going to be limited in gaining the broad and total support he needs."

"Jim, if you won't do it, who do you suggest should step into the position?"

I just stood there and looked directly at him as a smile slowly turned up one corner of my mouth. He blinked a couple of times and looked away. Then I put my hand on his shoulder and said, "Look, with your leadership experience and credibility having just served as the President of the association and my experience in knowing how to make it work, we'll make a great team."

I was counting on the fact that his motivation toward the youth in Greenbrier County was the same as mine and the other alumni. We all simply wanted an opportunity to enhance their education by helping them learn about the value of leadership skills based upon well founded principles. We wanted an opportunity to extend the same classic values that focused upon integrity, service and honor that we had learned in our youth at Greenbrier. Values that were sorely lacking emphasis not only in the public schools across America but in the halls of our highest officials. My friend looked back and like me a couple of years earlier agreed to accept the position unknowing of the great amount of responsibility and work that would befall him by saying "Yes". He nodded and said "OK Jim. I'll do it." I smiled broadly and shook his hand.

VI.

By early 2010 the Greenbrier Leadership Institute was picking up steam under the leadership of Executive Director Beaman Cummings. There was no set formal term for his role or mine. We agreed to be partners and recruited more from our alumni association with outstanding credentials to join us in the Institute.

We decided that he and I would stay together to build

the value and educational influence of the Institute as far as we could for the foreseeable future. In 2010 we expanded the programs to include not only students and teachers of the Greenbrier County Schools but offer educational resources beyond the Greenbrier County. The Institute also developed its first leadership training DVD as well as began to develop a strategy for offering online leadership development programs through a website.

With 'The Aviator' committed as well as the other talented men from our alumni association joining us, we looked forward to a long and successful legacy for the Greenbrier Military School.

The Light

'I am the light of the world. Whoever follows me will never
walk in
darkness, but will have the Light of life'
— *John 8 V.12*

I.

Soft lights of red, green and blue lit the banisters on stair cases
in the great foyer of the aged building. The overhead globes
were turned off. Outside the icy gusts whipped across the
steep slate roof of the old school house on the cold winter day
in late December 1953. But inside the warm building we were
comfortable. The scent of the decorated pine trees in each of
our classrooms intermingled with the odor of the oak wood of
the Victorian building.

We children, grades first through sixth were arranged
to stand in an orderly fashion on the stair cases outside of
our respective classrooms. In the preceding weeks since
Thanksgiving each grade had been rehearsed in the songs we
would sing. Because the staircases all led down into the center
of the foyer most of us could see each other. Some of the older
children held candles; the soft glow of which lit their faces.

Miss Gordon, the portly fourth grade teacher sat at an
antiquated upright piano that had been moved out into the
foyer. She raised her hand signaling the teachers to quiet their
students. Then she began to play the first piece to which we
would accompany her in song. It was 'O Come All Ye Faithful'.
We children sang loudly. But above the din Miss Gordon's

voice could be heard leading us as she banged away at her piano. Then 'It Came Upon the Midnight Clear' and following that 'Away in a Manger'. On we went through 'Hark the herald Angels Sing', 'Deck the Halls', and Joy to the World' until finally finishing with 'Silent Night'.

There's something especially innocent in the voices of children singing. The memory of those voices on that gray afternoon in Central School on School Street still brings warmth to the heart. Deeper still is the warmth stirred by what was behind the celebration. The moment was the product of a feeling and spirit that pervaded our culture during the Christmas holiday in those years. It was present not only in the communities, churches, homes and decorated shop windows in the streets of our towns; but it infused the hearts of men, women and children. It was a spirit which permeated our nation. Clearly etched on many of our government buildings and even our currency; 'In God We Trust'. That spirit provided stability and strength. It encouraged meaning as well as togetherness.

After returning home from school that day I asked my mother a question that I had been considering all day long. "Mom, why is it only at Christmas that people are so nice?"

"Well Jimmy, I think it's because they're most reminded at Christmas that we're supposed to be kind to one another and be joyful to be alive."

Mom was good at answering our deeper questions. Possibly that question, coming from her seven year old son was one she had heard before. As I sat next to her at the dining room table she worked on hand made ornaments that were part of a Christmas tradition she had initiated in our home. I would hand her beads, colored ribbons, and other garnishes used to produce the lovely decorations. And she and I would talk.

"Do you think Jesus knows we're still celebrating His birthday?"

She responded, "There're millions of people all over the

world right now that believe He does. That's another reason they're happier at this time of year."

While her reasoning and logic about many things escaped my seven year old mind, one thing was clear in those early years. It was that there was something very real and strong in the way many grownups felt about the mysterious character called Christ. Usually there was reverence when they spoke about Him. Even the movies in the early post war years such as 'It's a Wonderful Life', 'A Tree Grows in Brooklyn', 'A Christmas Carol', 'Miracle of 34th Street', 'White Christmas' and others treated Him in awe. And I also noticed that it was only His name and no other that made them feel profane when they used it out in anger.

Influenced by the Christian traditions, my child's mind began to ponder something beyond complete understanding of the most brilliant minds of any age. Who and what is God? As the panorama of life's experiences began to unfold in my childhood I believed in God; but I couldn't define or understand Him. That was a mystery no one could explain satisfactorily to me.

II.

Entering junior high school I began to question Christian teachings. I was attending Sunday school classes where we would study the stories in the Bible and talk about what they meant. Because of what appeared implausible in some of the stories I started to doubt the validity of a few parts of the Bible. Especially the Old Testament. The kind of events described in those stories did not happen in my world. They seemed so foreign. I was seriously wondering about many of the books of the Old Testament. They sounded too fantastic.

"Mom, do you really think there was a man named Jonah who was swallowed by a whale and lived inside it for three days and then came out alive?" I queried one day.

She responded, "Jim, what do you think is the message in that story?"

Her question prompted me to look for morals and lessons in Biblical stories. For awhile that placated me. But not for long. Some in the church made us feel that if we did question anything being taught by them, or any word in the Bible, it was due to a deficiency in us or a sinful nature. That made me all the more skeptical. And at this time, when many preteens begin to think and reason on their own, anything that appeared to stifle individual thought just fanned the flames of doubt in me.

By the age of thirteen I was uniformly rejecting organized religion. Though not God. I didn't think the two were mutually inclusive. I recognized that God was not religion and that religion did not create God. Religions were created by men and were so conflicted that it seemed no one of them could be completely correct. To me organized religion, as I observed in churches in those early years, appeared dogmatic. It also seemed to focus more upon promoting practices and rituals than I was comfortable with.

While I believed church encouraged higher moral behavior, it seemed to miss addressing something deeper. It seemed to lack answers to issues and questions spawned by a yearning for peace or meaning that was at the center of my developmental years between childhood and adulthood.

As I went off to college I was quite distanced from practicing religion. At the same time, because I had practically nothing or no one to share faith or interest in Christ and God, spirituality and related considerations fell out of my sphere of consciousness. My behavior degenerated as I no longer felt sure there was a divine force that was aware of my actions or thoughts. On one hand that was enormously freeing. On the other it was disconcerting. It seemed that I ultimately defined reality and what was moral in my world. I created my own reality. Without any faith based belief system beyond myself, my perspective was the only thing I had to go on. Even what I learned from my mother, my coaches and teachers and others whom I respected; it would all ultimately be filtered and accepted or rejected by my central perspective. There was no guide for me beyond that.

Without any sense of an eternal beyond the present, life had become primarily just a matter of survival without meaningful focus beyond temporary distractions. My life had to do with pursuit of interests and things that provided me whatever small sense of purpose or meaning I could wrest out of succeeding with. In sports, with friends and foes, and even with my family. There was no light to guide my path. I simply lived each day attempting to prevail against life rather than embrace and appreciate it. And in fact I soon realized that way of thinking was shared by many of my peers in the 'Baby Boom' generation. Especially the young men I knew.

In college, though I had no concrete understanding of existentialism, I was practicing it. All beyond me was meaningless and irrelevant. For my generation in the nineteen sixties many things made no sense. The war in Viet Nam; racial discord; the Cold War; and more. It was a turbulent and disorienting period. In April of 1966 Time Magazine published its infamous "Is God Dead?" story and cover which captured the spirit of doubt and alienation rampant in the youth of our nation. Though I still embraced conservative values, I rejected most of what I saw around me. Also in those years I often felt angry. Angry with the events from my childhood and in our home, with the war effort, and with our culture at large. The anger further served to promote alienation and distanced me even further from God.

While I was by nature basically kind and considerate to many others, it was still my self-focused will that guided my actions. I was at the center of my reality. God was something remote. There seemed nothing beyond me. I viewed other people as simply characters in my consciousness as though I was dreaming and they played a part in it. Sometimes there was a sense of fright that accompanied that perspective. I felt ultimately alone. It was in some respects analogous to being in a dark place stumbling around hoping to avoid falling into an abyss where nothing or no one could hear me because there was no one other than me.

III.

The events of my life in the quarter century between the iconic Time Magazine cover of 1966 and finally settling into middle age passed like a whirlwind. That time was a mixture of victories and heartbreaks that seemed to have very little connection to a just God. Those were years of simply fighting for or against things. Never going along with anything in life. Only battling life and the threats it posed to me or my children. And not feeling very much that God was present or aware of me and my plight. I believe this was a common feeling for many of the generation of my time.

However, by my mid-forties my perspective upon life and God began to change. By then I had enough experience to realize that while life appeared to not be fair there were some things that seemed consistent. For anyone. I had just read 'The Road Less Travelled' by M. Scott Peck. The book had referred directly to some truths I had experienced. Peck maintained that simply because life is not fair as humans define it, does not preclude there being laws and forces that ultimately work in reality; though we may not understand or comprehend them yet. That case has been proven countless times through human history as we continue to discover laws about the way things work where before they were a complete mystery and made no sense. In fact Peck maintained that some things can never be understood by scientific or rational thinking because they defy rationality. This is observed in quantum physics where none of the laws that hold true in Newtonian physics apply.

Additional reading in those years included 'Evidence that Demands a Verdict' by Josh McDowell and just about everything written by C.S. Lewis the great Christian apologetic of the Twentieth Century. What I read by Lewis did indeed make sense relative to my real life experience. And in fact direct experience still served as my guide. I could not believe in or accept anything simply because I wanted to believe in it or it sounded comforting. However, some of my Christian friends would argue about the need for blind faith in accepting Christ. I recall one such seminal debate around Christ involving the role of blind faith with a friend by the name of Tom.

Tom was a physicist with a MENSA level IQ. He was not only an extremely well educated man but he was well versed in theology. Not an easy opponent with whom to debate anything. Whether scientific or having to do with spiritual issues. At one point in a discussion, Tom asked, "Jim isn't there anything you believe though you have no absolute proof about it? For example, you have no absolute proof that if you lie down to sleep tonight your house won't burn with you it while you sleep; but you'll do it anyway."

"Tom I don't need absolute proof to take action. But I need enough information or knowledge to lead me to believe there is a reasonable chance the action is rational".

He responded, "Well that's my point. You have to have blind faith that things are a certain way even when you don't know for sure that they are."

"Not exactly, Tom. There's a difference between blind faith with no tangible proof and making a decision based upon the best knowledge available. I believe you're confusing the two."

Tom came back with, "But Jim, one's faith, spiritual perspective that is, can never be conclusively proven in every case. There has to be a willingness to simply believe in some things even though we don't see direct absolute proof."

"That's where we differ. My faith isn't based upon beliefs. It's based upon experience and it's grounded in rational observation. And that's why I'm so confident in it."

As the discussion ensued Tom could understand that I

didn't need blind faith to feel a strong connection with God or Christ. He accepted the fact that it was experiences in my life to that point that had provided the foundation for my acceptance of Christ. He went on with further questions. One of the more interesting ones was, "Well, how do you know that Christ was who He said He was if you never saw Him or any of His miracles?"

I liked the question because it offered me the opportunity to speak directly to why I was a Christian though I didn't practice organized religion. I began with the point that Christ did not found a religion. He simply encouraged others to come to God and maintained that He was God's instrument in this world to encourage that. It was others after Him that founded a religion based upon His teachings and role.

"Why do you maintain that you're not religious? I know you pray regularly and you read the Bible", Tom queried.

"I do. But I don't ascribe to any specific religious doctrine. I don't attend any church regularly. So you could say I'm a non-denominational Christian with no tie to one specific church. That's what I mean by not being religious."

Tom came back with, "OK. But if you're outside of a church and don't ascribe to any specific religious philosophy or doctrine, how come you have faith in Christ?"

That question allowed me to make reference to absolute proven facts about Christ that served as my basis for His role in my life and why I didn't rely upon traditional church teachings or basic apologetics. Some of the things I referenced included the fact that Christ is agreed to be by historians the most central presence in human history; accounts of miraculous actions on His part were corroborated even by His detractors; He is more reviled by sinister characters today and throughout history than any other which in effect makes Him the most significant spiritual force in history; the words and sayings attributed to Him are the most unique and well known of any age. I reminded Tom that these are all concrete facts; they're not simply "beliefs" or opinions.

I told Tom that though I had been a skeptic earlier in my life, when I became knowledgeable of these facts I was left with only two options. One was to ignore the reality of the facts about Him. The other was to accept Him for what He has proven to be. The single most powerful and positive event in human history. However, just realizing that fact was a long way from appreciating what it meant.

IV.

In any of the discussions and arguments I've observed in my life, never has any subject evoked as much ire or passion than questions and debates about God. God is an abstract concept, defined differently by a multitude of different persons and religious philosophies. But Christ is concrete. He is not abstract. He gives human form to the Divine Spirit. He actually lived and spoke. He was visible. He died. He promised to return. He spoke the most remembered words in history. He made the most fantastic claims in history.

His claims force me to either accept or reject Him completely. There's no middle ground. Because He claimed to be the Son of God He could only be insane, a preposterous liar, or Lord. There's no option beyond these three cases. So we are posed with examining His sanity. In fact there is nothing other than His incredible claim to indicate He was not sane. His behavior and speech was clearly rational as described by His followers and others. This indicates He was not insane. In respect to being a liar, He was described as the most moral and principled character of His times; and any times. There was nothing to indicate He ever lied to anyone about anything. He was never proven to be a liar in any case.

Though I had been highly skeptical for a time about Him, as I questioned and examined the facts, I finally realized that He had to be who claimed to be. That awareness about Him changed what and who I am. In essence I understood that if Christ was who He claimed, then God did know we are here and did care about us and our salvation enough to guide Christ in this world. I determined rationally that God came to speak directly to us and offer eternal life through Christ. As that fact sunk into my consciousness it made clear that I'm not alone and I'm not the center of reality. I don't define what is moral or right. And because I don't, it demands of me to seek the light of reality beyond myself.

Additionally, I recognized that both reality and truth are not within or defined by me. They are beyond me and the best I can do is to attempt to seek truth beyond myself. It was at that point in my life that I began to make decisions more rationally and act differently than before. While I'm still fallible and have negative aspects in my nature, I can connect with and be guided by something that is not fallible and has no negative aspects to its nature. I realize it's my Creator and source of life. And it is as aware of me as I am of it. Through prayer, reading the Bible and interaction with other Christians, I'm better informed, led and strengthened. When open to the way He speaks to us, not in words but through events I can experience Him.

One particularly memorable experience of Him occurred in late summer of 2009. I came home one evening discouraged and down as a result of some difficult events over the preceding months that culminated in an especially painful experience that evening. I got into bed and recited the 23rd Psalm from memory immediately before drifting off to sleep. That Psalm always seemed to give me strength and comfort. Early the next morning in the dim light I noticed the Bible was within reach. I thought about it for a moment and felt that since it was right there, I should open it to whatever page it would reveal by chance. It had over 2500 pages in it. My hand fumbled to no spot in particular. I looked at the print and was stunned. I was shocked to discover that I had opened the Bible exactly to the page with the 23rd Psalm. There was no page marker or anything about the binding of that Bible to increase the likelihood of opening it to that exact page. I knew it was not a coincidence. I was more than heartened by the moment. There have been many such moments in my life that encouraged me to accept that He is near.

As I accepted Christ I began to recognize that all of the best decisions and the most noble and worthwhile actions of my life were those that concerned themselves not at all with me. Nor what was most comfortable for me. All of the best decisions and actions were a function of putting others interests or needs before mine as Christ taught. In the case of my children. In the case of my stepchild. In the case of my father. In the case of reaching out or giving to others. In the case of the foundation. All of the best things in my life were a result of living and thinking the way Christ taught. All of the worst decisions I made and the sins I committed came in defiance of what He taught. This is the most conclusive fact of my life and experience.

In preparing this book while examining the vivid profiles of some of the people in my life I could see that His teachings were illustrated by the way each of these person's lives played out. Not that they necessarily followed Him. But the consequences, victories, and tragedies of their lives fit exactly the reality of life the way He defined it in His parables and teachings. Sam Trunzo, Dave Ritchie, my mother, Jack Shingleton, my children, Jennifer O'Neil, my father, and all of the players on the stage fit together into the kaleidoscope of reality as best described by Him. Each one that made the greatest contributions to me and others did so when they were in concert with His teachings whether they knew it or not. Tragedies for them were often a result of their actions when they did things He warned specifically against. Clearly the greatest tragedies that resulted from my own actions in life conflicted with His teaching as well. The greatest rewards were a direct result of making decisions in concert with His teachings.

Because of Him, there is a light in my life that illuminates the path toward truth and the ultimate reality. It provides a brighter and enlightened perspective on all experiences and questions I face across the panorama of my life. There is meaning and purpose. Everything that happened; everyone in my life and all of the joys and pains made sense when I grasped the reality of Him and what He taught. Because of Him my appreciation of others and my life has become worth far more than any pain or price I have endured or paid. The search for meaning and purpose that He encourages drove me to write the stories about some of the persons and events that shaped my reality that led me to Him. The light He has shone in my life has made me more grateful for all of these people and the life God gave me.

Epilogue

Though writing 'Profiles' was rewarding, attempting to get facts straight, many from years ago clouded by fading memories, was especially challenging. And having to guess at or create dialogue in some places compelled me to inject fiction into real life scenarios. While I tried to be as factual as possible, without such inferred dialogue, the stories would have not captured the drama of real life. Additionally a significant challenge was the effort involved in hundreds of hours of rewrites and edits that took seven years to complete. However, response to the initial draft of 'Profiles' proved all of the effort to be worthwhile.

'Profiles' was written primarily for my children and grandchildren to describe many of the important people and events that shaped and added value to my life which in turn largely influenced and possibly added value to their lives. Assessing the value of what we have in life, which is in essence our true concept of wealth, is determined only by our own individual perspective. Whether we perceive wealth in terms of relationships, health, adventure, financial or material, spiritual or anything else, it is a function of only what is important to us subjectively.

Writing 'Profiles' helped me realize that my wealth far exceeded what I hoped for in my youth. Not in material or financial terms, but in ways far more important. My most significant personal wealth is comprised of my loved ones, friends, adventures and the freedom to live life my way without having to yield to the will and direction of others. It also includes the many opportunities I've had to have been involved in the lives of a great number of people. Hopefully for the better.

While I was ultimately responsible for my decisions and actions the values, motives and choices that shaped my direction were largely guided or inspired by those people who took an interest in me and guided and encouraged me. To name everyone that enriched my life experience would be difficult. And describing the full scope and value of their influence, as well as my own influence in the lives of others, is not possible. Often we don't know how we impact others, whether for good or bad, or even the number we affect. Importantly, the persons who had the most positive influence upon me were those who encouraged me toward paths of service. I chose to write about them because the greatest rewards I've received along the way came by serving. In addition to describing those individuals in the nineteen chapters of 'Profiles' I must name additional important persons here in the Epilogue and their constructive roles for me.

The foundation of my being open to opportunities to serve was established by my mother. She modeled it. And she taught me to live by the Golden Rule as illustrated by Christ. While I didn't follow her example enough in the early going, I eventually realized that the most worthwhile things in our lives have little to do with accumulating material wealth or serving ourselves, but instead serving others. Trying to be more like her and embrace her Christian values led to opportunities that yielded the greatest returns that provided me fulfillment.

Mom was a very caring person and tried to encourage that quality in me. However, I had to learn the hard way that sometimes just caring about others, no matter how much we try with them does not necessarily lead to good ends. This was true in a few critical relationships for me. She tried to caution me that there are some people that no matter how much we care about them, or see the good in them they should be avoided. Not because they are bad, but because they just might not be good for us or we for them. Though such persons had significant impact upon the course of my life both positive and negative I chose not to include them. However to be fair, each of those persons had many positive attributes.

My first formal opportunity to learn about serving came in a leadership role when during my teen years when I was made a cadet officer at the Greenbrier Military School. I learned that effective leadership is first and foremost about service. The person who opened that door was a senior cadet officer, Beaman Cummings. I learned about leading and encouraging other cadets at a most formative period in their lives. This in turn had great positive value for the constructive formation of my own character and abilities.

Next, Jim Ummer, my best friend in college did more than anyone to that point to open the door to a professional path of service for me. After I graduated from college Jim practically moved mountains to gain my acceptance into graduate school at Michigan State University though I did not have the academic credentials. And it was at Michigan State where I met Jack Shingleton, the singular person who did the most to guide me on the practical path of service in my professional career.

Jack hired me into my first significant professional role of helping people with their careers and employment endeavors. Because of his faith in me and offering me the opportunity, I was inspired to become someone who like him might have a positive influence on the lives of others through their careers and work roles. He placed me in career development in 1971 at Oakland University and later brought me back to Michigan State University. Under his guidance, I worked with and counseled hundreds of students and graduates, assisting in career selection and employment. Later in those same years, he placed me in the role of directing the administration of job programs for thousands of Michigan State students.

Jack not only started me in the career development arena, but taught me important skills that served to increase my effectiveness in many contexts. From him I learned public speaking, how to handle the media, personnel assessment techniques, creative problem solving, time management, and most certainly self-confidence. He demonstrated how genuine confidence is a function of tenacity combined with doing what is right and principled. I've learned this is an unexcelled formula for success.

Because of my association and work with Jack in placement and career development, I have since had the opportunity to provide assistance to many persons, helping them define and develop their professional paths. Jack and I co-authored 'Mid Career Changes' published in 1990. As a product of Jack's influence I also wrote and produced many articles and video programs on careers and business success. And my professional path in management consulting would never have occurred without Jack directing, encouraging and mentoring me along the way.

After working in management consulting roles in two international firms immediately upon leaving MSU, Dr. Phillip Carter in the Graduate School of Business at Michigan State invited me to return there to teach. Because of him, from 1980 through 1991, I was privileged to have the opportunity to serve and teach a few thousand students in various management courses.

In conjunction with my faculty role at MSU I formed Management Services and Resources, a management consulting business. Over my 34 years to date with MSR, the most important doors to serve were opened by Dick Darios of Chrysler Corporation, Greg Morris of Fuller & Company, Jack Box of ONCOR International, and Jay Rhoden of Carter & Company. Though not appearing in the stories in 'Profiles', I mention each of these men because they helped me build the service platform of MSR which fostered a rewarding professional pursuit that has stayed with me the remainder of my life. As a result, I have now coached thousands of individual clients one on one. Also through MSR I was privileged to have conducted well over 100 practical seminars on leadership, sales, management, communications, and related professional topics.

In 2002 Steve Curtis invited me to co-found Lifecommercials.com, a Pro Life outreach that assists women in crises pregnancies to find options for allowing their child to live. At first I was reluctant, but at his insistence, I accepted the opportunity for fundraising, public relations, and coordinating various activities. The rewards of this volunteer role far exceeded any financial gain I have ever earned. A conservative estimate of women in crises pregnancies who decided against abortion as a direct result of our work as documented online to referral for alternatives to abortion reached the five figure range.

The many award winning commercials we produced and aired through our foundation Lifecommercials.com were seen by millions of viewers worldwide. As a result of that success, in 2006 CBN news anchor Lee Webb invited me to their world headquarters to be interviewed. My appearance during that quarter hour special feature about our foundation was broadcast to a worldwide audience. The number of unborn children saved by that outreach is not possible to estimate.

The life saving alternatives our foundation promoted not only enabled children to live but spared thousands of mothers from a lifetime of enormously painful regret. The success of Lifecommercials.com resulted in a sizable gift by an anonymous donor to fund a billboard campaign in Pittsburgh in 2007. This campaign was estimated by Lamar Advertising to have been viewed by over one million motorists just in Pittsburgh while the campaign was in full swing. There is no way to estimate the number of unborn children saved in Pittsburgh by that campaign.

Beaman Cummings, from my early GMS days resurfaced again much later in life. As the President of the Greenbrier Military School Alumni Association he partnered with me in 2008 to initiate the Greenbrier Leadership Institute. Lee

Martin, another former classmate of mine at GMS was the original stimulus for my willingness to serve the alumni association which led directly to creation of the Institute by me and Beaman.

To date hundreds of students, young men and women, as well as adults working and teaching in various venues in Greenbrier County, West Virginia, have been served by participating in our leadership development programs. Many more in other counties in West Virginia have also participated. Because of Beaman, Lee and others, the Institute continues to flourish as of this writing. Also Beaman and Lee served as catalysts for me to author the book 'Principle-Based Leadership' which is used as a text by our leadership students as well as in other settings nationwide.

Finally, my partner Cathy, who I met late in life, did not appear in any story in 'Profiles' as she did not grace my life until one year before the book was originally published. But she has since become the most positive influence by demonstrating more faith in and appreciation for me than anyone in my life. Her ever joyful nature and positive attitude lifts me continuously. She has unquestionably been the greatest catalyst for me to become the best man I am able.

In summary, all of the most significant blessings I've experienced in life are the direct result of knowing and being influenced by the persons I have profiled in each chapter as well as referred to in this epilogue. Thanks to each of these wonderful men and women I am more fortunate than I ever imagined I could be.